GRAMMAR EXPLORER 2B

Paul Carne

Series Editors: Rob Jenkins and Staci Johnson

NATIONAL GEOGRAPHIC LEARNING | CENGAGE Learning·

Australia • Brazil • Japan • Korea • Mexico • Singapore • Spain • United Kingdom • United States

Grammar Explorer 2B
Paul Carne

Publisher: Sherrise Roehr

Executive Editor: Laura Le Dréan

Managing Editor: Eve Einselen Yu

Senior Development Editors: Mary Whittemore, Eve Einselen Yu

Development Editor: Maureen Sotoohi

Associate Development Editor: Alayna Cohen

Assistant Editor: Vanessa Richards

Senior Technology Product Manager: Scott Rule

Director of Global Marketing: Ian Martin

Marketing Manager: Lindsey Miller

Sr. Director, ELT & World Languages: Michael Burggren

Production Manager: Daisy Sosa

Content Project Manager: Andrea Bobotas

Print Buyer: Mary Beth Hennebury

Cover Designer: 3CD, Chicago

Cover Image: BRIAN J. SKERRY/National Geographic Creative

Compositor: Cenveo Publisher Services

> For product information and technology assistance, contact us at
> **Cengage Learning Customer & Sales Support,**
> **1-800-354-9706**
>
> For permission to use material from this text or product,
> submit all requests online at **www.cengage.com/permissions.**
> Further permissions questions can be e-mailed to
> **permissionrequest@cengage.com.**

Student Book 2B: 978-1-111-35135-9

National Geographic Learning
20 Channel Center Street
Boston, MA 02210
USA

Cengage Learning is a leading provider of customized learning solutions with office locations around the globe, including Singapore, the United Kingdom, Australia, Mexico, Brazil and Japan.

Cengage Learning products are represented in Canada by Nelson Education, Ltd.

Visit National Geographic Learning online at **ngl.cengage.com**

Visit our corporate website at **www.cengage.com**

Printed in the United States of America
Print Number: 07   Print Year: 2022

CONTENTS

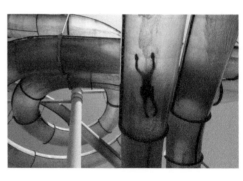

ACKNOWLEDGMENTS

The authors and publisher would like to thank the following reviewers and contributors:

Gokhan Alkanat, Auburn University at Montgomery, Alabama; **Dorothy S. Avondstondt**, Miami Dade College, Florida; **Heather Barikmo**, The English Language Center at LaGuardia Community College, New York; **Kimberly Becker**, Nashville State Community College, Tennessee; **Lukas Bidelspack**, Corvallis, Oregon; **Grace Bishop**, Houston Community College, Texas; **Mariusz Jacek Bojarczuk**, Bunker Hill Community College, Massachusetts; **Nancy Boyer**, Golden West College, California; **Patricia Brenner**, University of Washington, Washington; **Jessica Buchsbaum**, City College of San Francisco, California; **Gabriella Cambiasso**, Harold Washington College, Illinois; **Tony Carnerie**, English Language Institute, University of California San Diego Extension, California; **Ana M. Cervantes Quequezana**, ICPNA - Instituto Cultural Peruano Norteamericano; **Whitney Clarq-Reis**, Framingham State University; **Julia A. Correia**, Henderson State University, Arkansas; **Katie Crowder**, UNT Department of Linguistics and Technical Communication, Texas; **Lin Cui**, William Rainey Harper College, Illinois; **Nora Dawkins**, Miami Dade College, Florida; **Rachel DeSanto**, English for Academic Purposes, Hillsborough Community College, Florida; **Aurea Diab**, Dillard University, Louisiana; **Marta Dmytrenko-Ahrabian**, English Language Institute, Wayne State University, Michigan; **Susan Dorrington**, Education and Language Acquisition Department, LaGuardia Community College, New York; **Ian Dreilinger**, Center for Multilingual Multicultural Studies, University of Central Florida, Florida; **Jennifer Dujat**, Education and Language Acquisition Department, LaGuardia Community College, New York; **Dr. Jane Duke**, Language & Literature Department, State College of Florida, Florida; **Anna Eddy**, University of Michigan-Flint, Michigan; **Jenifer Edens**, University of Houston, Texas; **Karen Einstein**, Santa Rosa Junior College, California; **Cynthia Etter**, International & English Language Programs, University of Washington, Washington; **Parvanak Fassihi**, SHOWA Boston Institute for Language and Culture, Massachusetts; **Katherine Fouche**, The University of Texas at Austin, Texas; **Richard Furlong**, Education and Language Acquisition Department, LaGuardia Community College, New York; **Glenn S. Gardner**, Glendale College, California; **Sally Gearhart**, Santa Rosa Junior College, California; **Alexis Giannopolulos**, SHOWA Boston Institute for Language and Culture, Massachusetts; **Nora Gold**, Baruch College, The City University of New York, New York; **Ekaterina V. Goussakova**, Seminole State College of Florida; **Lynn Grantz**, Valparaiso University, Indiana; **Tom Griffith**, SHOWA Boston Institute for Language and Culture, Massachusetts; **Christine Guro**, Hawaii English Language Program, University of Hawaii at Manoa, Hawaii; **Jessie Hayden**, Georgia Perimeter College, Georgia; **Barbara Inerfeld**, Program in American Language Studies, Rutgers University, New Jersey; **Gail Kellersberger**, University of Houston-Downtown, Texas; **David Kelley**, SHOWA Boston Institute for Language and Culture, Massachusetts; **Kathleen Kelly**, ESL Department, Passaic County Community College, New Jersey; **Dr. Hyun-Joo Kim**, Education and Language Acquisition Department, LaGuardia Community College, New York; **Linda Koffman**, College of Marin, California; **Lisa Kovacs-Morgan**, English Language Institute, University of California San Diego Extension, California; **Jerrad Langlois**, TESL Program and Office of International Programs, Northeastern Illinois University; **Janet Langon**, Glendale College, California; **Olivia Limbu**, The English Language Center at LaGuardia Community College, New York; **Devora Manier**, Nashville State Community College, Tennessee; **Susan McAlister**, Language and Culture Center, Department of English, University of Houston, Texas; **John McCarthy**, SHOWA Boston Institute for Language and Culture, Massachusetts; **Dr. Myra Medina**, Miami Dade College, Florida; **Dr. Suzanne Medina**, California State University, Dominguez Hills, California; **Nancy Megarity**, ESL & Developmental Writing, Collin College, Texas; **Joseph Montagna**, SHOWA Boston Institute for Language and Culture, Massachusetts; **Richard Moore**, University of Washington, Washington; **Monika Mulder**, Portland State University, Oregon; **Patricia Nation**, Miami Dade College, Florida; **Susan Niemeyer**, Los Angeles City College, California; **Charl Norloff**, International English Center, University of Colorado Boulder, Colorado; **Gabriella Nuttall**, Sacramento City College, California; **Dr. Karla Odenwald**, CELOP at Boston University, Massachusetts; **Ali Olson-Pacheco**, English Language Institute, University of California San Diego Extension, California; **Fernanda Ortiz**, Center for English as a Second Language, University of Arizona, Arizona; **Chuck Passentino**, Grossmont College, California; **Stephen Peridore**, College of Southern Nevada, Nevada; **Frank Quebbemann**, Miami Dade College, Florida; **Dr. Anouchka Rachelson**, Miami Dade College, Florida; **Dr. Agnieszka Rakowicz**, Education and Language Acquisition Department, LaGuardia Community College, New York; **Wendy Ramer**, Broward College, Florida; **Esther Robbins**, Prince George's Community College, Maryland; **Helen Roland**, Miami Dade College, Florida; **Debbie Sandstrom**, Tutorium in Intensive English, University of Illinois at Chicago, Illinois; **Maria Schirta**, Hudson County Community College, New Jersey; **Dr. Jennifer Scully**, Education and Language Acquisition Department, LaGuardia Community College, New York; **Jeremy Stubbs**, Tacoma, Washington; **Adrianne Thompson**, Miami Dade College, Florida; **Evelyn Trottier**, Basic and Transitional Studies Program, Seattle Central Community College, Washington; **Karen Vallejo**, University of California, Irvine, California; **Emily Young**, Auburn University at Montgomery, Alabama.

From the Author: It has been an honor to work with National Geographic material in the preparation of this book. My thanks are due to my excellent development editors Maureen Sotoohi and Eve Einselen Yu, to Laura LeDréan, Tom Jefferies, Mary Whittemore, and the entire team at National Geographic Learning. The project has benefited from the expertise and enthusiasm of many experienced reviewers, and their contribution is also greatly appreciated. Finally, it has been an absolute privilege to work alongside my fellow authors, Daphne Mackey, Amy Cooper, and Sammi Eckstut. Hats off to you all!

Dedication: To Vicky, my wife and best friend, for her timeless love and support; to my wonderful sons, Thomas and Robin, for keeping me going; and last but not least, to my beloved border terrier, Bodhi, for his patience (sometimes!) and unflagging optimism throughout.

National Geographic images introduce the unit theme—real world topics that students want to read, write, and talk about.

UNIT **8** Consumer Society

Comparatives and Superlatives

▲ Cars in a scrap yard in Colombia.

Lesson **1**	Lesson **2**	Lesson **3**	Review the Grammar
page 206	page 213	page 220	page 227
Comparative Adjectives and Adverbs	Comparisons with (Not) As . . . As and Less	Superlative Adjectives and Adverbs	Connect the Grammar to Writing
			page 230

205

Units are organized in **manageable lessons**, which ensures students **explore, learn, practice,** and **apply** the grammar.

Each lesson begins with the *Explore* section, featuring a captivating National Geographic article that introduces the target grammar and builds students' knowledge in a variety of academic disciplines.

LESSON 1 **Comparative Adjectives and Adverbs**

EXPLORE

1 **READ** the article about consumer societies. Notice the words in **bold**.

What is a Consumer Society?

A *consumer* is a person who buys things, and a *consumer society* is a society that encourages people to buy and use goods.[1] Some people think that a consumer society provides people with **better** lives. People in consumer societies tend to live **more comfortably**. They eat a **wider** variety of food. They go to restaurants **more often**. They also buy a lot of products, maybe more than they need.

Products such as TVs, cell phones, and computers used to be luxuries.[2] Today people can buy these things **more easily than** ever before. The market for these goods is growing **faster** all the time. Consumer societies encourage people to buy **bigger** and **better** products. For example, **"smarter"** phones come out every year. In a consumer society, people are often buying **newer** and **more advanced** products. This creates a lot of waste. Nowadays, many people are thinking **more seriously** about the effects of consumer societies on the environment, and they are trying to become **more responsible** consumers.

[1] **goods:** items that can be bought or sold
[2] **luxury:** something that is expensive but not necessary

206

▼ A billboard, a traditional form of advertising

Comparisons with *(Not) As . . . As* **and** *Less* **LESSON 2**

EXPLORE

1 **READ** the excerpt from a discussion between the professor of a business class and a guest speaker. Notice the words in **bold**.

Online Reviews: ★ or ★★★★?

Professor: So, Dennis, what changes have you seen in marketing recently?

Dennis: Well, as you know, customers love to post online reviews of products these days. These reviews are now just **as important as** traditional advertising. Maybe even more important. TV advertising is **as useful as** it was before, of course. On the other hand, newspaper ads[1] are much **less** …

Professor: Hmm. That … who aren't …

Dennis: Really? I'm … online revie … write review … there might … shoppers a … **as** they use … ads. If a cu … **enthusiast** …

[1] **ad:** short for advertisement
[2] **endorse:** to say that you support …
[3] **enthusiastically:** to do somethin …

LESSON 3 **Superlative Adjectives and Adverbs**

EXPLORE

1 **READ** the article about a problem on Mount Everest. Notice the words in **bold**.

Mount Everest:
The Highest Garbage Dump in the World?

Most people know that Mount Everest is **the highest** mountain in the world. However, there is another fact that many people don't know: it has become one of **the dirtiest** mountains in the world.

Mount Everest is one of **the toughest** and **most exciting** mountains to climb on Earth. It is not **the coldest** or **the windiest** place on Earth, but it comes close! These challenges make it one of **the most attractive** mountains for serious climbers. Since 1952, over 3500 climbers have reached the top. Unfortunately, most of them have left equipment and trash on the mountain.

In fact, trash is now one of **the biggest** threats to the environment on Mount Everest. Local organizations have brought tons of trash down from the mountain. One of **the most interesting** projects handed over more than a ton of tin cans, glass bottles, and old climbing tools to artists in Nepal. The artists used the trash to create works of art. Then, they sold the art to raise money for local charities.[1] **The least expensive** work of art cost $17, and **the most expensive** one cost $2400.

[1] **charity:** an organization that raises money to help people

▶ The consumer society produces a lot of waste, even in the Himalayas. Here, a climber collects trash on Mount Everest.

220 COMPARATIVES AND SUPERLATIVES

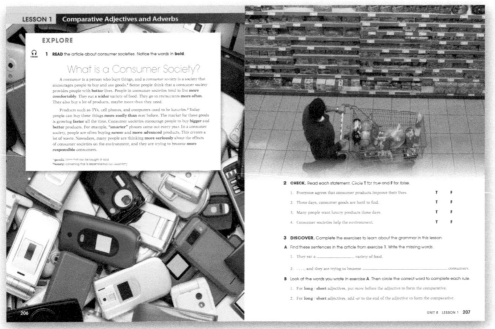

In the **Explore** section, students discover how the grammar structures are used in the readings and in real academic textbooks.

The **Learn** section features clear grammar charts and explanations followed by controlled practice of the grammar forms.

PRACTICE

9 Use the words in parentheses to complete the conversation with comparative adjectives or adverbs. Add *than* where necessary. In some cases, more than one answer is possible.

Matt: My phone is working (1) _worse than_ (badly) ever! And it's
(2) _____ (old) all the other phones I see, too.
I want a (3) _____ (modern) phone.

Lara: Take a look at my phone. It was (4) _____ (cheap) my
last phone, and I'm much (5) _____ (happy) with it. When I'm
traveling, I listen to music (6) _____ (often) I do when I'm at
home, so I wanted a phone with a (7) _____ (big) memory card.

Matt: Wow, it's much (8) _____ (nice) mine! The screen is a lot
(9) _____ (large), too. I want one like that!

Lara: Yeah, you need a big screen, because you watch videos on your phone
(10) _____ (frequently) I do.

10 Look at the charts comparing three laptop co[...]
the comparative form of the adjectives and a[...]

Product Details	T400
Screen size	15 inches
Weight	5.5 pounds
Amount of time on the market	18 months
Cost	$565

Customer Ratings	T400
Starts quickly	★ ★ ★
Runs reliably	★ ★ ★ ★ ★
Operates quietly	★ ★ ★ ★
Displays pictures well	★ ★ ★

1. (large / small) The screen of the T400 is __ le[...]
smaller than the XJ7's.

2. (light / heavy) The XJ7 is _____
the T400.

3. (new / old) The A-50 is _____
the XJ7.

4. (cheap / expensive) The T400 is _____
_____

5. (quickly / slowly) The T400 starts _____
_____ the A-50.

In the **Practice** section, students practice the grammar using all four skills through communicative activities that prepare them for academic work.

PRACTICE

8 Complete the sentences with the superlative form of the adjectives and adverbs in parentheses. Use *least* if *not* is included in the parentheses.

1. Kelly: I think people are too concerned about having (1) _the most modern_
(modern) cell phones. Cell phones contain some of (2) _____
(rare) minerals on Earth, but many people just throw their old cell phones away
when they buy a new one. This is (3) _____
(one of the / bad / thing) you can do! But if you recycle your old cell phones,
it's (4) _____ (one of the / good / thing) you can do.

2. Amir: My cell phone is (5) _____ (important / thing) I own. It's
(6) _____ (convenient / place) I have to keep information.

3. Brad: My new cell phone is a piece of junk! It was (7) _____
(not expensive) phone in the store. What a mistake! Also, the salesperson in that
store was one of (8) _____ (not helpful /
salesperson) I've ever spoken to.

9 **EDIT.** Read the article about trash in the desert. Find and correct eight more errors with superlatives.

Cameron's Camels

↓hottest
The Arabian Desert in the Middle East is one of the ~~most hot~~ environments on Earth, and it has
the less amount of rainfall. But to the camel, it is home. The camel is one of the most strong animals
in the world. Camels can go for many days with only a little food and water. When they do find water,
they probably drink the most quick of any land animal. Adult camels can drink about 25 to 30 gallons
(95–114 liters) in ten minutes. Unfortunately, finding water is not the seriousest problem camels face.
Most dangerous threat to camels comes from humans. Tourists in the desert leave trash behind. Camels
think the trash is food and eat it. This is very dangerous for the camels, because it can kill them.

One of the most polluted part of the desert is outside the city of Abu Dhabi. Each year, many

---

10 **APPLY.**

A Work with a partner. Use the words in parentheses to write superlatives. Then choose the correct answer to complete each fact on the quiz.

General Knowledge Quiz

1. _____ is _the highest mountain_ _____ (high / mountain) on Earth.
   a. Mount Kilimanjaro   b. Mount Everest   c. K2

2. _____ is _____ (fast / animal) in the world.
   a. the camel   b. the zebra   c. the cheetah

3. _____ is _____ (long / river) in the world.
   a. The Nile River   b. The Amazon River   c. The Yangtze River

4. _____ is _____ (wide / ocean) on Earth.
   a. The Pacific Ocean   b. The Atlantic Ocean   c. The Indian Ocean

5. _____ is _____ (small / continent).
   a. Africa   b. Antarctica   c. Australia

6. _____ is _____ (large / animal) on Earth.
   a. the elephant   b. the blue whale   c. the giraffe

7. _____ is _____ (cold / place) on Earth.
   a. Antarctica   b. Alaska   c. Canada

8. _____ is _____ (close / planet) to the sun.
   a. Mars   b. Venus   c. Mercury

B Check your answers at the bottom of this page. How many of your answers were correct?

C With your partner, write six more general knowledge facts like the ones from the quiz in exercise **A**. Use superlative adjectives and adverbs.

1. The Nile River is the longest river in the world.

D Use the facts from exercise **C** and quiz your classmates.

A: *This is the largest country in South America.*
B: *Is it Argentina?*
A: *No.*
C: *Is it Brazil?*
A: *Yes, it is!*

Answers: 1. b. Mount Everest, 2. c. the cheetah, 3. b. the Nile River, 4. a. the Pacific Ocean, 5. c. Australia, 6. b. the blue whale, 7. a. Antarctica, 8. c. Mercury

226 COMPARATIVES AND SUPERLATIVES

Students use their new language and critical thinking skills in the **Apply** section.

UNIT 8 Review the Grammar

Charts
8.1, 8.3–8.7

1 READ & WRITE.

A Read the information about the Greendex survey, and look at the chart. Then complete each sentence according to the information in the chart. Use the comparative or superlative form of the adjective or adverb in parentheses. For some sentences, more than one answer is possible.

Greendex↗

The Greendex is a survey of 1000 consumers in several countries. It asks consumers how they spend their money. Each consumer receives a score. High scores indicate "green," or environmentally friendly, attitudes. Low scores indicate environmentally unfriendly attitudes.

Greendex: Rankings

	Overall	Housing	Transportation	Food	Goods
Americans	44.7	31.5	54.9	57.0	44.2
Brazilians	55.5	48.9	67.1	57.5	53.8
British	49.4	35.9	62.7	62.2	47.1
Canadians	47.9	35.1	57.8	60.9	45.7
Chinese	57.8	48.2	69.0	63.7	56.8
Germans	51.5	40.3	61.9	61.9	47.1
Indians	58.9	51.4	67.3	71.1	57.3
Japanese	48.5	35.3	65.9	54.7	52.7
Mexicans	53.9	48.0	62.2	53.6	54.5
Russians	53.1	44.1	66.4	60.4	47.9

Transportation

1. The Chinese make ____the greenest____ (green) choices.

2. Americans are _____ (green) consumers.

3. British consumers make _____ (green) choices than Canadian consumers.

4. Mexican consumers are _____ (green) Japanese consumers.

Food

5. The British are _____ (concerned) the Chinese.

6. Indians are _____ (concerned) consumers.

7. Russians are _____ (concerned) Brazilians.

8. American

Review the Grammar gives students the opportunity to consolidate the grammar in their reading, writing, listening, and speaking.

Review the Grammar **UNIT 8**

Goods

9. Canadians don't buy goods _____ (responsibly) Mexicans do.

10. Indians buy goods _____ (responsibly).

11. Germans buy goods _____ (responsibly) Brazilians.

12. Americans buy goods _____ (responsibly).

B In your notebook, write four or five sentences based on the housing data from the Greendex chart in exercise A on page 227. Use comparative and superlative adjectives and adverbs. Use the sentences from exercise A to help you.

Mexicans make greener housing choices than Canadians.
Indian consumers are more concerned about green housing than German consumers are.

Charts
8.1–8.7

2 EDIT. Read the article about the results of the Greendex survey. Find and correct eight more errors with comparatives and superlatives.

The Greendex Survey: Some Overall Conclusions

- According to a recent Greendex survey, people in India were the ~~most green~~ greenest consumers in the world. They scored lower in transportation than the Chinese were, but they scored the highest than the Chinese in three other categories.

- Mexicans were more concerned about green transportation as green food or goods. For them, the low score of all was in the housing category.

- Germans scored highly in the transportation category than they did in the food category. However, they were least concerned about housing than goods.

- The Japanese were one of the least concerned nationality overall. They had one of the most bad scores in the housing category.

- Americans had the lowest overall score of all the nationalities in the survey. Food was the only category in which Americans did not score lower than the other nationalities.

Charts
8.1–8.4, 8.6

3 LISTEN & SPEAK.

🎧 **A** Listen to a professor discussing the Greendex survey with her students. Then complete the students' opinions about the survey.

Martin:

1. Most people think that their country is _____ the results show.

2. Many people think they buy goods _____ they really do.

3. We like to think we're trying _____ we can to be green.

Karin:

4. Life in the United States is much _____ without a car.

5. Cars that use less gas are becoming _____ in the United States.

6. Attitudes about the environment aren't changing _____ people think.

Andrew:

7. Most people want to make life _____ for themselves and their families.

8. Everyone wants an _____ life.

🎧 **B** Look at the sentences from exercise A. Then listen again. Do you agree or disagree with the students' ideas and opinions? Why, or why not? Write notes on your own ideas and opinions in your notebook.

C Work with a partner. Share your ideas and opinions from exercise B. Use comparatives and superlatives.

I agree with Martin's opinion about goods. People don't shop as carefully as they think they do.

Charts
8.1–8.7

4 WRITE & SPEAK.

A Look at the items in the box. Then rank the items from 1 to 8, with (1 = the least important and 8 = the most important).

____ a. a big car	____ d. a smart phone	____ g. plastic bags
____ b. stylish clothing	____ e. meals in restaurants	____ h. a gold watch
____ c. a computer	____ f. a TV	

B In your notebook, write six sentences about the items from exercise A. Use comparatives and superlatives and your own ideas and opinions.

I think a computer is less important than a smart phone.

C Work with a partner. Share your rankings from exercise A and your opinions from exercise B.

---

228 COMPARATIVES AND SUPERLATIVES

UNIT 8 REVIEW THE GRAMMAR **229**

Connect the Grammar to Writing

1 READ & NOTICE THE GRAMMAR.

A Before you buy something, do you compare it with similar products? Discuss your shopping habits with a partner. Then read the text.

The Best Sleeping Bag

I needed to buy a new sleeping bag for a winter camping trip. So, I went to a camping store and compared three different brands¹ of sleeping bags: Ultra Comfort, Snowy Down, and Northern Trek. I wanted to look at each sleeping bag very carefully. For winter camping, the Snowy Down had the highest rating. But in some ways, the other two sleeping bags were better. Of the three sleeping bags, the Snowy Down was the warmest, but it was also the most expensive. The Northern Trek cost less than the Snowy Down, but it was just as expensive as the Ultra Comfort. The Ultra Comfort was warmer than the Northern Trek. Finally, the Ultra Comfort was lighter than the other sleeping bags, so it was easier to carry.

I decided not to get the Northern Trek for camping outside. It wasn't as warm as the other sleeping bags. But we were having a mild winter, so I didn't need the warmest kind of sleeping bag. So I looked more closely at the lightest sleeping bag, the Ultra Comfort. That's the one I chose.

¹ **brand:** the commercial name for a product

> **GRAMMAR FOCUS**
>
> In exercise **A**, the writer uses comparatives and superlatives to discuss three sleeping bags.
>
> *The Ultra Comfort was **warmer than** the Northern Trek.*
>
> *. . . it was just **as expensive as** the Ultra Comfort.*
>
> *Of the three sleeping bags, the Snowy Down was **the warmest** and **most expensive**.*

B Read the text in exercise **A** again. Underline the comp[...] Then work with a partner and compare your answers.

C Work with a partner. Complete the chart with informati[...]

Product Details	Ultra Comfort	Snow[...]
Cost	as expensive as the Northern Trek	
Warmth		the war[...]
Weight		

230 COMPARATIVES AND SUPERLATIVES

Write a Product Review

2 BEFORE YOU WRITE. Think of a product that you plan to buy. Compare three different brands of this product. Complete the chart with information about each brand. Use the chart from exercise **1C** as a model.

Product Details	Product #1	Product #2	Product #3
Cost			

3 WRITE a review comparing the three different brands of the product you chose. Write two paragraphs. Use the information from your chart in exercise **2** and the article in exercise **1A** to help you.

> **WRITING FOCUS** Correcting Run-on Sentences
>
> A run-on sentence is an error that happens when two independent clauses are connected without a connecting word or correct punctuation.
>
> ✗ *I enjoyed my winter camping trip next year, I'll invite a few friends to join me.*
>
> To correct a run-on sentence, you can divide the run-on sentence into separate sentences.
>
> ✓ *I enjoyed my winter camping **trip. Next** year, I'll invite a few friends to join me.*
>
> You can also use a comma and a conjunction (*and, but, or*) between the two independent clauses.
>
> ✓ *I enjoyed my winter camping **trip, but** next year I'll invite a few friends to join me.*

4 SELF ASSESS. Read your review and underline the comparatives and superlatives. Then use the checklist to assess your work.

- ☐ I used comparative adjectives and adverbs correctly. [8.1, 8.2, 8.3]
- ☐ I used comparisons with *less* and *(not) as . . . as* correctly. [8.4, 8.5]
- ☐ I used superlative adjectives and adverbs correctly. [8.6, 8.7]
- ☐ I checked for and corrected run-on sentences. [WRITING FOCUS]

Connect the Grammar to Writing provides students with a clear model and a guided writing task where they first notice and then use the target grammar in one of a variety of writing genres.

Conjunctions and Adverb Clauses

▲ A bouvardia,
Lincoln, Nebraska, USA

233

EXPLORE

CD3-02

1 READ the article about a special kind of plant. Notice the words in **bold**.

What's for Dinner?

Most plants get the nutrients[1] they need to grow from soil. Some plants, however, grow in poor soil that doesn't provide the food the plants need. These plants have to attract **and** catch insects to stay alive. Plants that trap **and** eat insects are called carnivorous, **or** meat-eating, plants.

Many plants attract insects with bright colors **and** pleasant smells, **and** carnivorous plants **do too**. Some carnivorous plants also contain tasty liquids, **so** insects will come close **and** take a drink.

However, scientists have recently discovered something else that attracts insects to some carnivorous plants. These plants shine with a blue light. The light is ultraviolet,[2] **so** people can't see it. The light can't attract humans, **but** it is bright **and** attractive to insects.

Pitcher plants are among the most interesting "ultraviolet" plants. Their leaves form tubes that hold liquids. The blue light attracts insects to the edge of the plant's leaves, **and** some of them fall in. They try to escape, **but** the leaves have special hairs that stop them from climbing out. Soon the insects become a meal for the plant.

[1] **nutrient:** something in food that is necessary for life
[2] **ultraviolet:** a blue color that the human eye cannot see

▼ Carnivorous pitcher plants in the Morne Seychellois National Park, Mahe Island, Seychelles, Africa

2 CHECK. Match the beginning of each statement in Column A with the correct ending in Column B.

Column A

1. Ultraviolet light _____

2. Poor soil _____

3. Insects _____

4. Pitcher plants _____

5. Special hairs _____

Column B

a. does not provide enough nutrients for some plants.

b. keep insects inside the plant.

c. have leaves like tubes.

d. attracts insects to plants.

e. provide nutrients for carnivorous plants.

3 DISCOVER. Complete the exercises to learn about the grammar in this lesson.

A Read the pairs of sentences based on the article from exercise **1**. Then choose the correct answer for each question.

1. They have to attract **and** catch insects to survive.
   Many plants attract insects with bright colors **and** pleasant smells.

   How is *and* used in these sentences?   a. to add ideas   b. to show how ideas are different

2. The light is ultraviolet, **so** people cannot see it.
   Carnivorous plants grow in poor soil, **so** they do not get many nutrients from the ground.

   What type of idea follows *so*?   a. a result   b. a cause

3. The insects try to escape, **but** they are unable to get away.
   The light can't attract humans, **but** it is bright and attractive to insects.

   What type of idea follows *but*?   a. a similar idea   b. a different idea

B Work with a partner. Compare your answers from exercise **A**.

LEARN

9.1 Conjunctions: *And, Or, So, But*

1. Conjunctions connect words, phrases, or clauses.	Words: We're having <u>chicken</u>, <u>rice</u>, **and** <u>broccoli</u> for dinner tonight. Phrases: Do you want to go <u>to Paris</u> **or** <u>to Rome</u>? Clauses: <u>I like Texas</u>, **so** <u>I moved to Dallas</u>.
2. Use *and* to connect information that is similar. We also use *and* to add additional information.	You need flour, eggs, **and** sugar to make a cake. She likes to swim **and** play the drums.
3. Use *or* to talk about choices or alternatives.	Do you want pie **or** fruit for dessert? Tonight I'll watch TV **or** go to the gym.
4. Use *so* to show a result. *So* introduces a clause. Do not use *so* to connect words or phrases.	It was raining hard, **so** I took the bus. ⌞_____Cause_____⌟ ⌞_____Result_____⌟
5. Use *but* to show a contrast or a difference between people, places, things, or ideas.	She lived in Mexico for years, **but** she never learned Spanish.
6. Do not use a comma before a conjunction when it connects two words or phrases. Use a comma before a conjunction when it connects two independent clauses. An independent clause can stand alone as a complete sentence.	✓ Tennis is fun **but** difficult. ✗ Tennis is fun, but difficult. Mother's Day is May 11 this year, **and** it's my sister's birthday. Do you want to go out to eat, **or** do you want to stay home?

4 Circle the correct conjunction to complete each sentence.

1. Pitcher plants attract insects with bright colors, light, (**and**)/ **so** tasty liquids.

2. Plants get nutrients from the ground **or** / **so** from insects.

3. Insects go inside plants **but** / **and** drink the liquid.

4. The Botanical Garden is closed today, **so** / **but** we can't go.

5. Jamie knows a lot about nature, **and** / **but** he hasn't heard of pitcher plants.

6. Are you going to water the plants now **but** / **or** later?

7. Tasha didn't take care of her plants, **so** / **but** they died.

8. These flowers are beautiful, **or** / **but** they do not last a long time.

5 Complete the sentences with *and, or, so,* or *but.* Add commas if necessary.

1. Are you more interested in plants _____*or*_____ animals?

2. Bella loves flowers _____ she doesn't have a garden.

3. These plants require a lot of sunlight _____ water.

4. We worked hard in the garden _____ we were very tired.

5. The fruit on that plant looks delicious _____ it's poisonous. Don't eat it!

6. Do you want to visit the park _____ the zoo? We don't have time for both.

7. Sam bought flowers _____ a box of chocolates for his mother.

8. The flowers in the park were amazing _____ I took a lot of photos.

6 SPEAK. Work with a partner. Take turns making sentences by matching the beginning of each sentence with the correct ending.

1. English is difficult, but . . .	a. tea?
2. Last week, I went shopping and …	b. I don't play it very well.
3. Do you want coffee or . . .	c. I like it.
4. I have a headache, so . . .	d. went inside.
5. Is Rapid City in South Dakota or . . .	e. I bought some new shoes.
6. We parked the car and . . .	f. I took some aspirin.
7. I just finished a pizza, so . . .	g. Wyoming?
8. I like tennis, but . . .	h. I don't want anything to eat.

English is difficult, but I like it.

9.2   And + Too, So, Either, Neither

1. To show similarity in an affirmative statement and avoid repetition, use:
   a. *and* + subject + auxiliary verb* + *too*
   b. *and* + *so* + auxiliary verb + subject
 	
Be careful! The word order of clauses with *too* and *so* is different.
	a. Linda likes to swim, **and Luc does too.**
	b. Linda likes to swim, **and so does Luc.**
	
	Linda lives in Toronto, **and Luc does too.**
	Linda lives in Toronto, **and so does Luc.**

2. Use the same form for the auxiliary verb and the main verb.	I **went** to work, and so **did** Dante. Jackie **eats** meat, and I **do** too.

3. To show similarity in a negative statement and avoid repetition, use:
   a. *and* + subject + auxiliary verb + *either*
   b. *and* + *neither* + auxiliary verb + subject
Be careful! The word order of clauses with *either* and *neither* is different.
	a. Mae doesn't eat fish, **and Kim doesn't either.**
	b. Mae doesn't eat fish, **and neither does Kim.**
	
	I don't speak Greek, **and my parents don't either.**
	I don't speak Greek, **and neither do my parents.**

4. Do not use a negative auxiliary verb with *neither*.	✓ I don't play golf, and **neither does my sister.** ✗ I don't play golf, and <u>neither doesn't</u> my sister.

* Auxiliary verbs are sometimes called *helping verbs. Have, do,* and *will* are common auxiliary verbs.

7 Complete each sentence with *so, too, either,* or *neither* and the correct form of the auxiliary verb (*do, have, be,* or *will*).

1. Ellie likes to watch nature films, and _____*so do*_____ her children.

2. Franco's not watching TV, and _____ Mary.

3. I don't buy flowers often, and my sister

   _____.

4. We grew our own vegetables, and our neighbors

   _____.

5. Sid has finished his assignment, and

   _____ Olivia.

6. Eric won't be at the meeting tomorrow, and

   _____ his boss.

7. Carlos is from Mexico, and Vera _____.

8. I haven't seen that TV show, and _____ Paul.

> **REAL ENGLISH**
>
> Use *so* + an auxiliary verb + *I* to agree with an affirmative statement.
>
> > A: *I love San Francisco.*
> > B: **So do I**.
>
> Use *neither* + an auxiliary verb + *I* to agree with a negative statement.
>
> > A: *Tina has never been to Europe.*
> > B: **Neither have I**.

8 Choose the correct answer(s) to complete each sentence. For some sentences there is more than one correct answer.

1. Eddie arrived late, and _____.
   - (a.) so did I
   - (b.) I did too
   - c. neither did I

2. I haven't lived with my parents for a long time, and _____.
   - a. my sister has too
   - b. so has my sister
   - c. my sister hasn't either

3. Alicia was working last night, and _____.
   - a. Hans was too
   - b. neither was Hans
   - c. so was Hans

4. The restaurant won't be open, and _____.
   - a. so will the diner
   - b. neither will the diner
   - c. the diner will too

5. I speak French, and _____.
   - a. so does my sister
   - b. my sister does too
   - c. neither does my sister

6. Alex wasn't enjoying the movie, and _____.
   - a. so were we
   - b. we weren't either
   - c. neither were we

7. We like to ski, and _____.
   - a. so do our children
   - b. neither do our children
   - c. our children don't either

8. Jack will be on vacation next week, and _____.
   - a. Kate will too
   - b. Kate does too
   - c. so will Kate

PRACTICE

9 Complete each sentence with *and, or, so,* or *but* and a phrase or clause from the box. Add a comma if necessary.

learn to play it	go for a walk
~~the day after~~	she is free tonight
she doesn't like roses	the tickets are very expensive
I'm not hungry	a sleeping bag

1. Luisa is arriving tomorrow _or the day after_____.

2. Usha likes most flowers _____.

3. I had lunch an hour ago _____.

4. I'm going to buy a guitar _____.

5. The zoo is wonderful _____.

6. Before we go camping, I need to buy a tent _____.

7. Do you want to play tennis _____?

8. Lily has finished her project _____.

10 Replace the bold word in each sentence with *either, neither, so,* or *too.* Do not change the meaning of the sentence. Make any other necessary changes.

1. I've never had a garden, and **neither** has my brother.

   I've never had a garden, and _my brother hasn't either_____.

2. Uncle Steve likes working in the garden, and **so** does Aunt Jill.

   Uncle Steve likes working in the garden, and _____.

3. The yellow flowers aren't expensive, and the red ones aren't **either**.

   The yellow flowers aren't expensive, and _____.

4. I've read the article about plants, and Jane has **too**.

   I've read the article about plants, and _____.

5. Bill's not going to the lecture, and **neither** am I.

   Bill's not going to the lecture, and _____.

6. Chan doesn't like loud music, and his brother doesn't **either**.

   Chan doesn't like loud music, and _____.

7. The children enjoy baseball, and **so** do their parents.

   The children enjoy baseball, and _____.

8. I'll have time to help you, and Sally will **too**.

   I'll have time to help you, and _____.

11   **EDIT.** Read the fact file about the saguaro cactus. Find and correct seven more errors with conjunctions and *too, so, either,* and *neither.*

Fact File: The Saguaro Cactus

- Saguaros can reach a height of over 40 feet (12.2 meters), ~~so~~ *but* in their first ten years they only grow around one inch (2.54 cm).

- The fruit of the saguaro is red, so it contains around 2000 seeds. It is very tasty, but it is popular with local people.

- Saguaros grow arms, but they have room for a lot of flowers and fruit. This gives them a better chance to reproduce.

- The largest known saguaro is in Maricopa County, Arizona, in the United States. It is 45.3 feet (13.8 m) tall and 10 feet (3.1 m) wide.

- Saguaros live in the desert. There are hardly any rivers there, and it doesn't rain much neither. When it rains, saguaros store the rainwater inside their stems.

- Old western movies show saguaros in Texas and New Mexico, but Texas does not have any saguaros, and New Mexico does either.

- The saguaro used to provide both food or shelter for Native Americans.

- Bats help spread saguaro seeds, and birds do so.

▼ The saguaro is a type of cactus plant that grows in the Sonoran Desert of California, Arizona, and Mexico.

12 LISTEN & WRITE.

CD3-03

A Listen to a podcast about giant redwood trees. As you listen, circle the correct information.

1. a. Most of the world's giant redwoods are in **California** / **Montana.**

   b. Redwood trees also grow in **Iowa** / **Oregon.**

2. a. They grow to **379 feet** / **179 feet** tall.

   b. They can have a circumference of **26 feet** / **36 feet.**

3. a. Their leaves are **long** / **short**.

   b. Their leaves are **curved** / **flat**.

4. a. Their roots are **deep** / **shallow**.

   b. Their roots are very **weak** / **strong**.

5. a. The **tallest** / **shortest** trees are in deep valleys.

   b. The **youngest** / **oldest** trees are in deep valleys.

▼ People walking through a giant redwood tree tunnel, California, USA

B In your notebook, write five sentences about giant redwoods. Use the information from exercise **A** and the conjunctions from this lesson.

The giant redwood is found in California, and so are other types of redwoods.

C Work with a partner. Compare your sentences from exercise **B**.

13 APPLY.

A Complete each sentence with your own ideas.

1. I need to talk to my friend, but _I don't know where she is_____.

2. Do you want to go to the movies or _____?

3. I've packed my suitcase, so _____.

4. My new neighborhood is great! There are a lot of good restaurants and _____.

5. I left work early, so _____.

6. We can go to the pool or _____.

7. My car is not very fast, but _____.

8. The children finished their homework quickly, so _____.

B Work with a partner. Share your sentences from exercise **A**.

EXPLORE

1 **READ** the article about a volcano in Africa. Notice the words in **bold**.

Volcano Watching

Although Mount Nyiragongo in the Democratic Republic of the Congo looks beautiful, it is very dangerous. It is dangerous **because it is an active volcano**. It erupted[1] in 1977 and again in 2002. In 2002, 147 people died because of the eruption.

Scientists are studying Mount Nyiragongo very closely. They want to know when it will erupt again. This information is very important **since nearly a million people live nearby in the city of Goma**.

Ken Sims is a scientist who studies volcanoes. **Even though it was very dangerous**, in 2010 Sims and his team climbed down into the crater[2] of Mount Nyiragongo. Sims made this journey **because he wanted to collect new lava from the volcano**. New lava tells us more about the volcano than old lava. Sims hopes that the lava he collected will help predict the next eruption.

[1] **erupt:** explode
[2] **crater:** a large hole in the ground or in the top of a volcano

▼ View of lava from Nyiragongo Volcano, Democratic Republic of the Congo, Africa.

▲ A lava lake in the crater of Mount Nyiragongo

2 CHECK. Write a short answer for each question.

1. Why is Mount Nyiragongo dangerous?_____

2. Why are scientists studying Mount Nyiragongo very closely? _____

3. Who is Ken Sims? _____

4. What did Ken Sims do in 2010? _____

5. What can new lava help Ken Sims do? _____

3 DISCOVER. Complete the exercises to learn about the grammar in this lesson.

A Find these sentences in the article from exercise **1**. Write the missing words.

1. _____ Mount Nyiragongo in the Democratic Republic of the Congo looks
    beautiful, it is very dangerous.

2. This information is very important _____ nearly a million people live nearby in
    the city of Goma.

3. _____ it was very dangerous, in 2010 Sims and his team climbed down into the
    crater of Mount Nyiragongo.

4. Sims made this journey _____ he wanted to collect new lava from the volcano.

B Look at the words you wrote in exercise **A**. Then answer the questions.

1. Which words are used to introduce a contrast?

    _____ and _____

2. Which words are used to introduce a reason?

    _____ and _____

LEARN

9.3 Adverb Clauses: Cause

We got lost **because it was dark**.	
Main Clause — Adverb Clause	
Since it was raining hard, **we stayed home**.	
Adverb Clause — Main Clause	

1. An adverb clause shows a relationship, such as cause, time, or condition. It begins with a conjunction, such as *because*, *when*, or *if*.	**Since the weather was nice**, we went to the park. Adverb Clause (Cause) She's going to call us **when her train arrives**. Adverb Clause (Time) **If it's nice on Saturday**, we'll have a picnic. Adverb Clause (Condition)
2. Adverb clauses are dependent clauses. They cannot stand alone as complete sentences. Do not use an adverb clause without a main clause.	✓ I opened the window **because it was hot**. Main Clause — Adverb Clause ✗ Because it was hot.
3. An adverb clause of cause begins with the conjunction *because* or *since*. It tells why an action or event happened (its cause). The main clause tells the result.	I stayed home **because it was raining**. Result — Cause **Since it was raining**, I stayed home. Cause — Result
4. **Remember:** An adverb clause can come before or after the main clause. Use a comma when the adverb clause comes at the beginning of the sentence.	**Because I didn't know the answer**, I asked Meg. **Since the train was late**, we took a taxi.

4 Look at the underlined clauses in each sentence. Label each clause **C** for *cause* or **R** for *result*.

                           C   R

1. Since Mount Nyiragongo is so close, the city of Goma is in danger.

2. Scientists study volcanoes because they want to predict their eruptions.

3. The people of Goma are worried since there was a lot of damage after the last eruption.

4. Because some volcanoes don't erupt often, people don't worry about them.

5. Since volcanoes are so interesting, I like to read about them.

6. The film about volcanoes was popular because it had wonderful photography.

7. Since I'm afraid of volcanoes, I don't go near them.

8. Lava is dangerous because it is extremely hot.

5 Combine the sentences with the conjunction in parentheses. Do not change the order of the information. Add a comma if necessary.

1. There are around 1900 active volcanoes on Earth. It is important to study them. (since)

    Since there are around 1900 active volcanoes on Earth, it is important to study them.

2. My friend and I were in Sicily. We saw Mount Etna. (since)

3. Mount Etna is interesting. It erupts frequently. (because)

4. It was a hot day. We wore shorts and t-shirts. (because)

5. The volcano was very high. We didn't climb to the top. (because)

6. We had a wonderful view. It was a clear day. (because)

7. We climbed for several hours. We were very tired. (since)

8. My friend was excited. He found some lava. (because)

9.4   Adverb Clauses: Contrast

We took a walk **even though it was raining**.
— Main Clause — — Adverb Clause —

I like that restaurant **although it is quite expensive**.
— Main Clause — — Adverb Clause —

1. An adverb clause of contrast begins with the conjunctions *although* or *even though*. It introduces a contrast that is often surprising. The surprising information is in the main clause.	**Although golf is a popular sport**, I don't like it. — Adverb Clause — — Main Clause — I went swimming **even though the water was very cold**. — Main Clause — — Adverb Clause —
2. **Remember:** An adverb clause can come before or after the main clause. Use a comma when the adverb clause comes at the beginning of a sentence.	**Even though I was sick**, I went to work. **Although I wanted to go out**, I stayed home last night.

6 Combine the sentences using *although* or *even though*. Put the surprising information in the main clause. Add a comma if necessary.

1. The lava was hot. The scientist picked it up.

   Even though _the lava was hot, the scientist picked it up_ _____.

2. Erica looked everywhere. She couldn't find her book.

   Even though _____.

3. I am tired. I'm going to go to the gym.

   Although _____.

4. The book was useful. It was very old.

   even though _____.

5. Marsha likes her new apartment. It's very small.

   even though _____.

6. I went to bed early last night. I'm tired today.

   Although _____.

7. Mark didn't pass his math test. He studied hard.

   even though _____.

8. The movie was exciting. A lot of people left early.

   Although _____.

PRACTICE

7 Match the beginning of each sentence in Column A with the correct ending in Column B.

Column A

1. I visited Australia **because** _g_

2. We went on a hike **even though** ____

3. **Although** Nanette brought her camera, ____

4. **Since** the river is so fast, ____

5. Joe returned from vacation early **because** ____

6. **Although** the restaurant is famous, ____

7. I didn't finish the book **even though** ____

8. **Because** it was raining, ____

Column B

a. we were tired.

b. it's a dangerous place to swim.

c. it wasn't very long.

d. we didn't enjoy our walk.

e. the food isn't expensive.

f. he was sick.

g. my favorite cousin lives there.

h. she didn't take any photos.

8 Circle the correct conjunction to complete each sentence.

1. Keiko went to Brazil (because) / **even though** she wanted to see the Amazon rainforest.

2. **Although** / **Because** it wasn't dark in the rainforest, she couldn't see very well.

3. **Since** / **Even though** the desert is so hot and dry, not many people live there.

4. Alex went for a long walk **since** / **although** it was a beautiful day.

5. A lot of people were swimming in the lake **although** / **because** the water looked dirty.

6. **Since** / **Even though** it's warm and sunny, there are a lot of people at the beach today.

7. **Because** / **Even though** city parks are popular, they're usually crowded.

8. People like to go to city parks **although** / **since** they are easy to get to.

9 Combine each pair of sentences into one sentence with *since/because* or *although/even though*. Do not change the order of the ideas. Add a comma if necessary.

1. Marie wants to move to another city. She likes her hometown.

   Marie wants to move to another city although/even though she likes
   her hometown.

2. Dana likes her hometown. She wants to stay there for the rest of her life.

   _____

   _____

3. Miguel is good at basketball. He is tall and fast.

   _____

   _____

4. Alan is not very fast. He is good at basketball.

   _____

   _____

5. I studied math in college. It wasn't my best subject in high school.

   _____

   _____

6. My sister enjoyed history in high school. She decided to study it in college.

   _____

   _____

7. The children didn't eat much at the party. They didn't like the food.

_____

_____

8. Lin liked the food at the party. She didn't eat very much.

_____

_____

10 WRITE & SPEAK. Complete the sentences with your own ideas. Then share your sentences with a partner.

1. Many people like the ocean because _____.

2. Although the mountain was high, _____.

3. Since volcanoes can be dangerous, _____.

4. Computers are useful although _____.

5. Even though _____, I _____.

6. Because _____, my family _____.

7. My friend likes _____ because _____.

8. I don't like _____ although _____.

▼ The Sahara Desert

11 LISTEN & SPEAK.

CD3-05

A Listen to part of a lecture about the Sahara Desert and its relationship to the Amazon rainforest. Choose the correct information to complete each statement.

1. People don't connect the Sahara with the Amazon since the two places _____.

   a. have different climates   b. are a long way from each other

2. Sand contains minerals because it _____.

   a. comes from rocks   b. is in the desert

3. The Amazon needs lot of minerals since _____ there.

   a. it rains a lot   b. there are many plants

4. Sand travels from Africa to the Amazon because _____.

   a. the plants need it   b. that is the usual direction of the wind

5. The Sahara is helping new life to grow even though _____.

   a. it does not have many plants of its own   b. it is a very old desert

B Work with a partner. Tell your partner three things about the Sahara and the Amazon. Use the information from the lecture in exercise **A** and your own knowledge. Use *since, because, even though*, and *although*.

There are very few plants in the Sahara because it is so dry.

12 APPLY.

A Look at the notes about Manuel's favorite natural place. Then think about a natural place you have visited, such as a beach, a mountain, or a lake. Write notes about it in the chart.

Manuel's Favorite Beach	My Favorite _____
empty before 10:00 a.m.	
huge waves	
no restaurants or stores	
noisy in the afternoon	
people play games	
beautiful sunsets	

B In your notebook, write five sentences about the natural place you chose. Use your notes from exercise **A**. Use *because, since, although*, and *even though* to combine your ideas.

I usually go to the beach early because it is empty before 10:00 a.m.

Although the beach is popular, there aren't any restaurants or stores.

C Work with a partner. Share your sentences from exercise **B**. Ask follow-up questions to learn more about your partner's favorite natural place.

A: *Many people go to the beach to surf because there are huge waves.*

B: *Do you like to swim at the beach even though there are huge waves?*

EXPLORE

CD3-06

1 READ the article about the effects of noise on dolphins and whales. Notice the words in **bold**.

The Sounds of the Sea

Whales and dolphins use sound to locate food, find their way through the dark oceans, and communicate. Sometimes, however, human noise interferes with the sounds that whales and dolphins make. The result can be very harmful to these animals.

Underwater, sounds are louder and travel farther. Scientists believe that even distant noise from human activities can disturb dolphins and whales. This noise can come from ships, submarines,[1] and the equipment that is used to search for oil and gas. Underwater noise causes whales to increase how loudly they communicate. However, **if the underwater noise gets too loud, whales and dolphins will stop communicating.**

If dolphins and whales stop communicating, important information will be lost. For example, a dolphin that finds food won't be able to tell other dolphins. Mother whales will lose contact with their babies. Animals may die on the shore instead of finding their way across the sea.

What can we do to protect dolphins and whales? We can try to create less noise. Ships and submarines can avoid areas with a large number of these animals. Scientists also believe that a "curtain" of bubbles[2] around industrial sites will reduce noise underwater. **If we do nothing, dolphins and whales will suffer.**

[1] **submarine:** a kind of ship that can travel underwater
[2] **bubble:** a small ball of air found in a liquid

▲ Dolphins swimming off the coast of the Bahamas

2 **CHECK.** Read the statements. Circle **T** for *true* or **F** for *false*.

1. Whales and dolphins depend on sound for communication.   **T**   **F**

2. Ships cause problems for dolphins.   **T**   **F**

3. When dolphins can't hear, they can find their way correctly.   **T**   **F**

4. Mother whales don't need to be in contact with their babies.   **T**   **F**

5. Curtains of bubbles will make more underwater noise.   **T**   **F**

3 **DISCOVER.** Complete the exercises to learn about the grammar in this lesson.

A Find these sentences in the article from exercise **1**. Write the missing words.

1. However, if the underwater noise _____ too loud, whales and dolphins
   _____ communicating.

2. If dolphins and whales _____ communicating, important information
   _____ lost.

3. If we _____ nothing, dolphins and whales _____ suffer.

B Look at the words you wrote in exercise **A**. Then circle the correct answer to complete the statement. Discuss your answer with your classmates and teacher.

Will is used in _____.   a. clauses that begin with *if*   b. main clauses

LEARN

9.5 Adverb Clauses: Future Conditional

If you study hard, you'll pass the test.
— Adverb Clause — — Main Clause —

If she doesn't pass the course, she won't come back next year.
— Adverb Clause — — Main Clause —

1. A future conditional sentence includes an adverb clause of condition or *If*- clause and a main clause. The *If*- clause tells the possible condition. The main clause tells the result.	**If I go tomorrow,** I'll call you. — Adverb Clause — — Main Clause — (Possible Condition) (Result)
2. In a future conditional sentence, use the simple present in the *If*- clause. Use *will* or a form of *be going to* in the main clause.	If you **need** a ride, I **will drive** you. They **won't wait** if you **are** late. If you **don't leave** soon, you're **going to miss** the train.
3. Use a comma when an *If*- clause comes at the beginning of the sentence.	**If she wants to go,** we'll wait for her.

4 Circle the correct form of the verb(s) to complete each sentence.

1. If a dolphin **will find** / **finds** food, it will call other dolphins.

2. If humans **will make** / **make** a lot of noise, whales and dolphins will lose contact with each other.

3. Dolphins and whales **continue** / **will continue** to have problems if we don't do anything to help them.

4. If scientists **don't** / **won't** find a solution to the problem, the situation will get worse.

5. If you **watch** / **will watch** that documentary, you **learn** / **will learn** a lot about dolphins.

6. We **will be** / **are** late for class if we **aren't going to leave** / **don't leave** now.

7. Carol **gets** / **will get** good grades if she **keeps** / **will keep** working hard.

8. Tony **will help** / **helps** me with my assignment this weekend if he **will have** / **has** time.

5 Complete each sentence with the simple present or a future form of the verbs in parentheses.

1. If I _____go_____ (go) on the boat trip, I _____will bring_____ (bring) my new camera.

2. If you _____ (have) trouble with your homework, I _____ (help) you.

3. If it _____ (snow) a lot tonight, we _____ (not have) class tomorrow.

4. If the bank _____ (not call) me back, I _____ (be) angry.

5. If she _____ (go) to Singapore, she _____ (stay) with her cousin.

6. You _____ (miss) the bus if you _____ (not hurry).

7. If the tickets _____ (be) too expensive, I _____ (not go) to the concert.

8. If you _____ (want) to go downtown, I _____ (drive) you.

6 SPEAK. Work with a partner. Take turns completing the sentences.

1. If we have a lot of homework, . . .

2. If I pass this class, . . .

3. If it's sunny tomorrow, . . .

4. If I go to Rome, . . .

5. If I get up early tomorrow, . . .

6. If I call my family tonight, . . .

7. If you lend me twenty dollars, . . .

8. If we study together, . . .

If we have a lot of homework, I won't go out with my friends tonight.

9.6 Adverb Clauses: *If* and *When*

If we see a bear, I'll be scared.
  Adverb Clause   Main Clause

When they go hiking tomorrow, they'll take a lot of pictures.
        Adverb Clause   Main Clause

1. Use *if* in an adverb clause to talk about situations or events you think are possible, but you are not certain about.	**If dinner costs more than $50,** I'll pay with my credit card.
2. Use *when* in an adverb clause to talk about situations or events you are certain will happen.	**When the semester ends,** I will go to Miami.
3. **Remember:** Use a comma when an *If-* or *When-* clause comes at the beginning of the sentence.	**When I go to the grocery store,** I'll get some coffee.

7 Read each sentence. Does it describe a situation or event in the future that is certain or not certain? Complete the second sentence with an *if-* or *when-* clause. Add a comma if necessary.

1. Maybe the dolphin will swim too close to the shore.

    If the dolphin swims too close to the shore, it will have problems.

2. Maybe the whale will come near the boat.

    _____ we'll get some great photos.

3. I'm going to see Ray.

   _____ I'll show him the photos from our trip.

4. Maybe Noor will leave her job.

   I'll be surprised _____.

5. My parents are going to go to Paris.

   My parents are going to visit the Eiffel Tower _____.

6. The lecture is going to end soon.

   _____ I'll try to talk to the professor.

7. Maybe it will rain tomorrow.

   _____ we won't go hiking.

8. My brother is going to graduate.

   _____ he's going to work for my uncle.

PRACTICE

8 Complete the conversation using the words in parentheses. Add *if* or *when*. Then listen and check your answers.

Ivan: (1) _____ (I / not work) late tomorrow night, my wife and I are going to go see a movie. What are you doing this weekend?

Meg: My sister Carla is coming for a visit. (2) _____ (the weather / be) good, we're going to go hiking. (3) _____ (it / not be) good, we'll go shopping downtown.

Ivan: The weather report said it's going to be sunny all weekend.

Meg: Great! We'll go hiking, then!

Ivan: (4) _____ (you / get) out in the woods, you'll see a lot of wildlife, I'm sure. I always see interesting wildlife when I go hiking around here.

Meg: I know. I saw a lot of deer when I was hiking last weekend. I really hope we see some deer this weekend. Carla will be so excited (5) _____ (we / do). She loves deer.

Ivan: Really? Does she like bears, too? I hear there are a lot of bears around this year!

Meg: Bears? That sounds dangerous.

Ivan: Don't worry. (6) _____ (you / see) a bear, it probably won't come near you. In fact, (7) _____ (you / make) a lot of noise, it will probably run away.

Meg: Well, (8) _____ (we / go) hiking, we'll try to make a lot of noise, then!

9 WRITE & SPEAK.

A Read each statement. Then complete the second statement with an *If-* or *When-* clause. Add a comma if necessary.

1. Maybe there will be a storm tonight.

   If there is a storm tonight, _____ we're going to stay home.

2. It's possible that I'll miss two weeks of class.

   _____ I won't get a good grade.

3. My friend is going to arrive tonight.

   _____ I'll start cooking dinner.

4. Maybe I'll get a new job.

   I'll probably make more money _____.

5. You'll see me at the party tomorrow.

   I'll tell you all about my vacation _____.

6. I'll probably miss the train.

   I'll be late for my appointment _____.

7. My foot will probably still hurt tomorrow.

   _____ I won't play in the game.

8. The store is going to open in five minutes.

   _____ I'm going to buy a carton of milk.

9. I'm going to get home later.

   _____ I'm going to watch the news.

10. Maybe it will snow this afternoon.

    _____ our office will close early.

B Work with a partner. Compare your answers from exercise **A**. Then take turns completing the sentences with your own ideas. Use *if-* and *when-* clauses.

A: *If there's a good show on TV tonight, we're going to stay home.*

B: *If we're tired tonight, we're going to stay home.*

10 **EDIT.** Read the excerpt from an interview about the Sundarbans in Bangladesh and India. Find and correct five more errors with adverb clauses.

The Sundarbans

Jean: Today, I'm talking to Dr. Ruth Lowe, an expert on the Sundarbans region of Bangladesh and India. Dr. Lowe, if you ~~will be~~ *are* ready, we'll start the interview now. Can you explain why the Sundarbans are so important?

Dr. Lowe: Of course, Jean. First, the mangrove forests of the Sundarbans are home to wildlife such as the Bengal tiger. These forests also protect the region from serious storms that hit the coast every year. If the forests will disappear, millions of people will be in danger. Unfortunately, people are harming the Sundarbans. If they do not stop, they are in serious danger.

Jean: What exactly will happen if the mangroves will continue to disappear?

Dr. Lowe: Well, when people don't stop destroying the mangroves, the Sundarbans won't be able to protect towns and cities on the coast from storms. If the storms will hit these places, there will be a lot of damage, and people's lives will be at risk.

Jean: That sounds like a real problem.

Dr. Lowe: Well, yes, it really is . . .

◀ A Bengal Tiger in the mangrove forests of the Sundarbans

11 APPLY.

A Think about your future. What are some things you know will happen? What are some things you think will happen but are not certain about? Complete the chart with your ideas.

Things I Know Will Happen	Things I Think Will Happen
watch the hockey game on TV	go to Japan

B Write six sentences about your future using your notes from exercise **A**. Use adverb clauses with *if* and *when*.

If I have enough money this year, I'll go to Japan.

When I get home tonight, I'm going to watch the hockey game on TV.

_____

_____

_____

_____

_____

_____

C Work with a partner. Share your sentences from exercise **B**. Ask your partner follow-up questions for more information.

A: *If I save enough money this year, I'll go to Japan.*

B: *Interesting. Where do you want to go in Japan?*

Charts
9.1, 9.5, 9.6

🎧
CD3-08

1 Complete the conversation with the conjunctions in the box. You will need to use some conjunctions more than once. Then listen and check your answers.

| and | if | or | so | when |

Andy: Do you want to take the afternoon off (1) _____ *and* _____ go to the beach? It's a beautiful day, (2) _____ the beach is never crowded on Tuesdays.

Kerim: I'd like to come with you, (3) _____ I don't know if I can. I need to finish my science assignment. What time are you going?

Andy: It takes an hour to get there, (4) _____ I'm going to leave here at about one o'clock.

Kerim: OK. (5) _____ I work for a few hours now, I think I'll be able to finish it by then.

Andy: OK, great! I'll make some sandwiches for us. Do you want cheese (6) _____ turkey?

Kerim: Cheese, please! I'll call you (7) _____ I'm ready.

Andy: Take your time. We'll leave (8) _____ you finish.

Charts
9.2–9.4

2 Rewrite each sentence using the word(s) in parentheses. Do not change the meaning of the sentence. Make any other necessary changes.

1. John's flight was delayed, so he was upset. (because)

   John was upset because his flight was delayed.

2. My parents are going on vacation, and I am too. (so)

   _____

3. Lin didn't pass the exam, and neither did Brian. (either)

   _____

4. It was Anne's birthday, but she didn't go out. (even though)

   _____

5. Patricia enjoyed the trip, and so did her sister. (too)

   _____

6. I have a few days off, so I'm going to visit my uncle. (since)

   _____

7. Boris was sick, but he still went to work. (although)

   _____

8. Jane didn't go to the party, and Danny didn't either. (neither)

   _____

3 **EDIT.** Read the facts about lightning. Find and correct five more errors with adverb clauses and conjunctions. Sometimes there is more than one way to correct an error.

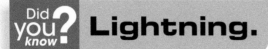

Lightning.

1. We do not see most lightning ~~even though~~ *because/since* it happens inside clouds.

2. Lightning usually strikes near the center of a storm, because it can also strike far from the center.

3. Rubber shoes do not protect people from lightning, and so do small buildings.

4. Lightning can travel through wires, although it's dangerous to use electrical equipment during a storm.

5. Lightning doesn't just happen during thunderstorms. People have seen lightning during forest fires, snowstorms, but volcanic eruptions.

6. Many people believe that lightning never strikes in the same place twice, so that is not true. Keep away from places that attract lightning.

4 **LISTEN, WRITE & SPEAK.**

CD3-09

A Read the statements in the chart. Then listen to two students discuss the differences between gorillas and chimpanzees. Decide if each statement is true for gorillas, chimpanzees, both, or neither. Put a check (✓) in the correct column.

	Gorillas	Chimpanzees	Both	Neither
1. They live in Africa.				
2. They have tails.				
3. They are intelligent.				
4. They eat meat.				
5. They are strong.				
6. They can be aggressive.				
7. They behave in a funny way.				

B In your notebook, write five sentences about gorillas and chimpanzees. Use the information from the chart in exercise **A** and conjunctions from this unit. Then work with a partner and compare your answers.

Gorillas live in Africa, and chimpanzees do too.

Connect the Grammar to Writing

1 READ & NOTICE THE GRAMMAR.

A How does your environment affect you? Work with a partner and discuss some of the things in your environment that affect your lives, such as storms, fires, or pollution. Then read the text.

Noise Pollution

Since we can't see, smell, or touch noise pollution, many of us don't notice it. People that do notice it think it's annoying, but they don't worry too much about it. However, noise pollution is all around us, and it sometimes causes some very serious problems.

Many things that we see every day cause noise pollution. Trucks, motorcycles, airplanes, loud machines, and power tools all make a lot of noise. Even music is noise pollution when people play it very loudly.

Noise pollution can cause a number of health problems. For example, it can lead to hearing loss. It can also lead to sleep problems. Near airports, people often wake up at night because the planes are so loud. They don't sleep enough, so they get sick more easily. Noise pollution also makes people feel stressed. Stress makes it difficult for them to concentrate, so they can't do their work very well. For example, if a child goes to a noisy school, he or she will probably get lower grades than a child in a quiet school.

These are just some of the ways that noise pollution affects our daily lives.

GRAMMAR FOCUS

In the text in exercise **A**, the writer uses *and* to connect information that is similar, and *so* to show a result.

> *Trucks, motorcycles, airplanes, loud machines, **and** power tools all make a lot of noise.*
> *They don't sleep enough, **so** they get sick more easily.*

The writer uses adverb clauses with *because* and *since* to show cause and effect relationships.

> ***Since** we can't see, smell, or touch noise pollution, many of us don't notice it.*
> *Near airports, people often wake up at night **because** the planes are so loud.*

B Read the text in exercise **A** again. Circle the conjunctions *and* and *so*, and underline the adverb clauses with *because* and *since*. Then work with a partner and compare your answers.

C In exercise **A**, the writer describes a situation in his environment that affects him and other people. He describes the causes of that situation and its results, or effects. Complete the chart on page **261** with causes and effects of noise pollution that the writer describes.

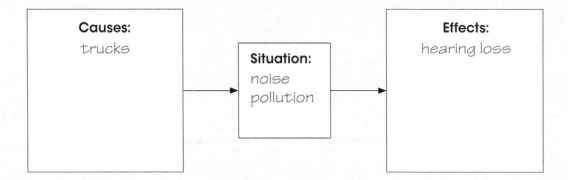

2 BEFORE YOU WRITE.

A Brainstorm a list of situations or events in your environment that affect you. Write a list of your ideas in your notebook.

B Choose one of your ideas from exercise **A** to write about. Think of the causes of this situation or event and its effects. Write notes in the chart. Use the chart from exercise **1C** as a model.

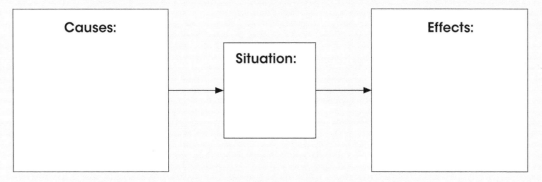

3 WRITE three paragraphs about your topic and its causes and effects. Use the notes from your chart in exercise **2B** and the article in exercise **1A** to help you.

WRITING FOCUS   Correcting Comma Splices

A comma splice is when two independent clauses are joined by a comma without a conjunction. To correct a comma splice, put a comma followed by a conjunction (such as *and*, *but*, or *so*) between the two independent clauses.

✗ Noise pollution is all around <u>us, it</u> sometimes causes some very serious problems.

      Independent Clause   Independent Clause

✓ Noise pollution is all around us, **and** it sometimes causes some very serious problems.

      Independent Clause   Independent Clause

---

4 SELF ASSESS. Read your text. Circle the conjunctions *and* and *so*, and underline the adverb clauses that show causes. Then use the checklist to assess your work.

☐   I used *and* to connect ideas and *so* to show results. [9.1]

☐   I used adverb phrases with *because* and *since* to show causes. [9.3]

☐   I used commas and conjunctions to join independent clauses to avoid comma splices. [WRITING FOCUS]

Gerunds and Infinitives

▲ A child plays on a water slide in Tucson, Arizona. Before water slides are open to the public, some people work testing them.

263

EXPLORE

CD3-10

1 READ the article about Jason deCaires Taylor. Notice the words in **bold**.

Jason deCaires Taylor

Combining work and play is not easy to do. However, British sculptor[1] Jason deCaires Taylor has succeeded **in doing** exactly that. As a child, Taylor often **went diving** for fun in Malaysia. He **enjoyed seeing** the beautiful colors of the coral reefs. He also **enjoyed swimming** with the fish that used the reefs as their home.

Over the years, more and more divers have visited coral reefs. The divers have sometimes damaged the reefs. **Saving coral reefs** became a passion of Taylor's. He has created underwater sculpture parks to draw[2] divers away from natural coral reefs. His sculptures also provided a base **for growing** new coral.

Taylor's largest work, *The Silent Evolution*, lies 30 feet (9 meters) under water near Isla Mujeres, Mexico. It consists of 400 life-size human figures. It took Taylor 18 months to create the statues. **Placing them** on the sea floor took another 120 hours. Before long, however, many different plants were growing on the figures, and Taylor's work was a success.

[1] **sculptor:** an artist who makes works of art from stone, wood, or metal
[2] **draw:** attract

▲ *The Silent Evolution*, Isla Mujeres, Mexico

2 CHECK. Read the statements. Circle **T** for *true* or **F** for *false*.

1. Taylor combines work and play.   **T**   **F**

2. Taylor went diving in Malaysia for work.   **T**   **F**

3. As a child, Taylor didn't like the ocean.   **T**   **F**

4. Taylor's sculptures helped the coral.   **T**   **F**

5. Taylor's sculpture, *The Silent Evolution*, is near Malaysia.   **T**   **F**

3 DISCOVER. Complete the exercises to learn about the grammar in this lesson.

A Find and complete these sentences in the article from exercise **1**. Write the missing words.

1. _____ work and play is not easy to do.

2. _____ coral reefs became a passion of Taylor's.

3. As a child, Taylor often went _____ for fun in Malaysia.

4. He enjoyed _____ the beautiful colors of the coral reefs.

5. His sculptures also provided a base for _____ new coral.

B Look at the sentences in exercise **A**. Then choose all of the possible correct answers to complete the statement.

In a statement, *-ing* forms can come _____ .

    a. before the main verb   b. after the main verb   c. after a preposition

LEARN

10.1 Gerunds as Subjects and Objects

Gerund as Subject		
Gerund	Verb	
Swimming	is	fun.
Not sleeping	was	difficult.

Gerund as Object		
Subject	Verb	Gerund
I	dislike	camping.
He	has stopped	working.

1. A gerund is the base form of a verb + -ing.* A gerund acts like a noun. It can be the subject or the object of a sentence.	Subject: **Running** is my favorite activity. Object: I enjoy **running**.
2. When a gerund or gerund phrase (gerund + object) is the subject of a sentence, the verb is always in the third-person singular.	✓ **Making new friends** takes time. ✗ **Making new friends** <u>take</u> time.
3. These are some common verbs that can be followed by gerunds:** avoid enjoy like consider finish mind dislike keep miss	They **avoided answering** the question. I **have finished washing** the dishes. We **miss seeing** you. What do you **enjoy doing** in your free time?
4. Put *not* before a gerund to make it negative.	We considered **not going** to the party.
5. *Go* + gerund is used in many expressions about activities. go camping go hiking go skiing go dancing go shopping go swimming	Did you **go running** today? Last week, I **went swimming** in the ocean. They **are going shopping** at the mall.

*See page **A1** for spelling rules for verbs ending in -ing.
See page **A5 for a longer list of verbs followed by gerunds.

4 Complete each sentence with the gerund form of the verb in parentheses.

1. Jason deCaires Taylor enjoys _____diving_____ (dive).

2. _____ (swim) around *The Silent Evolution* has become very popular.

3. We considered _____ (visit) Isla Mujeres.

4. Jerry enjoyed _____ (see) the underwater sculptures.

5. The divers avoided _____ (touch) the coral reefs.

6. _____ (take) photos underwater isn't easy.

7. We dislike _____ (go) to the beach when it's crowded.

8. I'm not in a hurry. I don't mind _____ (wait) for you.

5 WRITE & SPEAK. Complete the statements with a gerund. Use your own ideas. Then share your statements with a partner.

1. _____Skiing_____ is my favorite sport.

2. I enjoy _____ .

3. _____ is difficult.

4. I dislike _____ .

10.2 Gerunds as the Object of a Preposition

Preposition + Gerund		
We believe	**in working**	hard.
He has a good reason	**for missing**	class.
They are afraid	**of making**	a big mistake.

1. A gerund or gerund phrase can be the object of a preposition.	They're **excited about going** to Hawaii. He's **good at managing** people.
2. Gerunds are used after many noun + preposition combinations. Here are some common noun + preposition combinations: *choice between* *need for* *in danger of* *reason for*	They had a good **reason for being** late. We had a **choice between taking** the test on Monday or Tuesday.
3. Gerunds are used after many verb + preposition combinations. Here are some common verb + preposition combinations: *believe in* *succeed in* *dream about* *talk about* *feel like* *think about* *plan on* *worry about*	She **worries about finding** a job after college. Do you **feel like seeing** a movie tonight? I **succeeded in not looking at** my phone for two hours.
4. Gerunds are used in many adjective + preposition combinations. The verb *be* is usually used before the combination. Here are some common adjective + preposition combinations: *afraid of* *nervous about* *excited about* *sad about* *good at* *tired of* *interested in* *upset about*	Is she **sad about leaving**? I'm **nervous about giving** the presentation. I'm **tired of not feeling** well.
5. Use *by* + a gerund to tell how something is done.	I learned how to fix my bike **by watching** a video.

*See page **A5** for different patterns with gerunds.

6 Complete each sentence with the correct preposition and the gerund form of the verb in parentheses.

1. We planned _____*on seeing*_____ (see) the sights during our business trip.

2. Angela is interested _____ (take) a photography class after school.

3. I got good grades in college _____ (study) every night.

4. Mitchell is thinking _____ (go) to Montreal this summer.

5. My brother had to make a choice _____ (fix) his car or _____ (buy) a new one.

6. Nadine is very good _____ (solve) problems at work.

7. What was your reason _____ (leave) your job?

8. I'm tired _____ (study). Let's take a break.

9. Molly became a better tennis player _____ (practice) every day.

10. Steven likes swimming in pools, but he's afraid _____ (swim) in the ocean.

7 SPEAK. Work with a partner. Take turns completing the sentences with statements that are true about you. Use gerunds.

I feel like seeing a movie tonight.

1. I feel like . . .

2. I'm good at . . .

3. I'm not good at . . .

4. I'm afraid of . . .

5. I'm not interested in . . .

6. I'm interested in . . .

7. I worry about . . .

8. I often think about . . .

PRACTICE

8 Complete each person's story with the gerund form of the verbs in parentheses. Add a correct preposition when necessary. Then listen and check your answers.

CD3-11-13

Gail's Story

    Well, I had a choice (1) _between taking_ (take) a job at a bank in my hometown or

(2) _____ (become) a ski instructor. It was a very easy decision! I love

(3) _____ (ski), so (4) _____ (do) it as a job was a dream come true

for me. I enjoy (5) _____ (be) outdoors and (6) _____ (help) people.

I'm good (7) _____ (teach), too! I certainly don't miss (8) _____

(sit) in front of a computer all day. I feel really lucky. I've found the perfect job!

Nick's Story

    (9) _____ (find) a job isn't easy these days, but I finally found one. I work for

a sports website. I got the job (10) _____ (post) photos on the website. I'm

really good (11) _____ (take) action photos, and they needed a photographer.

When they saw my photos, they offered me the job immediately. I was very excited

(12) _____ (work) as a sports photographer, so of course I said yes. It's a fun

job. I really enjoy (13) _____ (get) up and (14) _____ (go) to work every day.

Miyoko's Story

    I'm really interested in (15) _____ (see) the world, so (16) _____

(leave) my teaching job to become a tour guide was a good choice for me. (17) _____

(travel) is stressful sometimes, so I make sure everything goes smoothly for my clients. It's such a

great job. I don't think I'll ever consider (18) _____ (go) back to teaching again!

9 READ, WRITE & SPEAK.

A Read the information and look at the chart. Then complete the statements with the correct information. Use gerunds.

> A large group of students between the ages of 11 and 16 answered the following question: *In a typical week, which of these activities are you most likely to do in your free time?* The chart gives information about their answers.

Free-Time Activities among 11- to 16-Year-Olds			
	All	**Girls**	**Boys**
Listen to music	87%	91%	83%
Watch TV/DVDs	87%	86%	87%
Go to a friend's house	84%	88%	81%
Text friends	75%	84%	66%
Talk on the phone	71%	83%	58%
Surf the Internet	68%	65%	71%
Go to the movies	66%	70%	62%
Play computer games	66%	45%	88%
Go shopping	64%	86%	41%
Read books or magazines	57%	67%	48%

Source: http://www.scotland.gov.uk/Publications/2005/09/02151404/14063   Poll figures: MORI

1. _Listening to music_____ is the most popular activity for girls.

2. _____ is 6 percent less popular among girls than it is among boys.

3. _____ is the least popular activity for boys.

4. _____ is 7 percent less popular among boys than it is among girls.

5. For all 11- to 16-year-olds, _____ (75%) is slightly more common than _____ (71%).

6. _____ is as popular as (87%) _____ for all students.

7. More 11- to 16-year-olds are interested in _____ (68%) than _____ (57%).

8. _____ is the most popular activity for boys and the least popular for girls.

B Work with a partner. Compare your answers from exercise **A**. Which statement in exercise **A** is the most interesting? Explain your answer to your partner.

10 LISTEN & SPEAK.

CD3-14

A Listen to eight people talk about their free-time activities. Take notes about each person's activities in your notebook.

CD3-14

B Complete each sentence with the gerund form of a verb you hear and other information about the speaker. Listen again if necessary. More than one correct answer is possible.

1. Elizabeth enjoys ___*going for a hike on weekends*_____ .

2. Frank is not interested in _____ .

3. Sandra doesn't mind _____ again.

4. Martin is apologizing for _____ party.

5. Roberto is afraid of _____ .

6. Lucia succeeded in _____ for a couple of hours.

7. _____ on the ship is Cindy's responsibility.

8. Sam can't think of a good reason _____ any longer.

C Work with a partner. Take turns making up more sentences about the people in exercises **A** and **B**. Use gerunds.

Elizabeth loves being outside in nature.

11 APPLY.

A Complete the questions with the words in parentheses. Add prepositions when necessary.

1. What have you ____*missed doing*_____ (miss / do) this year?

2. What have you _____ (stop / do) this year?

3. What are you _____ (interested / learn) to do?

4. What are you _____ (good / do)?

5. What are you _____ (terrible / do)?

6. What are you _____ (think / do) tonight?

7. What do you _____ (enjoy / do) on the weekends?

8. What is your main _____ (reason / take) English classes?

B Work with a partner. Ask and answer the questions from exercise **A**.

C In your notebook, write your own answers to the questions from exercise **A**.

I've missed seeing my friends this year.

EXPLORE

CD3-15

1 **READ** the article about Felix Baumgartner. Notice the words in **bold**.

The World's Highest Skydive

How **would** you **like to jump** out of a balloon way up in space? It sounds impossible, but Austrian skydiver Felix Baumgartner did exactly that! Baumgartner **wanted to become** a professional[1] skydiver from a very early age. He **learned to make** parachute[2] jumps and **started to skydive** when he was 16 years old. Baumgartner's goal was to set a record[3] for jumping from the highest altitude.[4] He also **hoped to become** the fastest skydiver of all time.

In 2012, Baumgartner got his chance. His childhood hero, the famous skydiver Joseph Kittinger, **helped** him **to prepare** for the historic jump. On October 14 of that year, Baumgartner flew a helium[5]-filled balloon to a height of 127,852 feet (about 24 miles, or 38.6 kilometers) above the surface of the Earth, and then jumped. On his trip back to Earth, Baumgartner **managed to reach** a record speed of 843.6 miles (1357.6 kilometers) per hour . . . faster than the speed of sound! After opening his parachute, the man known as "Fearless Felix" made a perfect landing on his feet, and lifted his arms in victory. His jump set new skydiving records for speed and distance.

Now Baumgartner **has decided to retire**. This will **allow** the next group of skydivers **to aim** for his records. He will soon **start using** his skills to help people in danger. He **plans to fly** rescue helicopters or **become** a firefighter.

[1] **professional:** doing something for pay rather than as a hobby
[2] **parachute:** a large, lightweight sheet attached to a falling person that unfolds in the wind and causes the person to fall slowly
[3] **record:** the best time, distance, speed, etc.
[4] **altitude:** distance above sea level
[5] **helium:** a gas that is lighter than air

▲ Felix Baumgartner jumps from a balloon 24 miles above Earth

2 CHECK. Choose the correct answer to complete each statement.

1. Felix Baumgartner became interested in skydiving _____.
   a. when he was very young
   b. after he learned to use a parachute
   c. as an adult

2. Baumgartner became a skydiver because _____.
   a. he wanted to learn new skills
   b. he wanted to set records
   c. he wanted to become famous

3. After Baumgartner landed, _____.
   a. he fell over
   b. he was very happy
   c. he became a professional skydiver

4. In the future, Baumgartner _____.
   a. won't skydive anymore
   b. doesn't know what he will do
   c. hopes to set more skydiving records

▲ Felix Baumgartner

3 DISCOVER. Complete the exercises to learn about the grammar in this lesson.

A Find these sentences in the article from exercise **1**. Write the missing words.

1. Baumgartner wanted _____ a professional skydiver from a very early age.

2. He learned _____ parachute jumps and started _____ when he was 16 years old.

3. He plans _____ rescue helicopters or become a firefighter.

B Look again at the sentences in exercise **A**. What words follow the main verbs *want, learn, start,* and *plan?* _____

LEARN

10.3 Verb + Infinitive

Subject	Verb	Infinitive	
I	learned	to speak	German.
They	wanted	to live	in Mexico.
We	need	to buy	a new computer.

1. An infinitive is the base form of the verb + *to*. An infinitive acts like a noun. It is often the object of a verb. Sometimes it is the subject of a sentence.

They decided **to take** the bus.
I want **to go** to the gym after work.

2. Certain verbs can be followed by an infinitive*:

agree	expect	need	refuse
appear	forget	plan	seem
ask	hope	pretend	want
decide	learn	promise	would like

She **hopes to visit Miami** soon.
He **seems to like** his new job.
I **forgot to call** Lucy.

3. Put *not* before an infinitive to make it negative.

She decided **not to go.**

4. *To* is usually not repeated when there is more than one infinitive in the sentence.

Farmers need **to wake up** early and **work** hard.

*See page **A6** for a longer list of verbs followed by an infinitive.

*See page **A6** for a longer list of verbs followed by an infinitive.

REAL ENGLISH

You can use *would you like* + infinitive to invite someone to do something.

Would you like to go to the movies?
Would you like to study together?

4 Put the words in the correct order to make sentences.

1. decided / the / jump / from / skydiver / to / space

   _____

2. wants / skydiving / brother / my / go / to

   _____

3. take / planning / is / Bruce / to / skydiving / class / a

   _____

4. seems / Shelly / sports / dangerous / love / to

   _____

5. not / pretended / be / to / Fred / about / nervous / skydiving

   _____

6. his / forgets / he / never / to / equipment / check

   _____

7. skydiving / friends / my / go / with / I / to / refused

_____

8. us / Kyle / stay / and / agreed / help / to

_____

10.4 Verb + Object + Infinitive

Subject	Verb	Object	Infinitive	
She	allowed	the children	to leave	early.
I	reminded	them	to arrive	on time.
They	will invite	their friends	to go	to the movies.

1. Some verbs are followed by an object + infinitive.* The object can be a noun or a pronoun. These verbs include:

advise	invite	teach
allow	order	tell
encourage	remind	warn

They don't **allow students to use** their phones.
We **invited our friends to go** to the movies.
I **told you not to be** late.

2. Some verbs can be followed by an infinitive or an object + infinitive, but the meaning is different. These verbs include:

ask	help	pay	want
expect	need	promise	would like

We **expect to be** there.
We **expect her to be** there.
We **want to come.**
We **want you to come.**

*See page **A6** for a list of verbs that can be followed by an infinitive or an object + infinitive.

5 Circle the correct words to complete each sentence. For some sentences, both choices are possible.

1. Jim and Marsha don't want (to do) / (their children to do) dangerous sports.

2. Our skiing instructor warned **not to go** / **us not to go** straight down the hill.

3. Ali's parents told **to come** / **him to come** home.

4. I would like **to stay** / **my sister to stay** a little longer.

5. The professor reminded **to finish** / **us to finish** our assignments by Thursday.

6. Irina would like **to paint** / **me to paint** the kitchen this weekend.

7. The police ordered **to leave** / **everyone to leave** the building.

8. The doctor has advised **to take** / **me to take** a few days off from work.

9. I expect **to be** / **you to be** on time for the lecture.

10. Do you allow **to borrow** / **your friends to borrow** your car?

11. This DVD teaches **to play / children to play** the piano.

12. They don't need **to wait / you to wait** any longer.

10.5 Verb + Gerund or Infinitive

Subject	Verb	Gerund	
I	started	driving	last year.
We	prefer	traveling	by train.

Subject	Verb	Infinitive	
I	started	to drive	last year.
We	prefer	to travel	by train.

1. Some verbs can be followed by a gerund or an infinitive.* Usually, there is no difference in meaning. These verbs include: *begin continue like prefer* *can't stand hate love start*	I **like to swim.** = I **like swimming.** They **love to dance.** = They **love dancing.**
2. Use *and* or *or* to connect two gerunds or two infinitives. You don't need to repeat *to* when you are connecting infinitives.	I like **swimming and playing** tennis. I prefer **to swim** or **play** tennis.
3. **Be careful!** Don't connect a gerund and an infinitive with *and* or *or*.	✓ She loves **cooking** and **traveling**. ✓ She loves **to cook** and **travel**. ✗ She loves <u>to cook and traveling</u>.

*See page **A6** for a list of verbs that can be followed by a gerund or an infinitive.

6 Complete each sentence with the infinitive or gerund form of the verb in parentheses. Use the gerund form for sentences 1–4. Use the infinitive form for sentences 5–8.

1. I like _____playing_____ (play) games.

2. I hate _____ (wait) in line.

3. I can't stand _____ (be) late for appointments.

4. I love _____ (give) parties and _____ (cook) meals for friends.

5. I've just started _____ (exercise).

6. This is a nice pool, but I prefer _____ (swim) in the ocean.

7. I began _____ (play) sports when I was very young.

8. I am going to continue _____ (live) where I am now for a long time.

7 SPEAK. Work with a partner. Student A reads a completed sentence from exercise **6**. Student B repeats the sentence using the alternative form, gerund or infinitive. Switch roles for each new item.

A: *I like playing games.*

B: *I like to play games.*

PRACTICE

8 Complete Lili's blog post with the gerund or infinitive form of the verbs in parentheses.

Lili's Blog | Welcome Mountain Lovers!
Enjoy! Share your adventures.

Sunday, March 28

I have always loved (1) _____to climb_____ (climb) mountains. I'd like
(2) _____ (visit) the Alps more often, but it's expensive. I plan
(3) _____ (go) back there as soon as I can. Last year, I went to
the Alps with my brothers. I always expect (4) _____ (have) a few
problems on the way up a mountain, but this time the weather was really bad. Halfway
up, we met some experienced climbers. They warned us (5) _____
(get) off the mountain as quickly as possible. My younger brother decided
(6) _____ (take) their advice. But my older brother is a very
experienced climber. Together we managed (7) _____ (reach) the top.

POSTED BY ERIK AT 10:56 PM

1 COMMENT:

Congratulations on (8) _____ (reach) the top.
I used to love climbing, but because of an illness, my doctor has advised me
(9) _____ (not continue) climbing mountains.
I will, however, continue (10) _____ (read) your blog!

---

9 PRONUNCIATION Read the box and listen to the examples. Then complete the exercises.

CD3-16

> | PRONUNCIATION | Infinitives |
> |---|---|
>
> In conversation, we usually pronounce the *to* of the infinitive as /tə/.
>
> **Examples:**
>
> We plan **to** visit California next year.
> Have you started **to** do your homework?

CD3-17

A Listen to the sentences and repeat.

1. I hope to take drum lessons in the fall.

2. I've started to learn kung-fu.

3. I've decided to quit running.

4. My parents like to dance.

5. He encouraged us to get there early.

6. I promised to buy all my friends ice cream.

7. I asked John to show us his new boat.

8. She told us to be quiet and finish our work.

B Complete the sentences with information about yourself. Then share your sentences with a partner. Practice pronouncing the *to* in the infinitive as /tə/.

1. I hope to _____.

2. I've started to _____.

3. I've decided to _____.

4. My parents like to _____.

5. Our teacher asked us to _____.

6. My friend invited me to _____.

CD3-18

10 LISTEN to Jenna talk to a friend about her trip to Australia. Complete the sentences about her story. Use the verbs in parentheses and the infinitive or gerund form of each verb you hear.

1. Jenna's brother ___*invited her to climb*___ (invite) down a slot canyon with him.

2. Jenna almost _____ (refuse) with her brother because she didn't have the right clothes.

3. Jenna _____ (love) at home in Colorado.

4. Jenna _____ (want) with her brother. That's really why she _____ (agree) the trip.

5. Jenna _____ (need) some climbing equipment from John's wife.

6. Jenna usually _____ (can't stand).

7. She _____ (not mind) down the slot canyon.

8. Jenna enjoyed the trip, but she still _____ (prefer).

11 WRITE & SPEAK.

A Complete the sentences with your own ideas. Use infinitives or gerunds as appropriate.

1. I hope *to learn how to skateboard someday* _____.

2. When it started to rain, I decided _____.

3. My parents taught me _____.

4. On weekends, I don't mind _____.

5. I often forget _____.

6. Next year, I'm going to continue _____.

7. I enjoy _____.

8. I like _____, but I prefer _____.

B Share your sentences from exercise **A** with a partner. Ask follow-up questions where possible.

A: *I hope to learn how to skateboard someday.*

B: *Is it very difficult?*

12 APPLY.

A Choose one of your interests or hobbies and write five or six sentences about it. Use either a gerund or an infinitive in each sentence.

Baking Cakes

I love baking cakes for special occasions.

Decorating cakes teaches you to be patient.

I hope to become a professional baker.

B Work with a partner. Share your sentences from exercise **A**. Ask follow-up questions for more information.

What type of cakes do you like to make?

EXPLORE

 CD3-19

1 READ the introduction and student presentation. Notice the words in **bold**.

Tiny Creatures in a Big Ocean

▲ Kakani Katija is a *National Geographic Society* Emerging Explorer.

Professor: Last week I gave you an assignment **to get** you thinking about your own future jobs. I asked you to research someone with an unusual job and gather **enough information to give** a presentation to the class. Yuri, would you like to go first?

Yuri: Sure. My hometown is **too far from the coast for me to go** there very often, but I've always loved the sea. That's why I chose a scientist who studies the oceans—Dr. Kakani Katija.

Dr. Katija researches the way warm and cold water mix and move in the oceans. She does this **to learn** more about the Earth's climate systems. The movement of water in the oceans has a big effect on our climate. So does the movement of living creatures, according to Dr. Katija.

A single whale is **too small to have** a big effect on the movement of water. However, millions of tiny creatures moving together in the same direction have **enough mass[1] to make** a difference. In fact, Dr. Katija believes that the movements of creatures in the ocean may influence our climate as much as the tides and wind do.

Dr. Katija's research provides important new reasons for protecting life in the oceans.

[1] **mass:** the amount of matter an object has

▼ A school of black-striped salema swimming together in the Pacific Ocean

2 **CHECK.** Choose the correct answer to complete each statement.

1. The professor gave this assignment because he wanted students _____.

   a. to learn about the ocean   b. to consider their futures

2. Yuri doesn't go to the coast often because _____.

   a. it isn't close to his home   b. he prefers to stay in town

3. Dr. Katija studies the oceans because she wants to understand _____.

   a. how the Earth's climate works   b. how sea creatures survive

4. _____ is very important to Dr Katija's research.

   a. The movement of single large creatures   b. The movement of small creatures

3 **DISCOVER.** Complete the exercises to learn about the grammar in this lesson.

A Look at the sentences based on the article from exercise **1**. Then answer the question that follows.

1. I gave you an assignment **to get** you thinking about your own future jobs.

2. She does this **to learn** more about the Earth's climate.

   What question does the infinitive answer in both sentences?

   a. What?   b. Why?   c. When?

B Look at the other bold phrases in the article. What verb form follows phrases with *too* and *enough*?

a. a gerund   b. an infinitive

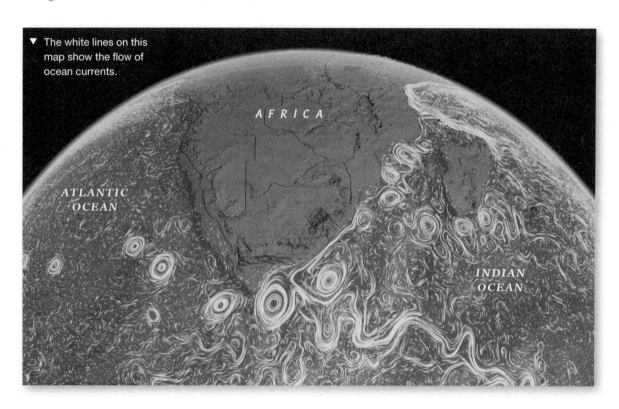

▼ The white lines on this map show the flow of ocean currents.

AFRICA

ATLANTIC
OCEAN

INDIAN
OCEAN

LEARN

10.6 Infinitives of Purpose

1. Use an infinitive to state a purpose or reason.	I went to the store **to buy** some food. (I went to the store because I wanted to buy some food.)
2. **Be careful!** Don't use *for* + an infinitive to state a purpose.	✓ She went online to find the information. ✗ She went online <u>for to find</u> the information.
3. We often use an infinitive in an incomplete sentence to answer questions with *Why*.	A: Why are you taking this class? B: **To learn** English.
4. **Remember:** *To* is usually not repeated when there is more than one infinitive in the sentence.	I use my phone **to talk** to people, **watch** videos, and **surf** the Internet.

4 Complete the sentences. Use infinitives of purpose.

1. The professor gave the assignment because he wanted to start a discussion about jobs.

   The professor gave the assignment ___to start a discussion about jobs___.

2. Yuri chose Dr. Katija because he wanted to show his interest in the ocean.

   Yuri chose Dr. Katija _____.

3. The scientist studies the oceans because she wants to understand climate systems.

   The scientist studies the oceans _____.

4. Dani went to the library because she wanted to do some research and finish her project.

   Dani went to the library _____.

5. Because he wanted to get a good grade, Jack studied all night.

   _____ Jack studied all night.

6. Louise used the Internet because she wanted to find some answers to her questions.

   Louise used the Internet _____.

7. Everyone worked hard on their assignments because they wanted to get good grades.

   Everyone worked hard on their assignments _____.

8. Some students stayed after class because they wanted to ask the professor questions.

   Some students stayed after class _____.

5 **SPEAK.** Work with a partner. Ask and answer *why* questions about the sentences in exercise **4**.

   A: *Why did the professor give the assignment?*

   B: *To start a discussion about jobs.*

10.7 *Too* + Infinitive

	Too	Adjective/ Adverb	For	Noun or Object Pronoun	Infinitive
Adjectives and Adverbs					
It's (not)		far		us	to walk.
It was (not)	too	difficult	for	Ken	to understand.
She's (not)		young			to drive.

	Too Much/ Too Many	Noun	For	Noun or Object Pronoun	Infinitive
Nouns					
There was	too much	noise		me	to study.
There are	too many	books	for	Alex	to carry.
I have	too much	work			to do.

1. Use *too* + infinitive in these patterns to tell why something is not possible.

   a. *too* + adjective/adverb + infinitive
   b. *too much* + non-count noun + infinitive
   c. *too many* + count noun + infinitive

   a. Jason is **too short to reach** the top shelf.
   b. I have **too much work to do** today.
   c. In New York, there are **too many museums to visit** in one day.

2. Use *for* + noun or object pronoun + infinitive to give information about "who."

   It's too dark **for me** to see.

6 Complete the sentences. Use *too, too much,* or *too many* and the words in parentheses. Add any other necessary words.

1. The businessman arrived _____too late to speak_____ (late / speak) at the meeting.

2. The report was _____ (long / read) while I was on the train.

3. Many doctors have _____ (patients / take) care of.

4. The secretary had _____ (work / finish) before the end of the day.

5. The taxi driver drove _____ (slowly / reach) the station in time.

6. Norman is _____ (experienced / make) a mistake like that.

7. Francine has _____ (e-mails / answer).

8. I have _____ (books / carry) in my backpack.

7 Complete the sentences. Use *too, too much,* or *too many* with the words in parentheses. Use infinitives. Add any other necessary words.

1. The teacher spoke ___too quickly for me to understand___ (quickly / me / understand).

2. The students have _____ (homework / the teacher / correct in one night).

3. My sister's job is _____ (work / one person / do).

4. A firefighter's job is _____ (dangerous / an inexperienced person / do).

5. The company received _____ (calls / the employees / answer).

6. A thousand dollars is _____ (money / John / spend) on a new camera.

7. Our teacher gave _____ (assignments / us / do) in one day.

8. This suitcase is _____ (old / me / take) on our trip.

10.8 *Enough* + Infinitive

Adjectives and Adverbs				
	Adjective/ Adverb	*Enough*	*For*	Noun or Object Pronoun	Infinitive
It's (not)	easy			students	to understand.
He spoke	loudly	enough	for	us	to hear.
It's (not)	cold				to snow.

Nouns				
	Enough	Noun	*For*	Noun or Object Pronoun	Infinitive
There was (not)	enough	time	for	me	to finish.
There is (not)		space			to exercise.

1. Use *enough* + infinitive in these patterns to tell why something is possible:
   a. adjective + *enough* + infinitive
   b. adverb + *enough* + infinitive
   c. *enough* + noun + infinitive

   a. I am **strong enough to lift** the heavy box.
   b. We will walk **quickly enough to arrive** on time.
   c. She has **enough talent to win** the contest.

2. **Remember!** Put *enough* after an adjective but before a noun.

   ✓ I'm **old enough to drive**.
   ✗ I'm <u>enough old</u> to drive.

   ✓ I have **enough money to buy** a car.
   ✗ I have <u>money enough</u> to buy a car.

3. Use *for* + a noun or object pronoun + infinitive to give information about "who."

   The TV screen is large enough **for everyone to see** it.

4. **Be careful!** Do not use *for* + infinitive.

   ✓ We don't have enough time **to eat** lunch before class.
   ✗ We don't have enough time <u>for to eat</u> lunch before class.

8 Complete the sentences. Use *enough* with the words in parentheses. Use an infinitive. Add any other necessary words.

1. This store hires ___enough salespeople to help___ (salespeople / help) its customers.

2. Tim didn't do _____ (well / get) the job.

3. We have _____ (staff / fill) the new orders.

4. The singer wasn't _____ (good / win) the competition.

5. Jun earns _____ (money / take) a vacation every year.

6. The children found the story _____ (easy / follow).

7. Do we have _____ (sugar / make) the cake?

8. The sofa was _____ (comfortable / sleep) on.

9 Complete the sentences. Use *enough* with the words in parentheses. Use an infinitive. Add any other necessary words.

1. The tour guide spoke _loudly enough for everyone to hear_ (loudly / everyone / hear).

2. There wasn't _____
   (time / me / finish) my report.

3. Maya's company is _____
   (small / everyone / know) each other.

4. The books weren't _____
   (light / him / carry).

5. My brother's house doesn't have _____
   (room / all of us / stay) overnight.

6. It was _____
   (warm / me / wear) shorts and a t-shirt yesterday.

7. The passengers boarded the airplane _____
   (quickly / the flight / leave) on time.

8. There weren't _____
   (books / every student / have) one.

PRACTICE

10 Complete the conversation with *enough, too, too much,* or *too many* and the words in parentheses. Use infinitives.

Anna: I applied for a job in Rome, so I need to improve my Italian. At the moment,
I make (1) _too many mistakes to work_ (mistakes / work) in Italy.

Caroline: Why don't you take an Italian class?

Anna: I am, actually, and I had my first class last night! It was tough! There was

(2) _____

(new vocabulary / me / remember). The teacher speaks quickly, but he is very clear.

It wasn't (3) _____ (fast /
me / follow). He says if he speaks (4) _____
(slowly / us / understand) every word, it won't be realistic.

Caroline: That's true. My sister and I used to get good grades in our high school German class,

but when we arrived in Berlin, everyone spoke

(5) _____ (fast / us / understand).

Luckily, we were there for a month, so we had

(6) _____ (time / get) used to it.

Anna: There are only five students in the class, though. I'm worried there may not be

(7) _____ (students / keep)

the class going.

Caroline: That's too bad. The subject is (8) _____
(interesting / attract) a lot of students!

11 LISTEN & SPEAK.

CD3-20

A Listen to each sentence. Then choose the sentence that has a similar meaning.

1. a. The computer is too expensive for us to buy.

    b. The computer is not too expensive for us to buy.

2. a. The police arrived quickly enough to catch the criminal.

    b. The police didn't arrive quickly enough to catch the criminal.

3. a. An hour was enough time for me to read the article.

    b. An hour wasn't enough time for me to read the article.

4. a. The text on this screen isn't big enough for me to read.

    b. The text on this screen is big enough for me to read.

5. a. The TV show wasn't on early enough for the children to watch.

    b. The TV show was on early enough for the children to watch.

6. a. The patient was too sick to have visitors.

    b. The patient wasn't too sick to have visitors.

7. a. Paul is too weak to run a marathon.

    b. Paul isn't too weak to run a marathon.

8. a. The video game wasn't easy enough for my little brother to play.

    b. The video game was easy enough for my little brother to play.

B Work with a partner. Take turns making up different ways to say the sentences in exercise **A**.
Try not to change the meaning. Use infinitives and different adjectives and nouns.

1. *We aren't rich enough to buy the computer.*

2. *The police arrived early enough to catch the criminals.*

12 EDIT. Read the article about langurs in India. Find and correct seven more errors with infinitives.

An Unusual Job for a Monkey

In the Great Indian Desert, it's too hot and dry for langur monkeys ˅to live comfortably all year round. That's why over 2000 of them come into the city of Jodhpur for to find something to eat. Local people like the langurs, so they bring food to sharing with the monkeys. It's enough easy for langurs to survive in the city, but it's not all fun and free food! Many of them have to work for a living . . . controlling other monkeys!

Langurs are welcome in Indian cities, but other kinds of monkeys aren't. There are too much of these monkeys to control, and they sometimes attack people to get food. Langurs scare other types of monkeys, so cities use them keep these monkeys away. In Delhi, for example, during a big sports event in 2010, 38 langurs patrolled[1] the streets, and the other monkeys were too much scared to stay in the area. The plan was successful enough for most people enjoying the event in peace.

▲ A langur is a type of monkey common in South Asia.

[1] **patrol:** make regular trips around an area to guard against trouble or crime

13 APPLY.

A Look at the notes in the chart about Lena's job. Then think of your job or the job of someone you know. In your notebook, make a chart like Lena's. What are the positive things about the job? What are the negative things? Write notes in your chart.

Lena's Job: Banker	
Positive Things	Negative Things
She makes enough money to take a vacation every year. The bank is close enough for her to walk to.	Her schedule is very busy. She often doesn't have enough time to eat lunch. She is usually too tired to go out with friends after work.

B In your notebook, write five or six sentences about the job you chose. Use your notes from exercise **A**. Use *too, enough*, and infinitives.

My job is too stressful. I often don't have enough time to finish all of my work.

C Work with a partner. Tell your partner about the job you chose.

Charts
10.1–10.6,
10.8

CD3-21

1 **LISTEN** to the conversation. Write the words you hear.

Milan: Sorry I've been too busy

(1) _____ together recently.

Amy: Yeah, you need (2) _____
more breaks!

Milan: I know. So, how is your hockey going?

Amy: Well, I'm getting better at

(3) _____ the puck,[1] but I still

don't skate very fast. The coach has advised

(4) _____ more training.

Milan: So, are you going to agree (5) _____ that?

Amy: Well, I don't mind (6) _____ hard, but I want to avoid

(7) _____ injured. I don't want (8) _____ my knee again.

It's still not (9) _____ for me to play at full speed.

Milan: Well, listen . . . I'm going to the park (10) _____ some exercise tomorrow

morning. Why don't you come along?

[1] **puck:** the small black disk that is used in hockey

Charts
10.1–10.3

2 Complete Nadia's blog entry about her job as a teacher. Use the gerund or the infinitive of
each verb in parentheses. In some cases you can use both forms.

I had a few different jobs in mind when I was young. I thought about

(1) ___studying___ (study) medicine because I love (2) _____

(help) other people, but (3) _____ (become) a doctor is hard

work! You need (4) _____ (study) for so many years. Also, I

wasn't sure I wanted (5) _____ (work) long hours like most

doctors seem (6) _____ (do). My final choice was between

(7) _____ (become) a nurse and (8) _____

(work) as an elementary school teacher. Well, (9) _____ (teach) won!

I started (10) _____ (teach) five years ago, and I know I made the

right choice. I really like (11) _____ (work) at my school. Sometimes

I don't have enough time (12) _____ (finish) all my work, but the

children are great. I love my job, and I love (13) _____ (know) that my

work makes a difference. That is very important to me.

Charts
10.1–10.5,
10.7, 10.8

3 Read each sentence. Then complete the second sentence so that it has a similar meaning to the first sentence. Use a gerund or an infinitive. In some cases, you can use either format.

1. I like to read magazines.

   I enjoy ___reading magazines___ .

2. It's fun to explore new places.

   _____ is fun.

3. The instructor told me to wait.

   The instructor asked _____ .

4. Dave wants to ski this weekend.

   Dave is interested _____ this weekend.

5. I hate to be late for work.

   I really dislike _____ .

6. Anna kept working.

   Anna continued _____ .

7. The meeting wasn't long enough to be useful.

   The meeting was too _____ .

8. I learned to swim from my father.

   My father taught _____ .

Charts
10.1–10.6,
10.8

4 **EDIT.** Read the article about Barrington Irving. Find and correct seven more errors with gerunds and infinitives.

Barrington Irving

In 2007, Barrington Irving became famous ⌄for ~~on~~ being the youngest person to fly solo[1] around the world. Irving was born in Jamaica and lived there until his parents decided move to Miami. Although life was not always easy, Irving has always been good at overcome difficulties. When he was 15, Irving met a professional pilot who invited him take a look at his plane. That was when Irving became interested in learning to fly. He didn't have money enough to go to flight school, so he earned money by washing planes. He practiced to fly in video games. When he was 23, Irving built his own plane and succeeded in flying around the world in 97 days.

After this success, Irving created exciting programs for to encourage children to learn about science, math, and technology. He believes in showing children that study hard brings success. If they do their best, no goal[2] is too difficult to achieve.

[1] **solo:** alone; without help from another person
[2] **goal:** something you hope to do that requires a lot of effort and work

5 WRITE & SPEAK.

A Write eight sentences about your work and activities you do in your free time. Use the words and phrases from the box or your own ideas. Use gerunds and infinitives.

afraid of	allow(ed) me to	ask(ed) me to	can't stand	enjoy
enough time to	exercising	go/went online to	interested in	prefer
relaxing	smart enough to	start(ed)	too much money to	too old to

Exercising is one of my favorite things to do.

I started to play the piano when I was six years old.

B Work with a partner. Share your sentences from exercise **A**. Then ask and answer as many questions as you can about each of your partner's sentences. Use gerunds, infinitives, and the other grammar from this unit in your questions and answers.

A: *Exercising is one of my favorite things to do.*

B: *What kind of exercise do you like to do?*

A: *I enjoy hiking.*

B: *Why do you enjoy hiking?*

A: *I like hiking because my apartment is near a canyon, so it's not too difficult for me to hike.*

Hikers pass through a slot canyon in Australia.

Connect the Grammar to Writing

1 READ & NOTICE THE GRAMMAR.

A Read the text. How did Carlos learn to do his job? Discuss your answers with a partner.

Abuela's Kitchen

When Carlos was five years old, he moved in with his *abuela*, or grandmother. She loved to cook, and Carlos spent a lot of time with her in the kitchen. Being in the warm kitchen with his grandmother was fun. She liked telling stories about her childhood, and Carlos enjoyed listening to her. He also enjoyed learning to cook by watching and helping her. In the beginning, most dishes were too difficult for him to make. First, he chopped vegetables and stirred beans. Then, he learned how to make soups and other simple dishes when he was seven. By the time he turned 13, Carlos was cooking full meals for his family and friends. He enjoyed making people happy with his food.

Eventually, Carlos realized that he had enough talent to become a chef. At the age of 18, he began working at a local restaurant. Then, 12 years later, after a lot of hard work, Carlos opened his own restaurant. He invited his family and friends to come to the grand opening. To honor his grandmother, Carlos named his restaurant Abuela's Kitchen.

GRAMMAR FOCUS

In exercise **A**, the writer uses gerunds and infinitives to explain the events of Carlos's life.

Gerunds:
Being in the warm kitchen with my grandmother was fun.
He enjoyed *making* people happy with his food.

Infinitives:
His grandmother loved *to cook*, and Carlos . . .
In the beginning, most dishes were too difficult for him *to make*.

B Read the text in exercise **A** again. Underline the gerunds and circle the infinitives. Then work with a partner and compare your answers.

C How did Carlos become a chef? Complete his timeline with the events from the text in exercise **A**.

Age: **CARLOS'S TIMELINE**

| 5 years old | 7 years old | 13 years old | 18 years old | 30 years old |

Event:

Moved in _____ _____ _____ _____
with Grandma _____ _____ _____ _____

2 BEFORE YOU WRITE.

A Think of someone you know well or know a lot about. In your notebook, brainstorm a list of important events in this person's life and his or her age when the event happened.

B Choose five or more events from your list from exercise **A**. Then complete the timeline. Use the timeline from exercise **1C** as a model.

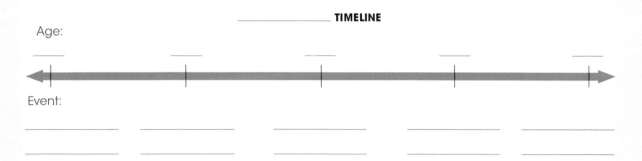

Age:

_____ **TIMELINE**

Event:

3 **WRITE** a short biography of the person you chose. Write two or three paragraphs. Use the information from your chart in exercise **2B** and the text in exercise **1A** to help you. Use gerunds and infinitives.

> **WRITING FOCUS**   Using *First* and *Then* to Show a Sequence
>
> Writers often use the words *first* and *then* at the beginning of a sentence to show the sequence of events, or the order in which the events happened. Use *first* for the first event. Use *then* for a later event.
>
> Use a comma after *first* or *then*.
>
> > **First,** *he chopped vegetables and stirred beans.* **Then,** *he learned how to make soups and other simple dishes.*

4 **SELF ASSESS.** Read your biography. Underline the gerunds and circle the infinitives. Then use the checklist to assess your work.

☐   I used gerunds correctly. [10.1, 10.2, 10.5]

☐   I used infinitives correctly. [10.3, 10.4, 10.5]

☐   I used *too* and *enough* with infinitives correctly. [10.7, 10.8]

☐   I used *first* and *then* to show sequence in my biography. [WRITING FOCUS]

Relative Clauses

▲ The men who fish on Inle Lake in Myanmar use a special technique to row their boats.

EXPLORE

CD3-22

1 **READ** the conversation about the town of Petra, Jordan. Notice the words in **bold**.

Petra and the Bedul Bedouin

Petra,
Jordan
AFRICA

Leo: I watched an old movie **that was on TV last night.** It was one of the Indiana Jones movies. There were wonderful old buildings in the story. They were in the Middle East somewhere, I think.

Jose: Oh, I wrote a report about those buildings for a history class. They're in Petra, Jordan. The buildings **which make up the oldest part of the city** are over 2000 years old. They are carved[1] into the hills.

Leo: Well, it certainly looks like a beautiful place. Does anyone actually live there?

Jose: Yes, I read about a Bedouin tribe **that has lived in the area for over 200 years**. They are called the Bedul. Until around 30 years ago, they had a simple life as farmers and traveled around with their animals. But Petra has become a popular tourist destination, so their lives have changed.

Leo: Oh really? How?

Jose: Well, many of the Bedul people have settled in a village. Some sell souvenirs[2] to the tourists **who visit Petra**. Others work as tour guides.

Leo: I see. Do any of them keep the old traditions alive?

Jose: Oh yes, there are still some Bedul people **who prefer to keep goats and grow crops**.

[1] **carve:** to cut from a solid material such as stone or wood
[2] **souvenir:** an object that helps people remember a place they visited

2 **CHECK.** Read the statements. Circle **T** for *true* or **F** for *false*.

1. Petra is a modern city. **T** **F**

2. The ancient buildings in Petra are on flat land. **T** **F**

3. The stone buildings are over 2000 years old. **T** **F**

4. The Bedul people have lived in the area for just a few years. **T** **F**

5. Many of the Bedul people have changed their jobs in the past 30 years. **T** **F**

3 DISCOVER. Complete the exercises to learn about the grammar in this lesson.

A Find these sentences in the conversation in exercise **A**. Write the missing words.

1. I watched an old movie <u>that was on TV last night</u>.

2. The buildings _____ _____ are over 2000 years old.

3. . . ., I read about a Bedouin tribe _____ _____.

4. Some sell souvenirs to the tourists _____ _____.

5. . . ., there are still some Bedul people _____ _____.

B Notice the missing words you wrote in exercise **A**. What words begin these clauses?

_____<u>that</u>_____ , _____ , _____

► The tower of ad-Deir Monastery in Petra, Jordan, with Bedouin children

LEARN

11.1 Subject Relative Clauses

After the Main Clause
We met the woman. <u>She</u> owns the shop.
We met the woman **who owns the shop.**
Subject Relative Clause

Inside the Main Clause
The tour was great. <u>It</u> left at noon.
The tour **that left at noon** was great.
Subject Relative Clause

1. A sentence with a relative clause* combines two sentences or ideas.	I met the man. He organized the tour. I met the man **who organized the tour.** *Relative Clause*
2. A relative clause describes a noun or a pronoun. It usually comes after the noun or pronoun it describes.	The people **that asked me about Jordan** have left. *Noun* We welcome everyone **who visits our home.** *Pronoun*
3. A subject relative clause begins with a relative pronoun (*that, which,* or *who*). Use *that* or *who* for people. Use *that* or *which* for places, things, and animals.	I know someone **who lives in Jordan.** Many people **that live here** speak French. The book **that's on the table** is Carla's. The photos **which show the Nile** are amazing.
4. In a subject relative clause, the relative pronoun is the subject of the clause. The relative pronoun is followed by a verb.	I like the guide **who showed** us the sites. She wants something **that will remind** her of her trip.

*Relative clauses are also called adjective clauses. Like adjectives, relative clauses describe nouns.

4 Underline the subject relative clause in each sentence. Draw an arrow from the relative clause to the noun or indefinite pronoun it describes.

1. The Bedul are people <u>who live near Petra, Jordan</u>.

2. Tourists that visit Petra buy souvenirs from the Bedul.

3. The Bedul used to be farmers who lived simply.

4. The building that is most popular with tourists is the Treasury.

5. The guides that show tourists around Petra are often Bedul.

6. The name *Petra* comes from the Greek word that means "stone."

7. The buildings that make up the old part of Petra are carved into the hills.

8. Anyone who wants to know more about Petra can find information on the Internet.

11.2 Subject Relative Clauses: Verb Agreement

1. The verb in a subject relative clause agrees with the noun it describes.	I have a friend **who likes traveling**. 　　　　　Noun　　　　Verb I have friends **who like traveling**. 　　　　　Noun　　　　Verb
2. **Be careful!** The verb in the main clause always agrees with the subject of the main clause.	Main Clause **The map** that shows the sites **looks** very old. Relative Clause
3. Do not repeat the subject in a relative clause.	✓ Where's the book **that has the map of Egypt**? ✗ Where's the book that <u>it</u> has the map of Egypt?

5 Complete the relative clause in each conversation. Use the simple present form of the verb in parentheses.

1. A: Have you seen the travel guide?

   B: I'm not sure. Is it the green book that _____is_____ (be) on the kitchen table?

2. A: What do you want to do this afternoon?

   B: I want to find some stores that _____ (sell) stone carvings.

3. A: Is there anyone who _____ (understand) French?

   B: Yes. I do. How can I help you?

4. A: Oh, no. I forgot my camera.

   B: Do you have a phone that _____ (take) good photos?

5. A: What kind of driver do you prefer, Ms. Jones?

   B: I prefer one who _____ (not talk) too much.

6. A: What sort of clothes are you taking on your trip?

   B: I'm just taking clothes that _____ (be) easy to pack.
   I can only take one suitcase.

6 Circle the correct form of the verb to complete each sentence.

1. The guide that told funny stories (**was**) / **were** the tourists' favorite.

2. Restaurants that offer a fixed menu usually **has** / **have** lower prices.

3. The boat trips that include a visit to the island **costs** / **cost** a lot of money.

4. The people who are complaining about the flight **has lost** / **have lost** their baggage.

5. The train that stops at every station **doesn't arrive** / **don't arrive** until 11:00 p.m.

6. The gallery that displays the work of local artists **has been** / **have been** open for two years.

7. I have some friends who **travel / travels** for a month every summer.

8. The bus that stops in front of the hotel **go / goes** to the museum.

PRACTICE

7 Complete the sentences. Write all possible relative pronouns (*that, which,* and/or *who*). Use the simple present form of a verb from the box.

allow	attract	~~explain~~	have	live	offer	tell	visit

1. Have you found any information <u>that / which explains</u> how Petra was built?

2. Do you know anyone _____ in Jordan now? I need a contact there.

3. Places _____ a lot of visitors are usually very busy on the weekends.

4. People _____ ancient cities often learn a lot from historical tours.

5. During the holidays, it's difficult to find hotels _____ cheap rates.

6. Sally needs a hotel _____ guests to bring their pets.

7. Guides _____ interesting stories are popular with tourists.

8. I want to stay in a hotel _____ a swimming pool.

8 PRONUNCIATION. Read the chart and listen to the examples. Then complete the exercises.

CD3-23

PRONUNCIATION	Reduced *That* in Relative Clauses

The full pronunciation of the vowel in *that* is /æ/, as in *cat*. When *that* is in a relative clause, the /æ/ often reduces to a schwa (/ə/) sound.

Examples:

Full Pronunciation (/thæt/)	Reduced Pronunciation (/thət/)
That's interesting.	The bus **that** took me to the airport was very old.
That building is over 100 years old.	Where is the hotel **that** offers free Internet?

CD3-24

A Write the relative pronoun *that* in the correct place in each sentence. Then listen and check your answers. Notice the pronunciation of *that.*

1. I like visiting places _ᵥthat are warm, sunny, and relaxing.

2. I have friends don't like to fly.

3. I don't like guides talk all the time.

4. My friend likes trips allow plenty of time to shop.

5. I don't buy souvenirs break easily.

6. My classmate likes places aren't very crowded.

7. I like to stay in hotels have exercise rooms.

8. My mother likes to eat in restaurants have fixed menus.

B Rewrite the sentences from exercise **A** in your notebook. Change the words after *that*. Use information about yourself and people you know.

1. I like visiting places that have guided tours.

C Work with a partner. Share your sentences from exercise **B**. Pay attention to the pronunciation of *that*.

9 LISTEN to the conversation about the World Cup in South Africa. Complete the conversation with the words you hear.
CD3-25

Neville: I've been reading an article about the World Cup
(1) _____that took place_____ in South Africa in 2010.
We watched some of it on TV. Do you remember?

Cindy: Oh, yes. Almost everyone
(2) _____ the games
had one of those awful musical instruments
(3) _____ a terrible noise.

Neville: Well, I suppose the people
(4) _____ them had
a good time. Anyway, this article is all about things
(5) _____ since the competition.

Cindy: And what does the writer say?

Neville: She says it was an event (6) _____
the South African people together. The people
(7) _____ it would be a big waste
of money were completely wrong. Researchers interviewed
people during and after the competition. Tourists
(8) _____ to South Africa for the
World Cup were very impressed, and most South Africans
(9) _____ to the researchers were very
proud of the way their country organized the Cup.

10 APPLY.

A Match each sentence in column **A** with the sentence from column **B** that defines the subject.

Column A

1. A vuvuzela is an instrument. __b__

2. Archaeologists are scientists. _____

3. A magnifying glass is a tool. _____

4. Statisticians are scientists. _____

5. A carving is a piece of art. _____

6. A spreadsheet is a computer program. _____

Column B

a. It allows you to organize numbers or data.

b. It is similar to a horn.

c. It is cut from stone, wood, or another material.

d. It makes small objects look bigger.

e. They study historic places and objects.

f. They calculate and analyze numbers.

B Combine the two sentences you matched in exercise **A**. Make the second sentence a subject relative clause.

1. _A vuvuzela is an instrument that is similar to a horn._

2. _____

_____

3. _____

_____

4. _____

_____

5. _____

_____

6. _____

_____

C In your notebook, write six sentences that define objects or jobs that you know about. Use subject relative clauses.

A doctor is someone who takes care of sick people.

D Work with a partner. Share your definitions from exercise **C** and let your partner guess which object or job you are defining.

A: *This is someone who takes care of sick people.*

B: *Is it a nurse? . . . A doctor?*

A: *Yes, it's a doctor. Now it's your turn.*

EXPLORE

CD3-26

1 READ the article about Lek Chailert. Notice the words in **bold**.

Chiang Mai, Thailand

AUSTRALIA

Lek Chailert and the Elephant Nature Park

The Elephant Nature Park is a rescue center that has taken care of sick elephants in northern Thailand since 1996. The park is in Chiang Mai Province, and the person who runs it is an extraordinary woman, Sangduen "Lek" Chailert.

Lek spent a lot of time with her grandfather as a child. He belonged to a tribe that lived in the forest. The time **that Lek spent with him** was very important to her. It helped her understand the wonders of nature. She created the Elephant Nature Park with her husband, Adam, and the organization has received international recognition.[1]

The elephants **that Lek rescues** come from all over Thailand. She often takes them from logging camps[2] when they are no longer useful. Others are sick, and some are elephants **which people have treated badly**. Lek's work also provides medical care for villagers who need it. The idea **Lek and her husband had** was to provide a safe place for elephants to live in peace. In fact, they are doing much, much more than that.

[1] **recognition:** praise and thanks for doing something good
[2] **logging camp:** a place where workers cut down trees and use elephants to move them

◄ Elephants that are born at the Elephant Nature Park will never have to work.

2 CHECK. Choose the correct answers.

1. What did Lek's grandfather help her do?

   a. create a park for elephants   b. understand the natural world   c. learn about his tribe

2. The Elephant Nature Park helps animals from _____ .

   a. Chiang Mai Province only   b. northern Thailand only   c. all parts of Thailand

3. Some elephants at the park _____ .

   a. are useful at logging camps   b. were treated badly   c. came from the Middle East

4. When does Lek take elephants from logging camps?

   a. when they can't work anymore   b. when they are sick   c. when they behave badly

5. What is the main purpose of the Elephant Nature Park?

   a. to teach people about elephants   b. to check on logging camps   c. to take care of elephants

3 DISCOVER. Complete the exercises to learn about the grammar in this lesson.

A Read the sentence. Then choose the two ideas it tells us about Lek and the elephants at the Elephant Nature Park.

The elephants that Lek rescues come from all over Thailand.

a. Lek comes from Thailand.

b. The elephants come from Thailand.

c. Lek rescues the elephants.

B Look at the sentence in exercise **A**. What is different about the word that comes after *that* in this clause and the word that comes after the relative pronoun in a subject relative clause? Discuss your answer with your classmates and teacher.

◀ Asian elephants at the Elephant Nature Park, Chiang Mai, Thailand

LEARN

11.3 Object Relative Clauses

After the Main Clause	Within the Main Clause
He is the doctor. You saw <u>him</u> last week.	The house is blue. She bought <u>it</u>.
He is the doctor **who you saw last week**.	The house **that she bought** is blue.
Object Relative Clause	Object Relative Clause

1. **Remember:** A sentence with a relative clause combines two sentences or ideas. In an object relative clause, the relative pronoun (*that, which, who,* or *whom*) is the object of the clause. The relative pronoun is followed by a subject and a verb.	The man is Vietnamese. You met him. The man **that you met** is Vietnamese. Object Relative Clause
2. Use *who, whom,* or *that* for people. Use *that* or *which* for places, things, and animals.	That is the woman **who / whom / that** I met last week. The book **that / which** I'm reading now is very good.
3. The subject and verb in an object relative clause agree.	I like the work **that she does**. Subject Verb I like the work **that they do**. Subject Verb
4. Do not repeat the object in an object relative clause.	✓ She has a job **that she loves**. ✗ She has a job that she loves <u>it</u>.

4 Complete the sentences. Write all possible relative pronouns (*that, which, who,* or *whom*) and the simple present form of the verb in parentheses.

1. The elephants ___that / which___ logging camps ___use___ (use) work very hard.

2. Many of the loggers _____ Lek _____ (meet) are concerned about their elephants.

3. Some of the elephants _____ Lek _____ (help) come from logging camps.

4. The forests of northern Thailand are not a place _____ many tourists _____ (visit).

5. The problems _____ Lek and her team sometimes _____ (find) are very serious.

6. The people _____ the park _____ (hire) all care about animals a lot.

7. The international recognition _____ Lek _____ (receive) regularly is helpful to the park.

8. Lek Chailert is a person _____ I _____ (admire).

11.4 Object Relative Clauses without Relative Pronouns

	Object Relative Clause			
	Object Relative Pronoun	Subject	Verb	
The people		I	met	were on the tour.
The film		we	watched	was about Indonesia.

1. The object relative pronoun (*that, which, who,* or *whom*) is often omitted from object relative clauses.	She is wearing a ring ~~that~~ I like. She is wearing a ring **I like**.
2. **Remember:** Do not omit the subject relative pronoun (*that, which,* or *who*) from subject relative clauses.	✓ I know a man **who owns ten cars**. ✗ I know a <u>man owns</u> ten cars.

5 Underline the object relative clause in each sentence. Then cross out the object relative pronoun.

1. Jan Peng is an elephant <u>~~that~~ people treated badly</u>.

2. Jan Peng worked in a camp that loggers built.

3. The trees which Jan Peng moved were large and very heavy.

4. As Jan Peng got older, the work that she was doing became too hard for her.

5. The people whom Lek interviewed about Jan Peng promised not to make her work again.

6. Jan Peng seemed afraid when she had to go with people that she did not know.

7. The team members that Lek brought to the logging camp took good care of Jan Peng.

8. Jan Peng liked the new home that Lek and her team provided for her.

6 Complete the object relative clause in each sentence. Write all possible relative pronouns (*that, which, who, whom,* or Ø for no relative pronoun).

1. The book _____ that / which / Ø _____ I am reading now is about Laos.

2. The animals _____ you see in zoos sometimes look sad.

3. The woman _____ we interviewed for the job last week works at a hospital.

4. Some animals _____ people keep as pets are dangerous.

5. The singer _____ I saw on the street has a great voice.

6. The man _____ we asked for directions was very helpful.

7. The doctor _____ I saw last week was very good.

8. The article _____ he wrote was about nature parks.

PRACTICE

7 Underline the object relative clauses in the sentences. Cross out the relative pronouns.

1. The notebook ~~that~~ I lost had important information in it.

2. The person that I talked to on the phone was rude to me.

3. The car that my sister bought is easy to drive.

4. Most of the people who I met on vacation speak German.

5. The doctor whom I called is not taking new patients.

6. The song which Alan was singing was beautiful.

7. The report that I'm writing is really difficult.

8. Do you have a map of the city that I can use?

9. Have you seen the books that I left on the table?

10. Meryl Streep is an actress whom I would like to meet.

8 LISTEN & SPEAK.

CD3-27-28

A Look at the photos and read the captions. Then listen to two students talk about the photos. Take notes below each photo.

Photo 1

▲ A traditional fisherman rows his boat on Inle Lake, Myanmar.

_____

_____

_____

Photo 2

▲ A floating garden on the surface of Inle Lake, Myanmar

_____

_____

_____

B Work with a partner. Compare your notes from exercise **A**.

CD3-27-28

C Read the pairs of sentences about the photos from exercise **A**. Then choose the sentence that gives the correct description of each photo. Use your notes to help you. Then listen again and check your answers.

Photo 1:

1. a. The photo the photographer bought looks like a ballet.
   b. The photo the photographer took looks like a ballet.

2. a. The technique the fisherman is using looks very difficult.
   b. The technique the photographer is using looks very difficult.

3. a. The boats the fisherman use are long and narrow.
   b. The boats the fishermen sell are long and narrow.

4. a. One challenge the fishermen have on Inle Lake is seeing over the tall plants.
   b. One challenge the photographers have on Inle Lake is seeing over the tall plants.

Photo 2:

5. a. The boats the local people build are made of wood and bamboo.
   b. The houses the local people build are made of wood and bamboo.

6. a. The farms the local people run produce enough food to live on.
   b. The farms the local people run produce enough food to sell in the city.

7. a. The fish they put in the lake are called Inle carp.
   b. The fish they catch from the lake are called Inle carp.

8. a. The fruits and vegetables the farmers grow come from floating gardens on the lake.
   b. The fruits and vegetables the farmers buy come from floating gardens on the lake.

D Work with a partner. Use relative clauses to tell your partner about one of the photos from exercise **A** on page 305. Use your notes from exercise **A** to help you.

The photo I'm looking at is of a fisherman on Inle Lake in Myanmar.

9 EDIT. Read the excerpts from a travel brochure. Find and correct five more errors with object relative clauses.

Kyoto

Kyoto was the capital of Japan for over a thousand years. It is a city which visitors find it fascinating.[1] In the eastern part of the city, there are many temples and gardens who you can see on a short walk. The Golden Pavilion is a beautiful building you can visit it in the northwestern hills. Another wonderful building in the center of town is Nijō-jō. This is a famous palace[2] whom every visitor wants to see.

¹ **fascinating:** very interesting
² **palace:** a large house that is the home of a very important person

Kuala Lumpur

The Malaysian capital, Kuala Lumpur (or "KL"), has changed a lot in the last 50 years. The historic buildings whom you can visit in Kuala Lumpur are now mixed with modern skyscrapers¹ such as the Petronas Towers. KL is a busy but friendly place, and the different cultures that you can experience them will make your visit fun.

¹ **skyscraper:** a very tall building

10 APPLY.

A Complete the sentences. Write a main clause for each object relative clause. Write true statements about yourself.

1. _____The last place_____ I visited on vacation _____was Washington DC_____ .

2. _____ I bought last week _____ .

3. _____ I admire most _____ .

4. _____ I met last year _____ .

5. _____ I really enjoyed _____ .

6. _____ I am looking at right now _____ .

7. _____ I owned as a child _____ .

8. _____ I called on the phone _____ .

B Work with a partner. Share your sentences from exercise **A**. Ask and answer follow-up questions.

A: *The last place I visited on vacation was Washington, DC.*

B: *How was it?*

A: *It was beautiful! Spring is the best time to visit.*

EXPLORE

1 **READ** the article about cyclists from the Isle of Man. Notice the words in **bold**.

Isle of Man, U.K.

Cycling and the Isle of Man

The Isle of Man is a small island between Great Britain and Ireland. The geography of the Isle of Man is perfect for cycling. Riding on the hills and valleys helps cyclists develop the strength **they are looking for**.

In 2011, a cyclist from the island, Mark Cavendish, became the World Road Race champion.[1] He also won several races in the famous *Tour de France*. Cavendish is an exciting cyclist **whose name is well known on the island**. He's the cyclist **everyone is talking about** now, but he's not the first to come from the island.

Rob Holden is another champion cyclist from the island. "The roads over here are difficult to ride," says Holden. "You do need to be tough."

There has been at least one successful cyclist from the island in each decade[2] since the 1950s. For an island **whose population is under 90,000**, this is an incredible[3] success story.

[1] **champion:** someone who wins an important competition
[2] **decade:** a period of ten years
[3] **incredible:** difficult or impossible to believe

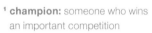

▲ Two mountain bikers descend toward Port Erin on the Isle of Man

2 CHECK. Read the statements below. Circle **T** for *true* or **F** for *false*. Then correct the false statements to make them true.

                                          ⌄ Ireland

1. The Isle of Man is between Great Britain and ~~Scotland~~.   **T**   **F**

2. The Isle of Man has hills and valleys.   **T**   **F**

3. The roads on the Isle of Man help cyclists become strong.   **T**   **F**

4. Mark Cavendish became the World Road Race champion in 2012.   **T**   **F**

5. The population of the Isle of Man is more than 90,000.   **T**   **F**

3 DISCOVER. Complete the exercises to learn about the grammar in this lesson.

A Find these sentences in the article from exercise **1**. Write the missing words.

1. Riding on the hills and valleys helps cyclists develop the strength **they are looking** _____.

2. Mark Cavendish is the cyclist **everyone is talking** _____ now.

B Look at the words you wrote in exercise **A**. Choose the correct word to complete the statement below.

These words are _____.   a. objects   b. prepositions   c. articles

11.5 Object Relative Clauses with Prepositions

	Object Relative Clause			
	Object Relative Pronoun	Subject	Verb + Preposition	
Did you find the book	that / which / –	you	were looking for?	
The man	that / who / whom / –	she	spoke with	is my boss.

1. A relative pronoun (*that, which, who,* or *whom*) can be the object of a preposition.

   The preposition usually comes after the verb in an object relative clause.

   The people were customers. I met **with them.**
   Preposition Object

   The people **that I met with** were customers.
   Object   Verb Preposition

2. **Remember:** The object relative pronoun is often omitted in conversation and informal writing.

   The people **who** I met with were customers.
   The people I met with were customers.

   The pen ~~that~~ I'm looking for is blue.
   The pen I'm looking for is blue.

3. In formal English, the preposition can come at the beginning of the object relative clause before *whom* (for people) or *which* (for things).

   The person **to whom we spoke** was helpful.
   The job **for which I applied** was new.

4. Do not use a preposition before *who* or *that*.

   ✓ The person **to whom** we spoke was helpful.
   ✗ The person <u>to who</u> you spoke is not here today.

   ✓ The job **for which** I applied was new.
   ✗ The job <u>for that</u> I applied was new.

---

4 Complete the sentences with an object relative clause. Use the words in parentheses. Only use a relative pronoun if one is given. More than one form of the verb may be correct.

1. Susanne enjoyed the race _____*that she rode in*_____ (that / she / ride in) yesterday.

2. The sport _____
   (that / Roberto / be / most interested in) is cycling.

3. The person _____ (whom / you / look for)
   is not in the office today.

4. Who are the students _____
   (you / be friends with)?

5. Who was the woman _____ (Valerie / talk to)
   when we saw her this morning?

6. What's the name of the company _____
   (your brother / work for) now?

7. The dress _____ (which / Sue / decide on) was very expensive.

8. He's the uncle _____ (I / not speak to) for many years.

9. Did you like the people _____ (you / work with)
   at your old job?

10. This is the article _____ (that / we / talk about) last week.

11.6   Relative Clauses with *Whose*

1. Use *whose* + noun at the beginning of a relative clause to show possession. *Whose* replaces a possessive adjective or a possessive noun (*his, her, their, its, Sam's,* etc.). *Whose* + noun can be the subject or the object of the relative clause.	The author writes beautifully. <u>Her</u> book won the award. The author **whose book won the award** writes beautifully. Subject Relative Clause She's the author. I just bought <u>her</u> book. She's the author **whose book I just bought**. Object Relative Clause
2. *Whose* can be used for people, places, animals, and things. A noun always follows *whose*.	That's the bakery. We love <u>its</u> cakes. That's the bakery **whose cakes we love**. Object Relative Clause
3. *Whose* often comes after *someone, anyone, no one,* and *everyone*.	She is someone **whose work interests me**. I don't know anyone **whose job involves travel**.
4. **Remember:** Do not repeat the subject or object in a relative clause.	✓ She is the artist **whose paintings are in the gallery**. ✗ She is the artist whose paintings <u>they</u> are in the gallery. ✓ The artist **whose painting I bought** is from Russia. ✗ The artist whose painting I bought <u>it</u> is from Russia.

5   Read the pairs of sentences. Circle the possessive adjective or possessive noun that the word *whose* in sentence b replaces.

1. a. Cavendish is an exciting cyclist. (His) success is not new to the island.

   b. Cavendish is an exciting cyclist **whose** success is not new to the island.

2. a. Sprinters are cyclists. Their job is to ride fast at the end of races.

   b. Sprinters are cyclists **whose** job is to ride fast at the end of races.

3. a. The cyclist lost the race. His bike wasn't working properly.

   b. The cyclist **whose** bike wasn't working properly lost the race.

4. a. The cycling team won the race. We saw the team's leader on TV.

   b. The cycling team **whose** leader we saw on TV won the race.

5. a. Is this the new bike shop? Was the bike shop's ad on the radio yesterday?

   b. Is this the new bike shop **whose** ad was on the radio yesterday?

6. a. I met a woman today. Her daughter works with my brother.

   b. I met a woman today **whose** daughter works with my brother.

7. a. We received a nice letter from the woman. We found her cat.

   b. We received a nice letter from the woman **whose** cat we found.

8. a. My sister has a dog. Its favorite food is ice cream.

   b. My sister has a dog **whose** favorite food is ice cream.

PRACTICE

6 Complete the sentences. Write a relative clause with a preposition or with *whose*.

1. The professor just walked in. You need his signature.

   The professor ___*whose signature you need*___ just walked in.

2. Steven Spielberg is a film producer. His movies have made millions of dollars.

   Steven Spielberg is a film producer _____ .

3. There's the school. My son goes to it.

   There's the school _____ .

4. Helen has a pet bird. Its name is Freddy.

   Helen has a pet bird _____ .

5. The salesperson was very helpful. Marianne spoke to her.

   The salesperson _____ was very helpful.

6. The student gets sick a lot. Her mother is a doctor.

   The student _____ gets sick a lot.

7. We had fun at the party. We went to it last night.

   We had fun at the party _____ .

8. The people are very nice. Lucy works with them.

   The people _____ are very nice.

7 **WRITE & SPEAK.**

A Write an object relative clause with a preposition. Use the words in parentheses and an appropriate verb form. More than one verb form may be correct.

1. The sport ___*Tim is interested in*___ (Tim / be interested in) is hockey.

2. I haven't seen the movie _____ (you / talk about) yesterday.

3. The job _____ (you / apply for) last week involves a lot of travel.

4. That's the place _____ (we / travel to) on vacation last year.

5. Everyone _____ (we / speak to) complained about the terrible weather.

B Complete the relative clauses with your own ideas.

1. I have a good friend whose house _____*is near the railroad station*_____ .

2. I'd like to join a gym whose members _____ .

3. The musician whose music I like the most is _____ .

4. Anyone whose English isn't very good _____ .

5. I know someone whose family _____ .

8 EDIT. Read the information about the Vikings of northern Europe. Find and correct five more errors with relative clauses.

The Vikings

The people that we think of ~~them~~ as Vikings were not in fact one group of people. They were different groups of people whose native countries they were in southern Scandinavia. The areas that they lived in them are now called Norway, Sweden, and Denmark.

▲ A painting of a Viking ship from Greenland approaching Newfoundland

In addition to the violence that they are famous for it, the Vikings were explorers whose love of the sea everyone know about. The Vikings were great travelers and traders. They sailed their small wooden ships as far as Russia to the east and North Africa to the south. They were also the first Europeans to reach America. The Vikings even settled for a short time in an area who Norse name was *Vinland*. Its modern name is Newfoundland, Canada.

9 APPLY.

A In your notebook, write five questions using the ideas in the box or your own ideas. Use relative clauses.

a musician or artist whose work you admire	something you are planning on
a restaurant whose food you enjoy	an interesting place you have been to
someone whose personality you like	a topic you know a lot about

Who's a musician or artist whose work you admire?

B Work with a partner. Take turns asking and answering your questions from exercise **A**. Use relative clauses in your conversation.

A: *Who's a musician whose work you admire?*

B: *Well, one musician whose work I have always admired is Baaba Maal.*

A: *I haven't heard of him. Where is he from?*

Charts
11.1–11.6

1 Combine the two sentences. Write one sentence with a relative clause.

1. These are the photos. My son took them on our vacation.

   These are the photos _that my son took on our vacation_.

2. That's the ancient building. I visited it yesterday.

   That's the ancient building _____.

3. The job was in Mexico City. Stefan applied for it.

   The job _____.

4. That's the man. I found his wallet.

   That's the man _____.

5. The TV show is about an archaeologist. She travels all over the world.

   The TV show is about an archaeologist _____.

6. We took a bus tour on Saturday. It was wonderful.

   The bus tour _____.

7. There's the museum. Our guide told us about it yesterday.

   There's the museum _____.

8. I bought some souvenirs for my family. They weren't very expensive.

   The souvenirs _____.

Charts
11.1–11.5

2 EDIT & SPEAK.

A Read the paragraph about Tanzania. Find and correct six more errors with relative clauses.

My country Tanzania

I come from the Tanga region of Tanzania, Africa. It is a

place ˄that is full of history and beauty. Tanga has many tourist

destinations[1] such as Mount Kilimanjaro that is famous around

the world. People whom go to see this mountain will never

forget it. There are guides which take people up the mountain. These trips can be

dangerous, so only people that they are physically fit should try to climb to the top of

the mountain. Another place is Zanzibar. This is a group of islands became famous

for its spices. These days, Zanzibar's economy depends more on tourism than on

spices. The Serengeti National Park also attracts a lot of tourists. Here you can go on

safari and see the many amazing animals live there.

[1] **destination:** a place that people go to or are going to

B Work with a partner. Use subject or object relative clauses to talk about three places in your city or country. Use the paragraph in exercise **A** as a model.

I come from Peru. It's a beautiful country that has a lot of interesting things to see. For example, . . .

Charts
11.1–11.6

3 LISTEN & SPEAK.

CD3-30

A Listen to the radio show. Complete the conversation with the relative clauses you hear.

▼ Hot-air balloon tours are the perfect way to see Cappadocia, Turkey.

Brian: Good evening, everyone. Brian Evans here with another vacation report. This week I'm in Cappadocia, Turkey, talking with some brave tourists about balloon rides. So, let's say hi to Scott from Toronto and Julie from Boston. Julie, tell us about your experience. How was the balloon ride (1) _____ ?

Julie: Oh, it was incredible, Brian! The balloon was huge and so colorful. The other people (2) _____ with me were really friendly and from all over the world. It was an experience (3) _____ ! The views were amazing!

Brian: Well, that's one satisfied customer! Now, Scott, what did you think about the company (4) _____ to go with?

Scott: Well, the pilot (5) _____ our balloon was excellent, and we had a guide (6) _____ from New Zealand, so his English was great.

Brian: Great! Any final words?

Julie: Yes! If you're a person (7) _____ travel and photography, you'll love Cappadocia! I hope the photos (8) _____ are half as beautiful as the real thing.

Brian: OK, there we have it. Thanks, and enjoy the rest of your vacation.

B Work in a small group. What kinds of activities do you like to do on vacation? Discuss your answers with your group.

1 READ & NOTICE THE GRAMMAR.

A How do you treat a cold? Discuss your ideas with a partner. Then read the essay.

COLD TREATMENTS AROUND THE WORLD

How do you treat a cold? I asked people from all over the world this question. They had many different answers.

The first group of treatments I learned about is made up of drinks. I spoke with a neighbor who is from Italy. She makes a tea that has sage and bay leaves in it. A Native American tea that my friend Deedee drinks is made from herbs and honey. A classmate whose grandparents are from Turkey also drinks tea with herbs and honey when he has a cold.

The second group of treatments consists of different kinds of food. My neighbor Wu from China eats a hot rice cereal she calls *jook*. The chicken soup that my friend Jason's grandfather from Hungary makes works well for him. The person whose remedy was most unusual was my friend Ray from Hawaii. He chews the bark[1] of a tree that grows there.

The last group of treatments involves activities. For example, some people I know sit in a room full of steam or take a hot shower. Some people put a hot stone on the place that hurts them. And sitting or lying in the sun is a remedy that many people use, too.

[1] **bark:** the skin of a tree

GRAMMAR FOCUS

In the essay in exercise **A,** the writer uses relative clauses to describe nouns.

I spoke with a <u>neighbor</u> **who is from Italy.**

He chews the bark of a <u>tree</u> **that grows there.**

B Read the essay in exercise **A** again. Underline the relative clauses and draw an arrow from each clause to the noun it describes. Then work with a partner and compare your answers.

C In the text in exercise **A,** the writer first tells us the topic of the essay. Then she names three groups within this topic and gives examples for each group. Complete the chart on page 317 with information from the essay.

Topic: Cold Treatments around the World		
Group 1: drinks	**Group 2:**	**Group 3:**
Examples: tea with sage/bay leaves	Examples:	Examples:

2 BEFORE YOU WRITE.

A Work with a partner. Make a list of topics that include groups or categories.

B Choose one of the topics on your list from exercise **A** and complete the chart below with your ideas. Use the chart from exercise **1C** as a model.

Topic: _____		
Group 1:	**Group 2:**	**Group 3:**
Examples:	Examples:	Examples:

3 WRITE a classification essay about your topic. Write one paragraph that introduces your topic and one paragraph for each of the groups within this topic. Use the information in your chart in exercise **2B** and the essay in exercise **1A** to help you.

> **WRITING FOCUS**   Using Transition Words
>
> Writers use transition words to lead their readers from one idea to the next. In a classification essay, the transition words *the first*, *the second*, and *the last* are often used.
>
> **The first** group of cures I learned about is made up of drinks.
> **The second** group of treatments I learned about consists of different kinds of food.
> **The last** group of treatments involves activities.

4 SELF ASSESS. Read your classification essay. Underline the relative clauses. Then use the checklist to assess your work.

- [ ] I used subject relative clauses correctly. [11.1-11.2]
- [ ] I used object relative clauses correctly. [11.3-11.4]
- [ ] I used object relative clauses with prepositions correctly. [11.5]
- [ ] I used relative clauses with *whose* correctly. [11.6]
- [ ] I used transition words to lead my readers from one idea to the next. [WRITING FOCUS]

Modals: Part 1

▼ Musicians in an alley covered with graffiti, São Paulo, Brazil

EXPLORE

CD3-31

1   **READ** the article about an artist who uses unusual material to create art. Notice the words in **bold**.

The Art of Trash

The famous French artist Edgar Degas said, "Art is not what you see, but what you make others see." In other words, art is not just something nice for you to look at. Art **is able to change** your beliefs, and maybe even your behavior.

German artist HA Schult agrees. For about four decades, Schult's art has helped to create an awareness[1] about society's wasteful consumerism.[2] One of his best-known works, *Trash People*, is an example. One thousand life-size human figures, all made of trash, make up *Trash People*. Since the 1990s, Schult has installed[3] these figures in several places around the world. Unlike many sculptors—who typically use stone, metal, or wood—his figures are made of old cans, electronics, and other kinds of everyday trash. His message is clear: people are too wasteful.

In 1999, people **were able to view** these figures in Red Square in Moscow. In 2001, visitors to the Great Wall of China **could see** them. From there, they traveled to the Pyramids of Giza in Egypt and many other places around the world. At first, some people **couldn't understand** his ideas. All they **could see** was trash. However, years later, you **can** still **find** Schult's army of trash people. If you **aren't able to see** them in person, you **can learn** a lot about them online. What do you think? Is his army winning the war?

[1] **awareness:** understanding
[2] **consumerism:** the act of spending money on goods and services
[3] **install:** to put together, put in place

▼ HA Schult's *Trash People* (2014)

2 CHECK. Circle the correct answer to complete each statement.

1. According to HA Schult, the purpose of art is to **please people** / **change people's behavior**.

2. One **hundred** / **thousand** life-size figures make up *Trash People*.

3. Schult wants people to think more about being **less wasteful** / **more creative** with trash.

4. *Trash People* is **not** / **still** traveling around the world now.

3 DISCOVER. Complete the exercises to learn about the grammar in this lesson.

A Find these sentences in the article from exercise **1**. Write the missing words.

1. Art ___is able to change___ your beliefs, and maybe even your behavior.

2. In 1999, people _____ these figures in Red Square in Moscow.

3. In 2001, visitors to the Great Wall of China _____ them.

4. At first, some people _____ his ideas.

5. If you _____ them in person, you _____ a lot about them online.

B Write the phrases you wrote in exercise **A** in the correct place in the chart.

	Present or Future	**Past**
Affirmative	is able to change	
Negative		

LEARN

12.1 Ability: *Can* and *Could*

Statements

Subject	Modal (*Not*)	Base Form	
I You	can can't	paint	with watercolors.
She They	could couldn't	speak	before the age of three.

Yes/No and *Wh-* Questions

Wh- Word	Modal	Subject	Base Form	
	Can	Lisa	sing?	
	Could	you	see	the stage last night?
What	can	babies	say	at age one?
When	could	you	speak	English well?

Short Answers

Yes, she **can**.
No, I **couldn't**.
Not much.
A few years ago.

1. *Can* and *could* are modals. Modals add meaning to a verb. Use the base form of a verb after affirmative and negative forms of modals.	We **can watch** TV when we finish dinner. You **can't see** the board. Maybe you need glasses. They **couldn't find** the museum, so they came home.
2. Modals do not change form. Do not add -*s/-es* to the end of modals.	✓ They **can see** the movie tomorrow. ✗ She can<u>s</u> see the sign.
3. To form questions, put the modal before the subject. Do not use *do/does*.	✓ **Can** you **understand** me? ✗ <u>Do you can</u> understand me?
4. To form negatives, use *not* after the modal. Do not use a form of *do*.	✓ He **couldn't understand** the teacher today. ✗ He <u>didn't could understand</u> the teacher today.
5. Use *can* to express ability or possibility in the present or future.	Larissa **can play** the violin beautifully. She **can sing** for us tomorrow night.
6. Use *could* to talk about ability in the past.	Jon **could paint** very well when he was young.

4 Complete the sentences. Use *can (not)* or *could (not)* and the words in parentheses.

1. HA Schult _____*can create*_____ (create) beautiful art from trash.

2. _____ (we / see) the exhibit today?

> **REAL ENGLISH**
>
> There are three correct ways to write *can + not*: *can not, cannot,* and *can't*.

3. Beethoven _____ (not hear) well, but he _____ (create) beautiful music.

4. Tim and Ria _____ (not discuss) modern art until they took an art history class. Now they _____ (talk) about different artists and movements.

5. Some people _____ (not understand) modern art.

6. A: _____ (van Gogh / write) beautiful music?

   B: No, but he _____ (paint) amazing pictures.

7. A: What _____ (da Vinci / do) well?

   B: He _____ (do) everything well!

8. Where _____ (I / buy) guitar strings around here?

5 PRONUNCIATION. Read the chart and listen to the examples. Then complete the exercises.

PRONUNCIATION	*Can and Can't*

In affirmative statements and questions, the /æ/ sound in *can* is reduced to a schwa (/ə/) sound. In negative statements and short answers, the /æ/ sound is fully pronounced.

Examples:

| I **can hear** you. | I /kən/ hear you. | **Can** you **see** me? | /kən/ you see me? |
| I **can't see** you. | I /kænt/ see you. | Yes, I **can**. | Yes, I /kæn/. |

CD3-32

CD3-33

A Listen to these students. Write *can* or *can't*.

1. My teacher _____ draw very well.

2. I _____ understand modern art.

3. My friends and I _____ get together often.

4. I _____ speak more than one foreign language.

5. In my opinion, art _____ change how people think.

B Work with a partner. Read the sentences in exercise **A** to your partner but say *can* or *can't* depending on what is true for you.

My teacher can't draw very well.

▶ HA Schult exhibition, *Under the Pyramids*, Egypt, 2002

12.2 Ability: *Be Able To*

Statements				
Subject	*Be*	*(Not) Able To*	Base Form	
I	am was			
You We	are were	able to not able to	attend understand	the performance. the presenter very well.
He She	is was			

1. You can also use *be (not) able to* + a base form of a verb to express ability.	They**'re able to read** the Chinese text. I**'m not able to hear** the speaker.
2. *Be able to* has the same general meaning as *can*, but it can be used in different past, present, and future verb forms.	We **were able to watch** the show recently. She **isn't going to be able to finish** the class. He**'ll be able to stay** until Friday.
3. Use *will be able to* for a future ability that will be new or learned; do not use *can*. If the ability is true or possible now, use *can* or *will be able to*.	✓ We**'ll be able to speak** French after the course. ✗ We <u>can speak</u> French after the course. I **can meet** you after work. I**'ll be able to meet** you after work.
4. **Remember:** To form *Yes/No* questions with *be*, put the form of *be* before the subject. To form *Wh-* questions, put the *Wh-* word + a form of *be* before the subject.	**Is** she **able to talk** now? **Were** you **able to finish** the project? **What are** you **able to see**? **Why wasn't** she **able to go**?

6 Complete the sentences. Use the correct present, past, or future form of *be able to* or *be not able to*.

1. Art is not what you see; it is what you _____*are able to*_____ make other people see.

2. The artist hopes his new painting _____ bring attention to the problem of poverty.

3. A: What _____ songwriters _____ do with a three-minute song?

   B: They _____ make people think and feel strong emotions.

4. Beethoven _____ hear, but he _____ create beautiful music.

5. Because of computers, artists of the future _____ work in new ways.

6. The lead actor is in the hospital, so he _____ appear in tonight's performance.

7. The director's last movie _____ influence people's opinions about the horrors of war.

8. Nowadays, people _____ see operas in movie theaters for a low price. Before, many people _____ experience them because they were so expensive.

9. After I return from my year in France, I _____ speak French and discuss art.

10. Now he has his own piano, so he _____ practice a lot more.

12.3 Past Ability: *Could* and *Was/Were Able To*

Could (Not)	Was/Were (Not) Able To
She **could walk** before she was one. We **couldn't dance** before we took the class. A: **Could** you **draw** well as a child? B: Yes, I **could**. / No, I **couldn't**.	She **was able to walk** before she was one. We **weren't able to dance** before we took the class. A: **Was** she **able to draw** well as a child? B: Yes, she **was**. / No, she **wasn't**.

1. Use both *was/were able to* and *could* to express general ability in the past.	Tara **could run** 10 miles when she was 20. As kids, we **were able to swim** every day.
2. Use *was/were able to* (but not *could*) to express ability related to one event in the past.	✓ She **was able to finish** the project last night. ✗ She <u>could</u> finish the project last night.
3. *Could* can be used to express ability related to one event in the past with: a. verbs of perception (*see, hear, understand*) b. negative forms (*couldn't*)	a. I **could understand** yesterday's lecture. b. She **couldn't finish** the project last night.

7 Circle all correct answers. Sometimes both answers are correct.

1. Nancy (**was able to**) / (**could**) sing beautifully as a child.

2. Patrice **wasn't able to** / **couldn't** go to the movies last night.

3. Bao **was able to** / **could** play the piano at the competition last year, but he **wasn't able to** / **couldn't** play in this year's competition.

4. A: **Were you able to** / **Could you** hear the speaker?

   B: No, I **wasn't** / **couldn't**.

5. George **was able to** / **could** buy a rare painting yesterday.

6. Most students **were able to** / **could** speak very well after the course.

7. When I turned ten, I **was able to** / **could** get my first laptop.

8. They **were able to** / **could** hear the doorbell even though the TV was very loud.

9. A: I need a few more tubes of this blue paint.

   B: Try the new art shop on Main Street. I **was able to** / **could** buy that color there last week.

10. I **wasn't able to** / **couldn't** finish my writing assignment during class. Luckily my teacher will let me finish it at home.

PRACTICE

8 Complete the first sentence with *can* or *could* and the verb in parentheses. Then rewrite the sentence using the correct form of *be able to*.

1. Chris _____ can play _____ (play) the piano fairly well.

    Chris is able to play the piano fairly well.

2. My parents _____ (not go) to the concert yesterday.

    _____

3. Tanya hasn't been practicing, so she _____ (not dance) next week.

    _____

4. A: _____ (you / understand) the actors last night?

    B: No, _____

    A: _____

    B: _____

5. I _____ (not find) the artist's biography on the website.

    _____

6. The children _____ (finish) their paintings tomorrow.

    _____

7. The professor _____ (not teach) the art class tomorrow.

    _____

8. I _____ (not hear) the movie because people were talking.

    _____

9 **LISTEN & SPEAK.**

A Complete the conversation. Use a verb from the box with the correct form of *be able to*.

come	do	not get	relax
create	~~not help~~	meet	not see

Director: Hi, Clare. I just got a call from Nomi, and she (1) _____ isn't able to help _____ us set up the art exhibit today. She's not feeling well. (2) _____ you _____ and help us?

Assistant: Sure, but I (3) _____ there until around two o'clock this afternoon. Is that OK?

Director: Two is fine. We (4) _____ a lot of work last night.

Assistant: Great. I'll see you then. By the way, who is the artist?

Director: His name is Yong Ho Ji.

Assistant: Oh, yes, I know his work. He (5) _____ such amazing sculptures with those old car tires. I really look forward to seeing his work. I (6) _____ his last exhibit because I was out of town. By the way, (7) _____ I _____ him? I'd love to ask him about his work.

Director: Sure. Once we set everything up, you (8) _____ and enjoy the reception. I'll introduce you then.

B Listen and check your answers.

C **ANALYZE THE GRAMMAR.** Work with a partner. Change the answers in exercise **A** to *can* or *could*. Find and circle the one item that must use a form of *be able to*. Then practice the conversation twice: once more formally and once less formally. Pay attention to the pronunciation of *can/can't*.

Hi, Clare. I just got a call from Nomi, and she <u>can't help</u> us set up . . .

▼ Korean artist Yong Ho Ji uses recycled tires to create his sculptures. This photo is from an exhibit on endangered species.

10 **EDIT.** Read the passage from a podcast. Find and correct five more errors with *can (not)*, *could (not)*, and *was/were (not) able to* for ability.

ABOUT ART: Podcast 22

Host: Welcome to the Guggenheim Museum in New York. This is Ava Paterson, and I'm talking to visitors here about this week's question: Can art ~~keeps~~ *keep* us young? What do you think, sir? Are people able fight the effects of aging with creative activities?

Man: Yes, I think so. My grandfather was able to organize his thoughts easily, and he thought art helped him. He was a painter. A lot of older people have trouble with their memories. People with Alzheimer's disease[1] sometimes can't remember their own families, for example. My grandfather was 93 when he died, and he can remember absolutely everything! The last time I saw him, I could ask him many questions about his life.

Host: And what do you think, miss? Can art have positive effects on people as they age?

Woman: Well, research shows that people are able to live longer in the future, but is art the reason? I'm not sure. I like to believe that it can help. I love to see and create art, so I hope when I'm older, I will able to think clearly.

[1] **Alzheimer's disease:** a disease that causes a person to lose their memory

▼ The Solomon Guggenheim Museum, New York City

🎧 **11 LISTEN.**
CD3-35

Listen to the conversations. Circle **T** for *true* or **F** for *false*.

1. The woman was able to understand the actors. **T** **F**

2. The woman is able to go to the museum on Friday. **T** **F**

3. The man isn't able to decide. **T** **F**

4. The man thinks he could draw better as a child. **T** **F**

5. The woman was able to enjoy the ballet. **T** **F**

6. The woman was able to help the man with his photos. **T** **F**

7. The woman will be able to see the concert. **T** **F**

8. The man wasn't able to finish his art exam. **T** **F**

12 APPLY.

A Work with a partner. Discuss the situations in exercise **11** and the topics in the lesson where people talked about ability (or inability). Write as many situations or topics as you can remember in your notebook.

seeing art at a museum, famous people and their abilities

B Choose four of the situations. Write two sentences using past, present, or future forms of *can, could,* and *be able to* for ability.

1. Situation: *looking at music videos online*

   I could enjoy the music. I wasn't able to understand the words.

2. Situation: _____

   _____

3. Situation: _____

   _____

4. Situation: _____

   _____

C Share your sentences in a group. Be sure to ask follow-up questions.

A: *I was looking at a music video online the other day. I wanted to learn the words, but I couldn't understand the singer.*

B: *What band was it? Often you can find song lyrics online. Just do a search for "lyrics" and the name of the band.*

EXPLORE

CD3-36

1 READ about a popular new type of *old* music in Argentina. Notice the words in **bold**.

Old Meets New in Argentinian Music

Radio Host: Today's show is about a new form of Latin American music whose roots[1] are in traditional music. You **may be** familiar with *cumbia*, but do you know *nu-cumbia?* You **might not know** it now, but you will very soon. Before we play you some music, we'd like to take some calls from a few of our listeners. Jana in Dallas.

Jana: Thank you for taking my call. When I was younger, I lived in Colombia and studied the language and history. In a music class, I first heard about *cumbia*. *Nu-cumbia* **must be** amazing because *cumbia* itself is so good.

Radio Host: So what can you tell our guests about *cumbia*?

Jana: Well, it's a musical tradition that originated[2] in Colombia and Panama around 100 years ago. I think drums **might be** one of the main instruments. It has a great beat for dancing.

Radio Host: Thank you, Jana. That's right. *Cumbia* originated in Colombia and Panama, but its popularity has since spread all over Latin America. Recently, a new form of *cumbia*—called *nu-cumbia*—has been growing in popularity in Argentina's capital, Buenos Aires. Before we play you some of this fantastic music, we have another caller. Miro from Miami.

Miro: Hi. I'm a DJ and I just wanted to say that *nu-cumbia* is not only popular in Argentina. One woman in particular, La Yegros, has become a hit in many countries. Her music is a mix of electronic sounds and *cumbia*-style melodies. She is a great performer, too. I think with artists like her, *nu-cumbia* **may become** even bigger. Soon, it **could reach** a much larger audience.

[1] **root:** beginning, origin
[2] **originate:** to begin to happen

◄ A DJ in a popular night club in Palermo, Buenos Aires, Argentina

2 **CHECK.** Read the questions.
Choose the correct answers.

1. Where did *cumbia* come from?

   a. Colombia and Panama

   b. Colombia and Argentina

2. When did *cumbia* start?

   a. recently

   b. 100 years ago

3. What is *nu-cumbia*?

   a. a new form of music

   b. a traditional dance

4. Who is La Yegros?

   a. a DJ from Miami

   b. a nu-cumbia performer

▲ La Yegros, 2013 album cover

3 **DISCOVER.** Complete the exercises to learn about the grammar in this lesson.

A Find these sentences in the interview from exercise **1**. Write the missing words.

1. You _____ be familiar with *cumbia*, but do you know *nu-cumbia*?

2. You _____ know it now, but you will very soon.

3. *Nu-cumbia* _____ be amazing because *cumbia* itself is so good.

4. . . . *nu-cumbia* _____ become even bigger.

5. Soon, it _____ reach a much larger audience.

B Use the words you wrote in exercise **A** to complete the statements.

1. The speaker uses _____, _____, and _____ to say
   something is (or isn't) possible. The speaker is not certain.

2. The speaker uses _____ to say something is probably true.

LEARN

12.4 Possibility: *May, Might,* and *Could*

Weak Possibility or Certainty
May (Not), Might (Not), and *Could*
The song **may become** a big hit. I don't know. We **might not go** to the show. We don't have tickets yet. He **could be** at lunch. I'm not sure. I'll check.

Strong Possibility or Certainty
Couldn't
The song **couldn't become** a hit. It's terrible. He **couldn't be** at lunch. He's in a meeting.

1. Use *may (not), might (not),* or *could* with the base form of a verb to express weak possibility in the present or future. The speaker is not certain.	He **may like** rock music. I'm not sure. I **may not go** to the party. I **might stay** home. We **could go** to a movie instead, perhaps?
2. Do not contract *may not* or *might not.*	✓ They **might not come** to the party. ✗ She <u>mightn't call</u>. She's been very busy.
3. **Remember:** *Could* is used for past ability as well as present and future possibility.	I **could climb** trees when I was young. We **could go** to the beach next weekend.
4. Use *could not/couldn't* when you are almost certain that an action or situation is not likely.	He **couldn't be** in Paris. He went to London. The baby **couldn't want** food. She just ate.
5. **Be careful!** Don't confuse *may be* and *maybe. Maybe* is an adverb and is usually at the beginning of a sentence.	✓ They **may be** home. ✓ **Maybe** they are home. ✗ They <u>maybe</u> home.

4 Change the sentences from certain to less certain. Use *may, might,* or *could.*

1. Alisha will become a great D.J. (could)

   Alisha could become a great D.J.

2. Eric Clapton plays the guitar better than anyone else. (might)

   _____

◄ A DJ in Catalonia, Spain

3. *The Nutcracker* is the best ballet I have ever seen. (may)

_____

4. That website provides free music. (might)

_____

5. The art gallery will become more successful next year. (could)

_____

6. His new movie will win a lot of prizes. (could)

_____

7. La Yegros will soon have a lot more fans. (might)

_____

8. Her latest album will surprise her followers. (may)

_____

5 **ANALYZE THE GRAMMAR.** What do these sentences with *could* express? Write **PP** for *present possibility*, **FP** for *future possibility*, or **PA** for *past ability*.

1. FP   Anti's new song <u>could win</u> the songwriting contest.

2. _____   I <u>couldn't go</u> to the jazz club last week.

3. _____   <u>Could you sing</u> well when you were a child?

4. _____   This album is awesome! It <u>could be</u> the best music I've ever heard.

5. _____   The movie about Mozart was confusing. I <u>couldn't understand</u> the story.

6. _____   This song is great. It <u>could become</u> a big hit.

7. _____   If you have trouble learning Romeo's lines, I <u>could help</u> you.

8. _____   Toni missed band practice. She <u>could be</u> ill.

6 **SPEAK.** Work with a partner. Make plans to do something after class. Use *could*, the ideas in the box, and your own ideas.

> REAL ENGLISH
>
> When making suggestions about possible future activities, we often use *could*.
>
> *We **could walk**. It's not far.*

| go to a movie | go to the theater |
| watch TV | try a new restaurant |

A: *We could go to a movie.*

B: *We could do that. Or we could try that new Turkish restaurant downtown.*

12.5 Logical Conclusions: *Must* and *Must Not*

Facts	Logical Conclusions
Jenna's songs are beautiful.	She **must practice** a lot.
Her songs are soft and slow.	She **must not like** hard rock.

1. Use *must* to express a logical conclusion (an idea you are almost certain is true, based on facts you know).	I heard you laughing. You **must be** happy.
2. Use *must not* to express a negative conclusion.	Barbara **must not eat** meat. She never buys it.

7 Complete the logical conclusions. Use *must* or *must not*.

1. She is one of the most popular musicians around. She _____ must _____ perform a lot.

2. They never listen to Bob Marley. They _____ like reggae music.

3. The music teacher is shouting. He _____ be angry.

4. Brian is listening to music. He _____ have any work to do.

5. Keiko's guitar sounds great! It _____ be an expensive one.

6. That song is on the radio all the time. The singer _____ be rich.

7. Junko has seen *Cats* six times. She _____ love musicals.

8. My brother gets bad grades in his music classes. He _____ work very hard.

PRACTICE

8 Read the conversation. Circle the correct answers.

Professor: OK, class, this week we are looking at world music and how you can use it in your own music. Have you all chosen a form of world music? Todd?

Todd: I'm sorry, Professor, I thought we were doing jazz this week . . .

Leo: Todd, sometimes I think you (1) **must not / couldn't** listen at all!

Professor: That's OK, Leo. We all make mistakes. Chen? How about you?

Chen: Um, I'm still trying to decide between two styles. I (2) **may / must** choose a Russian folk song, or I (3) **maybe / might** use some type of Indian music.

Professor: Hmm, they're very different. That (4) **must not / must** be a difficult choice. Either one (5) **must / could** be interesting.

Chen: Indian music (6) **could be / maybe** difficult to work into my style of music.

Professor: (7) **Maybe / Might** try listening to some songs by the Beatles. You (8) **may not / could not** realize it, but they combined Indian music with some of their music.

9 WRITE & SPEAK.

A Read each situation and write one positive and one negative logical conclusion.

Situation	Logical Conclusion
1. Carrie loves singing and dancing.	She must like performing for people. She must not be a shy person.
2. Maryam often listens to classical music.	
3. Matsu isn't playing with the band tonight.	
4. Julie spends hours practicing the guitar.	

B Work with a partner. Share your logical conclusions from exercise **A**. Decide which sentences are the best. Then share them with the class.

10 APPLY.

CD3-37

A Listen to five clips of music from different parts of the world. Write the number (1–5) next to the country you think the music is from.

United Kingdom _____   Portugal _____   India _____   Jamaica _____   Japan _____

B Work with a partner. Compare and discuss your answers from exercise **A**. Use *may (not), might (not), could (not),* or *must (not)* to explain your thoughts.

The first clip may be a Portuguese song. I think I recognized the language. It couldn't be from the United Kingdom. It doesn't sound English.

▼ A young Japanese woman plays a *taiko* drum during a musical performance.

CD3-38

1 **READ** three conversations that Peter, a fan, has outside a theater after a play. Notice the words in **bold**.

After the Show

Peter:	Excuse me! **May I come** through? I want to get some autographs.[1]
Security Guard:	No, you **can't come** through here. This area is only for the actors.
Peter:	Oh, I see. But this is the way they come out, isn't it? **Can I** wait here?
Security Guard:	Yes, **you can**, but **would you stand** over there by the wall, please, so you're not in the way?

****

Peter:	**May I have** your autograph, Mr. Lane?
Mr. Lane:	I'm sorry. I'm afraid I don't have time tonight. **Can I get** past, please?

****

Peter:	Hello, Ms. Garcia. I'm a huge fan of yours . . . I really loved the play. You were fabulous, as always! **Could I have** your autograph, please?
Ms. Garcia:	Yes, of course. **Can I borrow** your pen?
Peter:	Of course. Oh, and **will you sign** this program[2] for my sister?
Ms. Garcia:	Sure. What's her name?
Peter:	Frances. **Would you write** it on the front here?
Ms. Garcia:	Of course. I'm so glad you enjoyed the show.

[1] **autograph:** a famous person's signature, given to a fan or admirer
[2] **program:** a small book with information about a play or other event

2 CHECK. Read the statements. Circle **T** for *true* or **F** for *false*.

1.	Peter is standing near the actor's exit.	**T**	**F**
2.	The security guard asks Peter to stand somewhere else.	**T**	**F**
3.	Mr. Lane agrees to sign his autograph.	**T**	**F**
4.	Ms. Garcia has her own pen for signing autographs.	**T**	**F**
5.	Peter asks Ms. Garcia to sign the back of his program.	**T**	**F**

3 DISCOVER. Complete the exercises to learn about the grammar in this lesson.

A Find these questions in the conversations from exercise **1**. Write the missing words.

1. Excuse me! _____ I come through?

2. Yes, you can, but _____ you stand over there by the wall, please, so you're not in the way?

3. Yes, of course. _____ I borrow your pen?

4. Oh, and _____ you sign this program for my sister?

5. _____ you write it on the front here?

B Look at the questions in exercise **A**. Some questions ask for permission to do something yourself. Other questions ask someone else to do something for you. Complete the statements.

1. Questions _____ and _____ ask permission to do something yourself.

2. Questions _____, _____, and _____ ask someone else to do something for you.

LEARN

12.6 Permission: *May, Could,* and *Can*

Asking for Permission	Answers
May we **sit** in these seats?	I'm sorry. They're taken.
Could I **have** your autograph?	Sure. No problem.
Can I **borrow** your pen?	Of course.

Expressing Permission
You **may play** video games after all your homework is done.
We **can't play video games** until our homework is done.

1. Use *may, could,* or *can* + the base form of a verb to ask for permission.	**May** I **sit** here? **Could** he **use** this bike?
2. *Can* is less formal or polite than *may* or *could*. *May* is the most formal.	Hey Jim, **can** I **borrow** your bike? Doctor, **may** I **call** you at home?
3. Use *may (not)* or *can (not)* + the base form of a verb to express what is or is not permitted.	You **may watch** educational programs on TV. We **cannot watch** sitcoms or reality TV shows.
4. **Be careful!** When you use *could* to ask permission, it does not refer to the past.	**Could** I **use** your car tomorrow?
5. To answer questions using *can, could,* or *may,* use *can* or *may*. Do not use *could*. *Can* is more common. *May* is more formal.	A: **Could** my children **stay** at your house? B: Sure they **can**. A: **May** we **go** the library, Ms. Smith? B: Yes, you **may**. Please return by 4:00.

4 Complete the exercises.

A Circle <u>all</u> possible answers to complete the conversations.

1. A: Hey, Jim, (**may**) / (**can**) / (**could**) I ride with you to the show?

   B: Sure. I'll pick you up around six.

2. A: Excuse me, Mr. Evans, **may** / **can** / **could** I have your autograph?

   B: No, you **may not** / **can't** / **couldn't**. I'm afraid I'm in a hurry.

3. A: We **may** / **can** / **could** listen to Adele practice her new song. Her manager just said it was OK. We **may** / **can** / **could** sit to the right, over here.

   B: Great!

4. A: You **may** / **can** / **could** not go backstage tonight. The band is tired.

   B: OK.

5. A: Sam, **may** / **can** / **could** I ask your opinion about my new song?

   B: Of course, you **may** / **can** / **could**. Please play it for me.

6. A: Excuse me. You **may** / **can** / **could** not take photos here.

   B: Oh, I'm sorry. I didn't know.

B ANALYZE THE GRAMMAR. Work with a partner or your class. Discuss the possible situations in the conversations in exercise **A** and decide which modal you think is best.

In number 1, I think two friends are talking. It isn't very formal, so I would use "can" or "could."

5 SPEAK. Work with a partner. Take turns asking for and giving permission, using the words in the box. Use *May I, Can I,* and *Could I* at least once. Give affirmative and negative answers.

use your bike	sit here	change the TV channel
open a window	ask you a question	leave my car here

A: *Can I use your bike?*

B: *Sure. You can use it for an hour or so. I need it at 5:00.*

12.7 Requests: *Would, Could, Can, Will*

Questions
Would you **call** me later?
Could you **move** here, please?
Can you **come** here, please?
Will you **tell** me the problem?

Answers	
Yes, I **will**.	Sorry, I **can't**.
Of course.	I'm afraid I **can't**.
Yes, I **can**.	I **can't** right now. Hold on.
Sure, I'**ll** tell you later.	No, I'm sorry. I **can't**.

1. Use *would, could, can,* or *will* + the base form of a verb to ask someone to do something for you (i.e., to make a request).	**Would** you **help** me with this? **Could** you **wash** the dishes? **Can** you **come** to my house tomorrow? **Will** you **go** to the store for me?
2. Use *can* or *will* in short answers. Do not use *could* or *would*.	A: **Could** you **help** me with this? ✓ B: Yes, I **can**. ✗ B: Yes, I could.
3. An answer with *No* often sounds rude. Use phrases such as *I'm sorry* or *I'm afraid I . . .* to make them more polite.	A: **Can** you **help** me with this, Tim? B: **I'm sorry. I can't** at the moment. B: **I'm afraid** I'm busy right now.
4. *Would* and *could* are more polite than *will* and *can*.	**Could** you **tell** me my grade, Professor Ortega? **Can** you **text** me the homework, Tom?

6 Complete the exercises.

A Rewrite the informal questions with more formal modals.

1. Can you download the concert tickets?

   Could you download the concert tickets?

2. Will you help me practice my lines for the play?

   _____

3. Can you listen to me play the new song I just learned?

   _____

4. Will you rent the new Wes Anderson movie?

_____

5. Can you take our picture?

_____

B **SPEAK.** Work with a partner. Take turns asking and answering the questions in exercise **A**. Add *please* to the end of each question and use an appropriate affirmative or negative answer.

A: *Can you download the concert tickets, please?*

B: *Sure, I'll do it now.*

A: *Could you download the concert tickets, please?*

B: *Sorry, I can't. My Internet connection is down.*

> **REAL ENGLISH**
>
> To make any request more polite, add *please* to the end.
>
> Can you come here, **please**?
> Could you sign this, **please**?

7 **PRONUNCIATION.** Read the chart and listen to the examples. Then complete the exercises.

> **PRONUNCIATION**   *Could You* and *Would You*
>
> When *could* or *would* comes before *you*, the final *-d* blends with the *y-* sound in *you*, resulting in a softer /dʒ/ sound: /ˈkudʒu/ and /ˈwudʒu/.
>
> **Examples:**
>
> *Could you tell me the time?*   *Would you wait a moment?*
> *Could you speak a little slower, please?*   *Would you explain this word, please?*

CD3-39

CD3-40

A Complete the polite requests with *could* or *would*. Use the ideas in the imperative sentences in parentheses. Then listen and check your answers.

1. Could ___you tell me your full name?_____
   (Tell me your full name.)

2. Would _____
   (Lend me five dollars.)

3. Could _____
   (Repeat the last question.)

4. Would _____
   (Speak more slowly.)

5. Could _____
   (Tell me the time.)

6. Would _____
   (Raise your hands in the air!)

B Work with a partner. Take turns asking and answering the questions from exercise **A**. Give affirmative or negative answers. Pay attention to the pronunciation.

A: *Could you tell me your full name?*

B: *Sure. It's Jennifer Ann Reynolds.*

PRACTICE

8 Complete the conversations. Use appropriate modals and responses from this lesson and the words in parentheses. More than one answer may be correct.

Conversation 1

Photographer: Excuse me, ma'am. I'm working on a story for a local magazine. (1) ___Could I take___ (take) your picture in front of your stand?

Farmer 1: I'm sorry, but I'm busy right now.

Photographer: Oh, OK. No (2) _____. Have a good day.

Conversation 2

Photographer: Excuse me, sir, (3) _____ (you / let) me take your photo?

Farmer 2: Of (4) _____. (5) _____ (you / try) to get my stand in the photo?

Photographer: Sure. (6) _____ (you / stand) in front of the table? Good, uh . . . (7) _____ (you / move) to the right a little . . . That's great! And (8) _____ (you / smile)?

Farmer 2: Sure. So, (9) _____ (I / see) the photo?

Photographer: Of course, you (10) _____. Here . . .

Farmer 2: Wow, this is great! (11) _____ (you / send) it to me, please? I know my family would love to see it.

Photographer: (12) _____ problem. What's your e-mail address?

9 EDIT. Read the conversation between a student and a music professor. Find and correct five more errors with modals asking for or giving permission and making requests.

Kira:	Excuse me, Professor Howard, may I ~~to~~ speak with you?
Professor:	Yes, of course you may, Kira. What's the problem?
Kira:	Well, it's about my report on John Coltrane. I spent a lot of time researching his life. I'm surprised at the low grade I received. Would I ask you what I did wrong?
Professor:	Yes, of course. If I remember correctly, you wrote too much about his life and not enough about his music and its influence on jazz. Could you come to my office to discuss it?
Kira:	Yes, I could. May I come in tomorrow or Friday?
Professor:	Sure. May you come and see me on Friday around 1:00 p.m.?
Kira:	Um, I'm already seeing Dr. Stein then. Would we talk at 1:30?
Professor:	Yes, that's perfect, and would you please bring your report with you?
Kira:	Yes, I would. Thank you so much, Professor Howard. See you Friday.

▶ John Coltrane (1926–1967) American Jazz saxophonist, composer, and bandleader 1960

10 Complete the exercises.

A Read the conversation between a musician and a fan before a concert. Underline three questions that use the grammar from this lesson.

Megan: Hey, I'm looking forward to hearing you sing. <u>Can I help you set up your equipment</u>?

Angel: Thanks, that'll be great. Will you put the microphone stand on the stage for me?

Megan: Sure . . . Is this all right?

Angel: Yes, uh, could you move it forward just a little? It has to be in front of the speakers.

Megan: No problem.

B **SPEAK.** Work with a partner. Look at the underlined questions in exercise **A**. Ask each question using a different modal. Discuss which modal is more polite.

A: *"May I help you set up your equipment?" is more polite, I think.*

B: *I agree. You could also say, "Could I help you set up your equipment?"*

11 **APPLY.**

A Write two questions for each situation, one asking permission and one making a request.

1. You are buying something at a concert.

   _____

   _____

2. You are with a guitar instructor learning a new song.

   _____

   _____

3. You are on a bus or train.

   _____

   _____

4. You are in a movie theater.

   _____

   _____

B Work with a partner. Role-play the situations you have chosen. Take turns asking the questions and responding. Use the conversation in exercise **10A** as a model.

A: *Can I help you?*

B: *Yes, could I have two bottles of water, please?*

A: *Sure. That'll be eight dollars.*

B: *Forget it! That's much too expensive!*

▲ Graffiti in Buenos Aires, Argentina

Charts
12.1–12.5,
12.7

1 Circle the correct words to complete the conversation.

Rob: I (1) (can't)/ **might not** understand what's happening to this city! Everywhere you go, people are painting graffiti on the walls. It's terrible!

Devon: (2) **Will you / Must you** relax? Graffiti is a modern art form. When I was in Buenos Aires last year, I (3) **could / was able to** go on a special tour of the city's graffiti.

Rob: Really? When I look at graffiti, (4) **I may not / I'm not able to** see anything artistic.

Devon: Well, a lot of people (5) **can / must** like it, because I noticed the other day that a company here is now giving graffiti tours.

Rob: You (6) **will not / must not** be serious! When did *that* start?

Devon: I'm not sure exactly, but on their website, (7) **you must / you can** see that visitors take our city's graffiti very seriously. (8) **Will / May** you take the tour with me this weekend? (9) **May be / Maybe** after the tour (10) **you could / you'll be able to** appreciate graffiti a little better.

Charts
12.1–12.7

2 **LISTEN.** You will hear eight people. First listen and write the modal and base form you hear. Then listen again and choose the correct meaning.

CD3-41

1. _couldn't see_   (a.) I wasn't able to see well.   b. I may not be able to see well.

2. _____   a. I don't know if he likes it.   b. It's clear he doesn't like it.

3. _____   a. I'll definitely buy a novel.   b. I could buy a novel.

4. _____   a. I can teach you.   b. I'd like you to teach me.

5. _____   a. She might become good.   b. She will become good.

6. _____   a. He will have the ability.   b. He will be allowed.

7. _____   a. I might be able to hear.   b. I was able to hear.

8. _____   a. Do I know how?   b. Would you let me?

3 **EDIT.** Read the conversation. Find and correct six more errors with modals and similar expressions expressing ability, probability, requests, permission, or logical conclusions.

Christine:	What is your favorite art form, Joan?
Joan:	Oh, ballet, without a doubt. I must ~~spending~~ *spend* half my money on ballet tickets!
Christine:	Really? Could you explain why?
Joan:	I appreciate the skill of the dancers. They must not work very hard to make it look so easy.
Christine:	So, who is the best dancer you've seen?
Joan:	Last summer, I could get tickets to see South Korean ballerina Hee Seo dance in New York. She is amazing! She is able communicate many emotions just with her movements. I think she could become one of the best ballet dancers of all time. This summer she is going to appear in *Swan Lake*, which I love. Unfortunately, I maybe out of the country then. If I'm here, I'm going to get tickets for the first night.
Christine:	Would you to let me know when they go on sale? From what you say, I'm sure Hee Seo might be amazing to watch.

4 **SPEAK.**

A Brainstorm a list of hobbies or other activities related to art and music. Write things that you have experience with or hope to learn more about.

Visual Art	Music	Other Art Forms
painting drawing	playing guitar jazz music	ballet acting

B Work with a partner. Discuss the questions. Talk about your experience with art and/or music. Use the chart you completed in exercise **A** to help you with ideas.

1. Can you play a musical instrument? Which one? How well?

2. What could you do as a child that you can't do now? What can you do now that you couldn't do five years ago?

3. If you could make a request to a famous artist or musician, who would it be? Tell your partner your request.

4. Could you be a famous artist one day? If so, what type of artist? If not, why not?

Connect the Grammar to Writing

1 READ & NOTICE THE GRAMMAR.

A What are some different types of reviews you've read? Tell a partner. Then read a review of the movie *Gravity*.

Go See *Gravity*!

Would you like a new view of the world? Then go and see the movie *Gravity*. This powerful movie could change the way you see your world. In fact, it might turn your view of the whole universe upside down.

In *Gravity*, disaster strikes two astronauts while they are on a space walk. They aren't able to get back to their ship, and they will probably not survive. Because *Gravity* is a 3-D movie, viewers can experience floating in space along with the astronauts. You may feel off balance as you watch the screen. You will feel like you are with the astronauts and have no control.

After I saw *Gravity*, I couldn't look at the world in the same way. I was able to see my place in the world. The world is so large, and I am so small. Watch and you too might leave the movie with a new sense of your place in the universe.

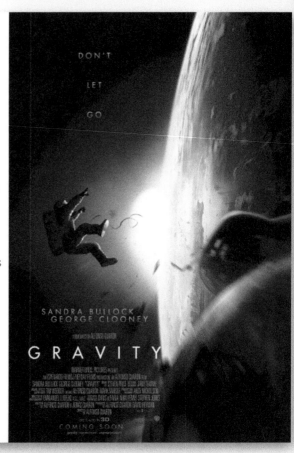

GRAMMAR FOCUS

In the review in exercise **A**, the writer uses modals to discuss ability and possibility in the past, present, and future. Be aware that each modal has different meanings and uses.

Past: *After I saw* Gravity, *I **couldn't look** at the world in the same way.*
Present: *. . . viewers **can experience** floating in space along with the astronauts.*
Future: *This powerful movie **could change** the way you see your world.*

B Read the review in exercise **A** again. Find four more modals or similar expressions used to discuss ability and possibility in the past, present, or future. Write them in the chart.

Past	Present or Future
	. . . movie could change the way you see . . .

C Complete the outline with information from the review in exercise **A**. Discuss your answers with a partner.

Title/Name: _Gravity_

Main characters: _____

Basic idea: _Disaster strikes while they are on a mission._

Setting (place): _____

Artistic quality: _3-D movie,_ _____ ,

Possible effects on viewer: _could change your view of the world,_

_____

_____

_____

_____

2 BEFORE YOU WRITE.

A Think of a movie, book, or musical artist that has had an effect on your life by changing your ideas, feelings, or behavior. In your notebook, brainstorm a list of the possible effects that your chosen topic might have on other people.

B Make an outline like the one in exercise **1C**. Complete the outline with information about your movie, book, or musical artist.

3 WRITE a review. Use the information from your outline in exercise **2B** and the model in exercise **1A** to help you.

| WRITING FOCUS | Using Italics or Quotation Marks for Titles of Works |

Use *italics* for the titles of movies, books, paintings, television series, and other longer works of art.

Then go and see the movie **Gravity**.

Use quotation marks (" . . .") for titles of short stories, poems, songs, single television shows, and shorter works of art.

"The Journey" is a short story about space.

4 SELF ASSESS. Read your review. Underline the modals. Then use the checklist to assess your work.

☐ I used *can, could,* or *be able to* to discuss ability. [12.1, 12.2]

☐ I used *may, might,* or *could* to discuss possibility. [12.4]

☐ I used *must* or *must not* to state logical conclusions. [12.5]

☐ I used italics and quotation marks correctly for titles of works. [WRITING FOCUS]

Modals: Part 2

▲ Two young Brazilian men practice capoeira in a New York park at sunset.

EXPLORE

CD4-02

1 **READ** the conversation on an online forum about judo. Notice the words in **bold**.

I'm a FEMALE judo player. Ask me anything!

Submitted 6 months ago by Judo_Gal

Hi, forum! I am a female, and I have been practicing judo for 15 years. I'm happy to answer your questions.

Concerned Dad: Hi Judo_Gal. My daughter wants to take judo lessons, but I'm concerned about safety. Should I be?

Judo_Gal: No. You really **don't have to worry** too much. Judo means "the Gentle Way." Players do not try to hurt their opponents.[1] Of course, you **have to be** careful. Sometimes players throw each other, and accidents can happen.

Concerned Dad: Do they kick, too?

Judo_Gal: No. Judo players **cannot kick** each other. In fact, there are several moves that players **must avoid**. For example, players **may not punch**[2] each other or **touch** their opponent's face. They also **have to keep** their hands away from their opponent's legs.

Concerned Dad: Can you hold your opponent's jacket? You **can't do** this in other martial arts.

Judo_Gal: Yes, you are allowed to hold the outside of your opponent's jacket, but you **can't put** your hands inside a sleeve.

Concerned Dad: Thanks for your answers. Just one more question. Why do you think practicing judo is good for young people?

Judo_Gal: Well, it was great for me. Judo players **must be** very disciplined. I learned quickly to follow rules and manage my time. They **must not ignore** their coaches, and they **must** always **behave** respectfully. These are great lessons for people at any age!

[1] **opponent:** a person who takes the opposite side in a fight, game, or contest
[2] **punch:** to hit with a closed hand

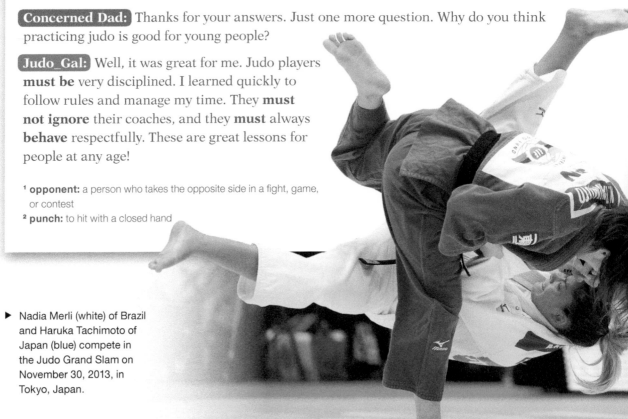

▶ Nadia Merli (white) of Brazil and Haruka Tachimoto of Japan (blue) compete in the Judo Grand Slam on November 30, 2013, in Tokyo, Japan.

▲ Female karate players watch a karate competition during the First Women's Olympics of Afghanistan in Kabul, November 6, 2006.

2 CHECK. Read the statements. Circle **T** for *true* or **F** for *false*.

1. Judo is a sport for men only.   **T**   **F**

2. Judo is very dangerous.   **T**   **F**

3. Judo players can throw each other.   **T**   **F**

4. It's OK to hit each other in the face in judo.   **T**   **F**

5. Judo_Gal believes judo is just for fun.   **T**   **F**

3 DISCOVER. Complete the exercises to learn about the grammar in this lesson.

A Find these sentences in the online forum from exercise **1**. Write the missing words.

1. You really _____ worry too much.

2. Of course, you _____ be careful.

3. Judo players _____ kick each other.

4. For example, players _____ punch each other . . .

5. They _____ ignore their coaches, . . .

6. . . . and they _____ always behave respectfully.

B Look at the sentences in exercise **A**. Write the number of each sentence in the correct place according to its meaning.

1. Necessary or required action or behavior: __2__ and _____

2. Unnecessary action or behavior: _____

3. Prohibited action or behavior: _____, _____, and _____

LEARN

13.1 Necessity: *Must* and *Have To*

Must
You **must arrive** on time. They **must finish** by the end of the day.

Have To
She **has to arrive** on time. We **have to finish** by the end of the day. I **had to leave** before class ended.

Questions with *Have To*
Do you **have to leave**? **Does** she **have to go**? Why **do** we **have to** be early? What **did** he **have to do**?

Short Answers
Yes, I **do**. **No**, she **doesn't**. Because it's polite. He **had to** apologize to the coach.

1. Use the modal *must* or the similar expression *have to* + the base form of a verb to mean *need to*.	Players **must start** at the same time. A soccer team **has to score** goals to win.
2. *Must* is common in formal situations, such as when expressing rules or laws as an authority.	Drivers **must wear** seat belts. You **must be** quiet during the test.
3. *Have to* is common when talking about something you need to do yourself.	My child is sick. I **have to leave** early. We **have to be** on time. Hurry!
4. *Have got to* is an informal way to say something is necessary. It is common in conversation, and it is usually contracted.	Hurry up! We**'ve got to** go. She**'s got to leave** now or she'll be late.
5. To express that something was necessary in the past, use *had to*. *Must* and *have got to* cannot be used for the past.	✓ We **had to go** to the store earlier. ✗ We <u>must go</u> to the store earlier. ✗ We <u>had got to go</u> to the store earlier.
6. For questions, use a form of *do* + *have to*. *Must* and *have got to* are not usually used in questions.	**Do** I **have to stay** home? **Does** he **have to attend** every class?

4 Circle the correct answers to complete the conversations. In some cases, both answers are possible.

1. **Official:** Excuse me. You (1) (**must**) / (**have to**) leave cell phones in a locker.

   Player: Sorry, sir.

2. **Player:** Do we (2) **must** / **have to** join a specific group?

   Official: Yes, you (3) **must** / **have to** check this list and find your group.

3. **Player:** Excuse me, where do we (4) **must** / **have to** sign in?

   Official: You're late. You (5) **must** / **had to** sign in by 9:00 a.m. this morning.

4. **Friend 1:** Sorry, I couldn't call you. I (6) **must** / **had to** put my cell phone in a locker.

   Friend 2: Oh, yeah. Did you (7) **have to** / **had to** apologize to the coach?

   Friend 1: Yes. I (8) **have to** / **had to** do extra exercises, too. My arms hurt!

5. **Player 1:** Hey, you (9) **'ve got to** / **got to** be careful.

   Player 2: Sorry. I'm tired. I (10) **had got** / **had** to wake up early this morning.

5 Read the club rules. Then complete the five conversations. Use the words in parentheses and the correct form of *must* or *have to*.

▼ A boy practices kung fu in Shaolin, People's Republic of China.

Club Rules

1. Arrive on time! Never be late for a lesson.
2. Do not wear watches or jewelry on the mat.
3. Put long hair in a braid or a ponytail.
4. Do not wear shoes on the mat.
5. Bring a clean suit to class.

1. **Instructor:** _____Students must arrive_____ (students / arrive) on time.

2. **Student:** _____ (we / take off) our watches?

   Instructor: Yes. _____ (you / remove) jewelry, too.

3. **Lisa:** Jen, do you have a hair band? I always forget that _____ (we / wear) our hair up.

   Jen: I know. _____ (it / be) in a braid or ponytail. Here's a band.

4. **John:** Tim, _____ (you / remove) your shoes before practice.

   Tim: Oh yeah. Thanks. I almost forgot.

5. **Mother:** Remember, _____ (you / bring) a clean suit to class.

   Daughter: I forgot! Where is it? _____ (I / hurry) or I'll be late.

▼ Children practice kung fu at the Ta Gou Academy, Shaolin, Henan Province, People's Republic of China.

13.2 Prohibition (*Must Not, May Not, Can't, Couldn't*) and Lack of Necessity (*Not Have To*)

Prohibition	Lack of Necessity
You **must not do** that. It's not allowed. They **must not leave** work before 5 p.m.	I **don't have to take** the test. It's not necessary. He **doesn't have to go**, but he can if he wants to.

1. To express that an action is prohibited, use *must not*.	Players **must not speak** during the match.
2. *May not* and *can't* are also used to express prohibition. *Can't* is more informal. Use *couldn't* to express past prohibition.	Players **may not start** until they hear the bell. You **can't drive** without a license. I **couldn't drive** before I was 16.
3. To express that an action is not necessary, use *don't have to*.	He **doesn't have to go** to class. It's a holiday.
4. To say that something was not necessary in the past, use *didn't have to*.	They **didn't have to** take tennis lessons because they already knew how to play.
5. **Be careful:** There is no negative or past form of *have got to*, so the expression is not used for prohibition or lack of necessity.	✗ I <u>have not got to</u> go. ✗ I <u>had got to</u> go yesterday.

6 Circle the correct answer to complete each sentence.

1. In some sports, players (**must not**)/ **do not have to** talk during play. Silence is required.

2. Players **must not** / **don't have to** ignore the rules. It's important to play fairly.

3. Monica **must not** / **doesn't have to** go to practice this evening. It's her night off.

4. You **can't** / **don't have to** be late, or you'll be in trouble.

5. Jim **must not** / **didn't have to** play his best to beat me. I played terribly!

6. You **must not** / **don't have to** cheat! No one will want to play with you if you do.

7. In many sports, players **may not** / **don't have to** play the whole game, but often they do.

8. In the past, girls **couldn't** / **didn't have to** compete in many sports.

9. We didn't **have to** / **have got to** be at school until 8:00 yesterday morning.

10. In soccer, you **may not** / **don't have to** use your hand to score a goal. It's against the rules.

7 WRITE & SPEAK. Work with a partner. Write one thing that is prohibited and one thing that is not necessary in your class or school. Then share your answers with your class.

Prohibited: *We must not speak while someone else is speaking.*

_____

Not Necessary: *We don't have to write essays in class.*

_____

PRACTICE

8 PRONUNCIATION. Read the chart and listen to the examples. Then complete the exercises.

CD4-03

PRONUNCIATION	Reduced Forms of *Have To*, *Has To*, and *Have Got To*

Have to, *has to*, and *have got to* are usually reduced.

Pronunciation:	Examples:
have to = /ˈhæftə/	You don't **have to** go already, do you?
has to = /ˈhæstə/	She **has to** play better next week.
has got to = /sˈgatə/ or /zˈgatə/	It **'s got** to stop. He **'s got** to see that.
have got to = /vˈgatə/	We **'ve got to** leave early.

CD4-04

A Listen to the reduced pronunciation. Complete each sentence with the full form.

1. You _____have to_____ practice a lot to become good at any sport.

2. My friend _____ stop watching football! It takes up all his time.

3. I _____ get new running shoes. Mine have a hole in them.

4. Students don't _____ know all the answers.

5. A student _____ be responsible.

6. Did you _____ study a lot last weekend?

B Work with a partner. Take turns saying the sentences in exercise **A**. Then use your own ideas after *have to* and *have got to*.

You have to <u>practice speaking a lot to become fluent</u>.

9 Complete the exercises.

A Circle the correct answers to complete the conversation.

Sunil: Hi, Jay. It's Sunil. I can't find my schedule. When (1) (do we have to) / **have we to** be at the ice rink for tomorrow's game?

Jay: Hi, Sunil. Um, 3:15 or 3:30, I think. I'll have to check. It's right here on my phone. Hold on . . . Uh, no, I was wrong—we (2) **must not** / **don't have to** be there until 4 p.m.

Sunil: Thanks. I (3) **got** / **'ve got** to remember these things! Are you feeling confident?

Jay: To be honest, I'm nervous. We were terrible last week.

Sunil: Yeah, you're right . . . but we (4) **must** / **had to** compete without our best player.

Jay: Well, Kurt is still sick, and a sick player (5) **can't** / **hasn't got to** play. The coach says we (6) **can't** / **don't have to** stay on the team if we do badly again tomorrow.

Sunil: Why (7) **does he have** / **has he** to say things like that?

Jay: I guess it's his job! Look, I (8) **'ve got to** / **had to** go—I have a ton of homework to do.

CD4-05

B Listen to the conversation and check your answers.

10 Look at Rosa's *To Do* lists. Write six sentences. Use modals and similar expressions of necessity, lack of necessity, and prohibition.

Last Weekend

> **To Do List**
>
> 1. ☑ New diet! No sweets all weekend!
> 2. ☒ Meet study group at library. CANCELED!!
> 3. ☑ Work 8-noon Sat.

This Weekend

> **To Do List**
>
> 4. ☐ No work! Day off!
> 5. ☐ Don't forget tennis practice!
> 6. ☐ Write draft of essay.

1. (eat) _Rosa couldn't eat sweets all weekend._

2. (meet) _____

3. (work) _____

4. (go) _____

5. (forget) _____

6. (write) _____

11 SPEAK.

A Complete the chart with activities in your life. Use the *To-Do* lists in exercise **10** as a guide.

	Necessary	**Not Necessary**	**Prohibited**
Last Weekend			
This Weekend			

B Work with a partner. Share the information in your chart. Use modals and expressions of necessity, lack of necessity, and prohibition.

I have to work on Saturday this weekend.

12 LISTEN.

A Listen to the radio feature about Folk Racing. Choose the correct answers to complete the sentences.

Folk Racing

1. In Finland, Folk Racing drivers _____ adults.

   a. have to be

   b. don't have to be

   c. must not be

2. If your child is under five years old, she _____.

   a. can compete

   b. has to compete

   c. may not compete

3. You _____ a good driver to be in a Folk Race.

   a. must be

   b. don't have to be

   c. cannot be

4. To drive a car in a Folk Racing competition, you _____ a special license.

   a. don't have to have

   b. must have

   c. must not have

5. If you want to do Folk Racing, you _____ a car.

   a. must have

   b. don't have to have

   c. must not have

6. In 2013, the price of a car _____ more than 1400 euros.

   a. couldn't be

   b. had to be

   c. didn't have to be

B Complete the sentences about Folk Racing. Use modals and similar expressions of necessity, lack of necessity, and prohibition.

1. If you want to drive in one of these races, you _____*have to*_____ go to Finland.

2. In Finland, a four-year-old _____ wait very long to drive in a race.

3. Last year we forgot to get a special license, so we _____ join the race.

4. He spent 2000 euros on his car. He _____ compete in Folk Racing.

5. Drivers in Folk Racing _____ spend a lot of money on their cars.

6. You _____ forget to have fun!

13 **EDIT.** Read the article about Lynn Hill, a well-known rock climber. Find and correct five more errors with modals and similar expressions of necessity and prohibition.

▲ Lynn Hill rock climbing in California, USA

         don't have to
You ~~may not~~ be an expert rock climber to enjoy Yosemite National Park, but it doesn't hurt. According to climbers, if you want the best views, you must to climb some of the park's famous mountains. If you are a climber, you have to visit Camp 4, the base camp where many famous climbs have started.

    Lynn Hill arrived at Camp 4 for the first time as a 15-year-old in the 1970s. She was a gymnast, so she hadn't to learn to control her movements. She soon showed great ability.

    In her thirties, she came back to Camp 4 with a goal. To reach her goal, she had got to 'free climb' the challenging route—the Nose, within 24 hours. Free climbing means it's just you and the rock. You have to put your hands and feet into cracks in the rock, and you don't have to use ropes or other equipment. At times during her climb, Hill must hang by just her fingers. She completed her famous climb in 23 hours.

14 **APPLY.**

A Work with a partner. Brainstorm other competitions you know about (e.g., marathons, car racing). Then choose one, and write 4-5 sentences about it.

You must be very healthy and strong.
You don't have to be a professional athlete.
You cannot compete if you haven't trained and qualified.
You must wear a number on your shirt.

B Read your sentences to another pair of students and let them guess what you wrote about.

A: *You must be very healthy and strong. . . .*
B: *Is it a running race, maybe a marathon?*
A: *Yes, it is!*

EXPLORE

1 **READ** the conversation. Notice the words in **bold**.

Man versus Horse

Denise: Hey, coach! I was wondering if I could ask you about my training plans. I'm **supposed to run** in the "Man versus Horse" race in Wales in a few months. I'm not sure how to prepare.

Coach: The *what*? What is the "Man versus Horse" race? That sounds crazy!

Denise: I know. It's a tough race; it's about 23 miles long. I don't think you can really beat the horses, but it**'s supposed to be** fun trying.

Coach: I've never heard of it! Sounds interesting. So what are your training plans?

Denise: The course has a lot of hills, so I'm planning to do my training on hills.

Coach: Well, you **shouldn't run** on hills all the time. Hills are important, but you **ought to run** on flat surfaces as well. And you **should take** at least one rest day a week . . . two if you include a really long run in the schedule.

Denise: OK. That's good to know. I was wondering, **should** I **run** the full race distance before the event?

Coach: Yes. In fact, you **should do** at least one run that's longer than the race. It'll be good for your confidence. So, you **are supposed to keep** away from the horses, right?

Denise: Yes, of course! They say you **shouldn't get** too close to them if you can avoid it.

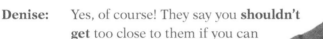

▼ "The "Man versus Horse" competition takes place every year in Llanwrtyd Wells, Wales.

359

2 CHECK. Read the statements. Circle **T** for *true* or **F** for *false*.

1. Denise thinks the "Man versus Horse" race will be easy.   **T   F**

2. She thinks she will enjoy the race.   **T   F**

3. The race is not on flat land only.   **T   F**

4. The coach thinks training only on hills is a good idea.   **T   F**

5. The coach advises Denise to run further than 23 miles in her training.   **T   F**

6. The organizers tell runners to stay close to the horses.   **T   F**

3 DISCOVER. Complete the exercises to learn about the grammar in this lesson.

A Underline the modal or similar expression in each sentence. Then circle the main verb.

1. I'm supposed to (run) in the "Man versus Horse" race in Wales in a few months.

2. Well, you shouldn't run on hills all the time.

3. Hills are important, but you ought to run on flat surfaces as well.

4. And you should do at least one run that's longer than the race.

5. So, you are supposed to keep away from the horses, right?

B Which sentences in exercise **A** give advice? Which sentences express the speaker's belief or expectation? Write the number of each sentence according to its meaning.

1. Advice: __2__ , _____ , _____

2. Expectation: _____ , _____

▼ Runners at the start of the "Man versus Horse" competition in Llanwrtyd Wells, Wales, UK (June 2013)

LEARN

13.3 Advisability: *Should* and *Ought To*

Should	Ought To
You **should exercise** regularly to stay fit. He **shouldn't play** in the game. He's sick.	You **ought to exercise** regularly to stay fit.

1. Use *should* or *ought* to + the base form of a verb to give advice or to say that something is a good idea.	People **should help** each other more. You **ought to call** your mother.
2. Use *shouldn't* to say that something isn't a good idea. It is uncommon to use *ought not to*.	You **shouldn't be** mean to your sister.
3. Use *should* in questions.* *Ought to* in questions is uncommon.	**Should** we **help** them?

*See Chart 12.1 on page **322** to review forming statements and questions with modals.

4 Read the advice sheet for runners. Then complete the sentences. Use *should, shouldn't,* or *ought to.* If there is more than one correct answer, write both.

5th Annual Hartfield 3-Mile Family Fun Run

Advice for Adult Runners
- Register online to ensure a place. Space is limited.
- Don't wait until the day of the race to register. You may be too late!
- Ask for a map if you want to check out the course.
- Wear something light; you don't need special running clothes.

Notes for Parents
- We don't advise children under five to run this distance.
- Drinking a little water before the race is a good idea.
- Walking to the finish is allowed if your child doesn't want to run all the way.
- Please don't make children train too hard for the race.

---

1. A: __Should__ I sign up early to be sure to get a place in the run?

   B: Yes, you __should/ought to__ register online.

2. You _____ register on the day of the race.

3. If you want to check out the course, you _____ ask for a map.

4. This is a "fun run," so you _____ buy special running clothes. You _____ wear something light.

5. Children under five _____ run this distance.

6. Runners _____ drink a little water before the race starts.

7. If your child gets tired, you _____ push them. It's OK to walk.

8. Children _____ train for the fun run only if they want to.

5 SPEAK.

A Match each piece of advice on the right with a situation on the left. Some advice may work for more than one situation.

Situation	Advice
1. I'm so tired! __c__	a. Join our swimming club.
2. I need information about ice hockey. _____	b. Try another sport.
3. I'm afraid of the water. _____	c. Don't train so hard!
4. I don't enjoy basketball anymore. _____	d. Look on the Internet.

B Work with a partner. Take turns reading the situations from exercise **A** and giving advice using *should* or *shouldn't*.

A: *I'm so tired!*

B: *You shouldn't train so hard.*

> **REAL ENGLISH**
>
> *Should* and *ought to* have similar meanings, but we use *should* much more frequently.

13.4 Expectations: *Be Supposed To*

Present and Future
A: You **aren't supposed to walk** on the grass. B: Oh, I didn't realize that. I'm sorry.
She's **supposed to call** in a few minutes. It's **supposed to rain** tonight. Bring an umbrella.

Past
A: He **wasn't supposed to arrive** until 10. B: Well, I guess he's early. Let's say hello!
He **was supposed to call**. Maybe he forgot. It's sunny! How nice. It **was supposed to rain**.

1. To express a future expectation, use *am/is/are* + *supposed to* + the base form of a verb.	I'm **supposed to arrive** a few minutes early. The package **is supposed to arrive** later today. You're **supposed to use** a new ball for each game.
2. To talk about something that was expected but did not happen, use *was/were* + *supposed to* + the base form of a verb.	A: They **were supposed to be** here by noon. B: Maybe they are stuck in traffic.

6 Complete the sentences with the correct form of *be supposed to* and the verb in parentheses.

1. We _____are supposed to be_____ (be) at football practice early today. We should hurry.

2. You _____ (not kick) other players in soccer.

3. A: _____ that runner _____ (win) the race?

   B: Yes, he is. His times have been faster than everyone else's.

4. My mother _____ (call) me tomorrow.

5. Alex _____ (not arrive) last night, but he got on an earlier flight, and he got here at 10 p.m.

6. Peggy _____ (go) on vacation tomorrow, but she's sick.

7. Ken is always at the gym. _____ he _____ (train) so hard?

8. I _____ (drive) Steve to the big game yesterday, but my car broke down.

9. We are late! We _____ (arrive) at 7:00.

10. Players _____ (not wear) jewelry during the game, but they sometimes do.

7 WRITE & SPEAK.

A Complete the sentences. Use your own ideas.

1. I'm supposed to _____ .

2. Students aren't supposed to _____ .

3. As a child, I was supposed to _____ , but I didn't.

4. I wasn't supposed to _____ , but I did.

B Work with a partner. Share your sentences from exercise **A**. Ask follow-up questions.

A: *I'm supposed to be on a diet this month. I'm not supposed to eat sweets or drink soda.*

B: *Why? Are you training for something?*

PRACTICE

8 Circle all correct answers. Sometimes both answers are correct.

1. A: Professional athletes **shouldn't** / **aren't supposed to** make so much money.

   B: I disagree. They **should** / **ought to** make as much as they can.

2. The game **should** / **was supposed to** start at 2 p.m., but it was delayed by half an hour.

3. If you're interested in action photography, you **ought to** / **are supposed to** borrow my camera. It's great for sports shots.

4. Dev **isn't supposed to** / **shouldn't** run on his bad ankle. He could get hurt.

5. **I'm supposed to** / **ought to** be at baseball practice in ten minutes, but I won't get there with all this traffic!

6. You **ought** / **should** not wear glasses when you play soccer.

7. I fell yesterday, and my shoulder hurts. I **ought to** / **should** see a doctor.

8. I can't believe we lost the game! That team **shouldn't** / **wasn't supposed to** be very good.

9 Look at the photo and read the caption. Complete the conversation with the phrases from the box. Use each phrase only once.

should I try	shouldn't worry	it's supposed to be
ought to learn	should I call	ought to provide
are supposed to use	should call	~~was supposed to be~~

Gina: Christine (1) ___was supposed to be___ here 15 minutes ago. Where is she? She (2) _____ us if she is going to be late.

Myoko: We have time. You (3) _____ so much. Our start time is an hour away.

Gina: (4) _____ her and ask if she's changed her mind?

Myoko: Oh, Gina, you (5) _____ to relax a bit more! She'll be here soon. So, are you looking forward to going hydrosphering for the first time?

Gina: Yes, I am. (6) _____ really exciting when you are riding inside the ball. I'm a little bit nervous. I think they (7) _____ more safety information.

Myoko: I agree. Don't forget that you (8) _____ the safety straps when you are in a hydrosphere by yourself for the first ride.

Gina: I won't forget. I'm really excited about the second ride when we'll be together in the same hydrosphere. (9) _____ to take some photos?

Myoko: Yes, of course. Oh, look. Here comes Christine now . . .

▼ Hydrosphering is a sport invented in New Zealand in the 1990s. People hydrosphere by rolling down hills inside a large, plastic ball called a hydrosphere.

10 EDIT. Read the answers to an online survey. Then find and correct six more errors with modals and other similar expressions of advisability and expectation.

Survey: Are Sports Out of Control?

This month's online survey was about the state of modern sports. Here are some of the replies we received to our questions.

1. Should top athletes ✗ earn millions of dollars a year?

Tim in Texas: No, I think it's gotten crazy. There ought to be a maximum salary in every sport.

Gene in Georgia: Yes, I think so. Athletes should earn a fair amount. Sports stars are supposed provide entertainment for millions of people. That is worth a lot of money. Also, college athletes don't earn any money, but they risk a lot. They should to get paid, too.

2. Should there be so much advertising in sports?

Tim in Texas: I understand the need for advertising—sports are a very expensive business. However, there ought to be more control.

Gene in Georgia: Sports supposed to be attractive to fans, and advertising adds a lot of color to events. There shouldn't be more control.

3. Should children compete or ought they just have fun?

Tim in Texas: Small children are suppose to enjoy sports. They ought to concentrate on learning skills, not winning games.

Gene in Georgia: All sports supposed to produce stars for world championships. If we want that to happen, then competition should start as early as possible.

---

11 APPLY.

A Work with a partner. Discuss the questions in exercise **10**. In your notebook, take notes about your answers and your partner's answers.

Question 1

A: *All sports are different. Each sport should make its own rules about players' salaries.*

B: *I agree. Sports stars are like movie stars. They should earn as much as they can.*

B Write two sentences for each question. Write about your ideas and your partner's.

Question 1

My answer: Top athletes are supposed to be "superhuman." Their salaries should be more than the average person's, too.

My partner's answer: Top athletes . . .

Charts
13.1–13.4

1 Circle <u>all</u> correct answers. Sometimes more than one answer may be correct.

1. You (**may not**) / (**can't**) / (**must not**) bring food into the stadium.

2. Tom **can't** / **doesn't have to** / **shouldn't** join the club. He is below the minimum age.

3. We **don't have to** / **must** / **have to** return the tickets by today, or we'll lose our money.

4. Lori and her friend **didn't have to** / **shouldn't** / **weren't supposed to** play tennis yesterday. Their match was canceled.

5. I **have to** / **must** / **'m supposed to** practice tonight, but I have a headache. I might not go.

6. The team isn't very good. The coach **ought to** / **has to** / **should** find better players.

7. The referee **must** / **had to** / **has got to** act fast when a fight started during the game last night.

8. You **don't have to** / **may not** / **can't** sit there. That seat is reserved for the coach.

Charts
13.1–13.4

🎧
CD4-08

2 **LISTEN** and circle the answer that is similar in meaning to the sentence you hear.

Example: 1. You hear: *I am supposed to play softball tomorrow.*

1. (**People expect me**) / **I have permission** to play softball tomorrow.

2. It's **a good idea** / **necessary** for me to speak to the coach immediately.

3. We **should** / **must** buy three tickets for the game.

4. I **must** / **should** ski more often.

5. I **went** / **didn't go** swimming yesterday as planned.

6. The referee **must** / **ought to** write a report after the game.

7. The players **have got to** / **ought to** receive free tickets for their families.

8. It wasn't **necessary** / **a good idea** for us to train hard for the race.

9. Tennis players **do not have to** / **can't** touch the net.

10. Speaking while the coach is talking is **prohibited** / **not necessary**.

Charts
13.1–13.4

3 **WRITE.** Read the tennis serving tips. Then write four sentences in your notebook about the tips. Use one modal or similar expression for each of the following: necessity, prohibition, advice, and expectation.

You shouldn't practice during a game.

Tennis Serving Tips	
1. Do not practice during a game.	3. Don't throw the ball too high.
2. Don't throw the ball straight up.	4. Keep your eye on the ball.
	5. Relax and enjoy serving!

4 **EDIT.** Read the tips about serving. Use the information in exercise **3** to find and correct seven more errors with modals and similar expressions of necessity, prohibition, advice, and expectation.

Perhaps, like many tennis players, you love playing the game, but hate serving. Well, good news! You don't have feel that way anymore! We asked our readers to share their advice on serving like a pro. Here are the results.

• You shouldn't practice during a competition. You ought practice your serve only when you don't have to worry about winning or losing.

• You got to relax. Serving ought to be easy, but it can be very difficult if you are nervous.

• You must take your eye off the ball! You should watch it all the way from your hand until you hit it.

• You shouldn't throw the ball too high. You're not supposed wait a long time for the ball to drop. If you do that, you are throwing it too high.

• You don't have to throw the ball straight up. Instead, you should to throw the ball slightly to your right, if you are right-handed. Left-handers should throw to the left.

• You must not be afraid of your serve. It's the only time in tennis that you have complete control of what happens. Serving supposed to be fun!

5 **SPEAK.**

A In your notebook, take notes about tips you would give a beginner about one of the activities in the box or your own idea. Use modals of necessity, prohibition, advice, and expectation. Use exercise **4** as a model.

> Cycling: going uphill   Swimming/Running: breathing
> Basketball: shooting a basket   Soccer: scoring a goal

B Work with a partner. Share your ideas from exercise **A**.

All cyclists ought to ride up hills regularly. When you approach a hill, you should increase your speed on the flat road. If the hill is steep, you must choose a low gear. On very steep hills you've got to be ready to stand on your pedals, if necessary.

Connect the Grammar to Writing

1 READ & NOTICE THE GRAMMAR.

A Think of a sport that you enjoy. Tell a partner your sport and your reasons for liking it. Then read what one student wrote about snowboarding.

Try Snowboarding!

We all know we are supposed to exercise to stay in shape, but sometimes going to the gym can become boring. That's when you have to find a new challenge. If you live in an area with mountains and snow, you definitely ought to try snowboarding.

First of all, snowboarding is great exercise. It strengthens your muscles and it's good for your heart. Of course, you must take things slowly at first; you can't expect to fly down a mountain like an Olympic snowboarder on your first day. Like any activity, you must practice to become more advanced. You shouldn't start on steep[1] hills, for example. First you have to learn to control the board on small hills.

Another great thing about snowboarding is that it is easy to get started. Instructors are easy to find, and you don't have to buy a lot of equipment. In fact, you should rent a board at first. Then, if you enjoy it, you can buy your own equipment.

With snowboarding, you don't have to worry about a lot of rules because there aren't any! Snowboarding is a fairly new sport, but it has quickly become very popular. Try snowboarding today! You won't regret it!

[1]**steep:** not flat; a steep hill will cause a skier or snowboarder to go very fast.

GRAMMAR FOCUS

In the text in exercise **A**, the writer uses modals and similar expressions to express necessity and advisability.

Necessity:	*That's when you **have to find** a new challenge.*
	*. . .you **must take** things slowly . . .*
Advisability:	*. . . , you definitely **ought to try** snowboarding.*
	*You **shouldn't start** on steep hills, for example.*

B Work with a partner. Find at least one more example for each meaning.

Necessity: _____

Advisability: _____

C In exercise **1A**, the writer introduces the topic and states his opinion. He gives two reasons and supports, or explains, those reasons. Complete the diagram to show his writing plan.

Topic: Snowboarding →	Opinion:
Reason 1: *great exercise* →	Support/Explanation:
Reason 2: →	Support/Explanation: Instructors are easy to find, and you don't have to buy a lot of equipment.

2 BEFORE YOU WRITE.

A Work with a partner. Choose a sport to write about and discuss your opinion with your partner. You may decide to write about a sport you <u>don't</u> like.

B In your notebook, draw a diagram like the one in exercise **1C**. Complete the diagram with your topic, your opinion, and two reasons. Then support or explain your reasons.

> **WRITING FOCUS   Writing a Clear Introduction**
>
> When writers set out to write an opinion essay, their goal is to get readers to agree with their ideas. It's a good idea to start an essay strongly by doing the following.
>
> - **Relate to your readers**: *We all know we are supposed to exercise to stay in shape, but sometimes going to the gym or running can become boring. That's when you have to find a new challenge.*
>
> - **State your opinion clearly:** *If you live in an area with mountains and snow, you definitely ought to try snowboarding.*

3 WRITE an opening paragraph that names your sport and states your opinion. Then write one paragraph for each reason. Use the information from your chart in exercise **2B** and the text in exercise **1A** to help you.

4 SELF ASSESS. Read your text. Underline the modals and similar expressions. Then use the checklist to assess your work.

☐ I used *must* or *have (got) to* for necessity and *don't* or *doesn't have to* for lack of necessity. [13.1, 13.2]

☐ I used *should* or *ought to* for advisability. [13.3]

☐ I used *be supposed to* for expectation. [13.4]

☐ I wrote a clear introduction by relating to my reader and stating my opinion clearly. [WRITING FOCUS]

14 Innovations

Verbs

▲ In 1964, people considered the AT&T picture phone to be an exciting new invention.

371

EXPLORE

CD4-09

1 **READ** the article about driverless cars. Notice the words in **bold**.

Cars without Drivers

We **live** in a modern world with constant technological innovation.[1] These new ideas often **raise** difficult moral[2] questions. "Driverless" cars, which **drive** their passengers around automatically, are a good example. When the technology first **appeared**, it was just one more amazing modern invention. Now, four U.S. states **allow** driverless cars on certain roads. Nevada, Florida, California, and Michigan have all **passed** laws that **permit** them. Several cities in Belgium, France, and Italy **are** also **planning** for them.

▲ People in a driverless car

Do you feel safe knowing that the cars around you **might** not **have** drivers? In a dangerous situation, a driver **must react**[3] instantly. A car without a driver **has** only its computer program.

So what **happens** if a child **runs** in front of a driverless car? The child's life is in danger, and the situation **requires**[4] an instant response. **Will** the driverless car **change** direction and **put** its passengers in danger? Or **will** it **continue** toward the child because that **reduces** the risk to the car's passengers? If the machine **makes** the morally wrong choice, who is to blame . . . the car company or the helpless passenger?

[1] **innovation:** the process of developing new and improved ideas, methods, and products
[2] **moral:** related to what is right or wrong
[3] **react:** speak or move when something happens
[4] **require:** need

2 CHECK. Choose the correct answer to complete each sentence.

1. In the writer's opinion, modern inventions _____.

   a. are always a good thing   b. can cause new problems   c. do not affect our lives

2. According to the article, driverless cars are _____.

   a. allowed everywhere   b. allowed in some places   c. not allowed anywhere

3. In the example of the child, the writer worries that the driverless car may not _____.

   a. realize danger   b. stop   c. make the right decision

4. According to the article, in an accident involving a driverless car, it is difficult to know _____.

   a. exactly what happened   b. who is responsible   c. if the passenger had a choice

3 DISCOVER. Complete the exercises to learn about the grammar in this lesson.

A Find the following verbs in the article in exercise **1**. Write the direct object that follows each verb. If the verb does not have a direct object, write **✗**.

1. raise _difficult moral questions_

2. drive _____

3. appeared _____✗_____

4. allow _____

5. must react _____

6. has _____

7. happens _____

8. requires _____

9. Will . . . change _____

10. makes _____

B Look at the verbs without direct objects in exercise **A**. Can you add a direct object to any of these verbs? Discuss your answer with your classmates and teacher.

LEARN

14.1 Transitive and Intransitive Verbs

Verbs				
	Subject	Verb	Direct Object	
Transitive	Jen and Joe	**rented**	**a car**	on their vacation.
Intransitive	They	**arrived**		in the evening.

1. A transitive verb is followed by a direct object (DO). The direct object is a noun or pronoun that experiences the action of the verb. It often answers questions with *who* or *what*.

   Jon **lost** his car keys.
   _{DO}

   A: **What** did John lose?
   B: **His car keys.**

2. An intransitive verb is not followed by a direct object. It is often followed by a prepositional phrase or an adverb. Here are some common intransitive verbs:

arrive	fall	live	sleep
come	go	travel	wait

   We **arrived** after dark.
   Prepositional Phrase

   They **waited** quietly.
   Adverb

3. Some verbs can be both transitive (T) and intransitive (I). Here are some common examples:

begin	close	open
call	continue	start
change	drive	stop

   He **is driving** his new car.
   She **drives** to work.

   He **opened** the door.
   The door **opened.**

4 Underline the verb in each sentence. Write *T* if the verb is transitive or *I* if the verb is intransitive. If the verb is transitive, circle the direct object.

1. __T__ Eve always tries (the latest things.)

2. _____ Last week, she tested a driverless car.

3. _____ She traveled to the beach in the car.

4. _____ She slept for about 30 minutes.

5. _____ Then, a dog ran in front of the car.

6. _____ Luckily, the car didn't hit the dog.

7. _____ Eve went to the store.

8. _____ She arrived safely.

9. _____ However, she didn't like the car.

10. _____ Eve won't buy a driverless car.

5 Read the pairs of sentences and notice the verbs in bold. Write *T* if the bold verb is used transitively or *I* if the verb is used intransitively. Circle the direct object of each transitive verb.

1. a. __T__ The boss **started** (the meeting) with an announcement about the new product.

   b. __I__ The meeting **starts** at 9:30. Don't be late.

2. a. _____ The gas station **closes** at 6 p.m.

   b. _____ **Close** the windows. It looks like it's going to rain.

3. a. _____ They **drove** the new car.

   b. _____ They **drove** carefully.

4. a. _____ My class **began** at 3:00. I'm late.

   b. _____ The teacher **began** the class a few minutes late.

5. a. _____ We **continued** the class the next day.

   b. _____ The lecture **will continue** on Wednesday.

6. a. _____ Someone **called** while you were out.

   b. _____ Someone **called** us late last night.

7. a. _____ They **opened** the car door carefully.

   b. _____ The car doors **open** automatically.

8. a. _____ **Has** the design **changed**?

   b. _____ **Have** you **changed** your tires recently?

▲ Doors open automatically in many taxis in Japan.

14.2 Direct and Indirect Objects with *To* and *For*

	Direct Object	To/ For	Indirect Object
He sent	an e-mail	to	his parents.
She bought	a gift	for	her brother.

1. Some transitive verbs are followed by a direct object + *to/for* + an indirect object (IO).	She showed **the article** to **her friend**. 　　　　　　　DO　　　　　　IO I often get **the mail** for **my neighbor**. 　　　　　　DO　　　　　IO
2. **Remember:** A direct object experiences the action of the verb. It often answers the question *what* or *who*.	We like **our teacher**. A: **Who** do they like? B: **Their teacher**.
3. An indirect object is usually a person who experiences the action indirectly. It answers the questions *to who(m)* or *for who(m)*.	He sent the package to **his parents**. A: **Who** did he send it to? B: **His parents**. I bought a gift for **my brother**. A: **Who** did you buy it for? B: **My brother**.
4. Here are some common transitive verbs that use *to* or *for*: 　a. *to: explain, give, offer, send, show, tell* 　b. *for: buy, fix, keep, make, get, provide* 　c. either *to* or *for: bring, take*	 a. Dr. Lin **showed** the results **to the students**. b. They **made** dinner **for their children**. c. Jim **brought** the report **to his boss**. 　Jim **brought** snacks **for the team**.

6 READ, WRITE & SPEAK.

A Circle the correct words to complete the article.

Nicolas Appert Changed the Way People Eat

▲ Nicolas Appert

At the end of the eighteenth century, the French general Napoleon Bonaparte needed help. He needed to provide healthy food (1) **to** / **for** his soldiers. Often food would go bad before it reached them. The French government offered a prize (2) **to** / **for** the inventor who could discover a solution, but for 15 years no one could solve the problem (3) **to** / **for** the government. Then in 1809, the French chef Nicolas Appert showed his ideas (4) **to** / **for** the government authorities. He recommended using glass bottles and high temperatures to keep food safe (5) **to** / **for** people. In 1810, after testing his idea, the government gave the prize (6) **to** / **for** Appert. Now the government could send fresh food (7) **to** / **for** the army when it was far away. Strangely, Appert didn't know why this process worked. He couldn't explain the reasons (8) **to** / **for** anyone, but his innovative ideas changed the way people eat.

▼ Modern-day canning jars

▼ An Appert canning jar

B Look at items 1–8 in exercise **A**. Write the verb and object that comes before *to* or *for*.

1. _provide healthy food_
2. _____
3. _____
4. _____

5. _____
6. _____
7. _____
8. _____

C In your notebook, use five of the phrases from exercise **B** and *to* or *for* to write new sentences with your own ideas. Then share your sentences with a partner.

The parents <u>*provide healthy food*</u> *for their children.*

14.3 Direct and Indirect Objects: Word Order with *To* and *For*

1. With some transitive verbs, it is possible to omit *to* or *for* and put the indirect object before the direct object. Here are some common examples:	1. We bought some batteries **for** Timothy.
bake buy leave make sell show bring get lend pass send write	2. We bought **Timothy some batteries.**
2. Put *to* or *for* + indirect object after the direct object. Do not put it before the direct object.	✓ He brought some flowers **to my mother.** ✗ He brought <u>to my mother</u> some flowers.
3. When the indirect object is a pronoun, it is common to put it before the direct object and omit *to* or *for*.	My cousin owes **me money.** IO DO Jamal showed **us the city.** IO DO
4. When the direct object is a pronoun, it always comes before the indirect object. Do not omit *to* or *for*.	✓ She got **them** for her sister. DO IO ✗ She got <u>her sister them.</u>

7 Rewrite the sentences without *to* or *for*. Remember to change the order of the direct and indirect objects.

1. I lent my e-book reader to my cousin.

   I lent <u>my cousin my e-book reader.</u>

2. Marie bought the latest smartphone for her husband.

   Marie bought _____

3. Mike sent the new product design to his boss.

   Mike sent _____

4. Did you leave the new Internet password for me?

   Did you leave _____

5. Eva e-mailed her homework assignment to her professor.

   Eva e-mailed _____

6. Diane showed the article about robots to her friend.

   Diane showed _____

7. My parents got a new tablet for me.

   My parents got _____

8. I gave the files to my coworker.

   I gave _____

8 Complete the paragraphs. Put the direct object (DO) and indirect object (IO) in the correct order. Add *to* or *for* if necessary.

Paragraph 1

For graduation, my parents bought (1) _____*me a car*_____ . My brother sometimes
            (DO: a car / IO: me)

lends (2) _____ , and he knows what I like. So my parents showed
            (DO: his car / IO: me)

(3) _____ first to be sure I would like it. Of course, I loved my new car!
            (DO: it / IO: my brother)

I sent (4) _____ . He wrote (5) _____ about his
            (DO: a photo of it / IO: my grandfather)   (DO: a nice e-mail / IO: me)

first car.

Paragraph 2

I try to make (6) _____ for her birthday every year. I don't often buy
                (DO: a card / IO: my sister)

(7) _____ from a store. It takes quite a lot of thought, so I never send
            (DO: a card / IO: her)

(8) _____ . I prefer to bring (9) _____ in person.
            (DO: the card / IO: her)   (DO: it / IO: my sister)

PRACTICE

9 Choose the correct ending(s) for each sentence. If no ending is necessary, choose Ø.
Sometimes there is more than one correct answer.

1. Sometimes new ideas can cause _____ .

   (a.) problems   (b.) difficulties   c. at the beginning

2. The new product appeared _____ .

   a. last week   b. customers   c. all over the country

3. The latest computers use _____ .

   a. Ø   b. quietly   c. less electricity

4. Alison sent _____ .

   a. her friend some photos   b. to her friend some photos   c. some photos to her friend

5. When Hassan heard the news, he didn't react _____ .

   a. immediately   b. the situation   c. Ø

6. The children can cook _____ .

   a. their own meals   b. Ø   c. very well

7. The movie started _____ .

   a. on time   b. Ø   c. an argument among my friends

8. We waited _____ .

   a. Ø   b. outside   c. the teacher

10 READ & SPEAK.

A Circle the correct answers to complete the conversation. Circle Ø if you do not need *to* or *for*.

Drone Delivery?

Misha: What are you doing, Deena?

Deena: I'm doing some shopping online. I want to get some presents (1) **to / for / Ø** my family. There are several birthdays in my family in the next few weeks. My cousin is first. I'm going to buy (2) **to / for / Ø** her this e-reader. Oh no, wait . . . they can't deliver it (3) **to / for / Ø** her house until next week. That's too late.

Misha: Did you hear about the companies that are planning to send (4) **to / for / Ø** customers their goods by drone, sometimes even the same day?

Deena: Drones? You mean those automated flying machines? I don't believe it!

Misha: Well, it's true. Several companies are considering using drones to send orders (5) **to / for / Ø** their customers. It sounds a bit crazy, I know. Look, I'll show (6) **to / for / Ø** you the article. . . . Here's a picture of one. Amazing, huh?

Deena: Um, I'm not so sure. I'm planning to order some expensive dishes (7) **to / for / Ø** my mother. I don't think I'd ever trust one of those machines to bring them (8) **to / for / Ø** me safely!

◄ A delivery drone that may someday be used to deliver packages to customers in as little as 30 minutes

B Work with a partner. Discuss the questions.

1. Do you think it's a good idea for drones to deliver things to people? Why, or why not?

2. What are possible problems with delivering things by drone?

3. Would you send people gifts by drone?

11 WRITE & SPEAK.

A Complete each sentence with a direct object and an indirect object. Use your own ideas.

1. I always go online to buy _____*food*_____ for ____*my cats*____ .

2. I sent _____ a(n) _____ recently.

3. Can you show _____ to _____?

4. I would like to get _____ a(n) _____ .

5. Last week I brought _____ to _____ .

B Work with a partner. Share your sentences from exercise **A**.

A: *I always go online to buy cat food for my cats.*

B: *Is it cheaper online?*

12 LISTEN.

CD4-10-13

A Listen to four students talk about different historical innovations. Write the correct date under each invention.

1. Rail Travel
George Stephenson

2. The Dishwasher
Josephine Cochran

3. The Circular Saw
Tabitha Babbitt

4. The Printing Press
Johannes Gutenberg

1825 _____

_____   _____   _____

CD4-10-13

B Listen again. Complete the chart with the verbs and objects you hear.

	Subject	Verb	Object
1. Rail Travel	Stephenson	*changed*	the way we travel
	He	operated	
2. The Dishwasher	Cochran		dishwashers for her friends
	She	started	
3. The Circular Saw	Babbitt		a large circular saw
	Men		large straight saws
4. The Printing Press	Gutenberg		books
	The printing press	changed	

C In your notebook, write sentences about each person using the verbs and objects in exercise **B**.

George Stephenson changed the way we travel.

13 **EDIT.** Read the conversation about a recent innovation in eyewear. Find and correct six more errors with transitive and intransitive verbs and with *to* and *for*.

Markus: Hey, Dave, I told ~~to~~ you how much I like my new phone, right? It gives me all the information I need when I'm away from my computer. Well, I just watched a video about a new pair of glasses that does the same thing. They show for you the same information as your phone, but right in front of your eyes!

Dave: Oh yeah, Mira sent me a photo of hers a couple days ago. Her parents got a pair her. I don't understand the attraction. Can you explain me it?

Markus: Well, I guess they make life easier for people.

Dave: Are you serious? . . . I'm pretty sure they'd give a headache to me, and I really don't mind checking my phone for information. Are you seriously going to get a pair? I'm sure they will cost a lot of money you.

Markus: Maybe, but I can't wait to get some.

Dave: I guess I won't need to buy a pair—you can lend to me yours!

14 **APPLY.**

A Read about the picture phone. Underline the verbs.

> The inventor <u>made</u> the picture phone for people who wanted more meaningful communication. The invention looks unusual, but nowadays people can easily talk to and see their friends and family on their phones or computers.

B Look at the photos of unusual inventions from the past and read the captions. In your notebook, write a short paragraph about each. Use the paragraph in exercise **A** as an example.

▲ Amphibious Bike, 1932

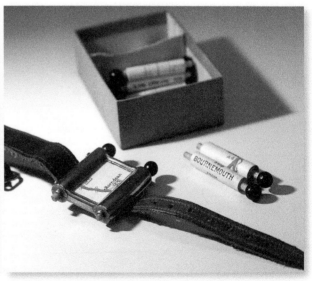

▲ Route indicator watch, 1926

EXPLORE

1 **READ** the transcript from a podcast about innovations in brain research. Notice the words in **bold**.

Podcast 23   Innovations: Wearable EEGs

Larissa: Hello! This is Larissa coming to you from State University with this week's *Tech Talk* podcast. On today's show, we have the president of the Tech Club here to **talk about** another exciting innovator. Welcome, Jamil!

Jamil: Thank you, Larissa. Today I'd like to tell you about a woman named Tan Le. She's a pioneer[1] and co-founder of a company that created the first ever portable[2] EEG and BCI (brain-computer interface). It's a lightweight headset that reads your brainwaves. Basically, it reads and interprets your thoughts and sends the information to a device, such as your laptop or mobile phone.

Larissa: So, anyone can **hook** their brain **up** to a device? What do we use it for?

Jamil: Well, for one thing, Tan Le hopes that it can help people who are injured or ill. For example, with this technology a person could soon be able to control an electric wheelchair[3] simply by **thinking about** turning left or right. There's a great TED talk about it online if anyone wants to **find out** more . . .

Larissa: Sounds fascinating. I'll definitely **check** that **out**. I imagine application developers[4] will **figure out** a lot of different ways to use the technology.

Jamil: Yes, definitely. That's the plan.

Larissa: So, I've heard that Tan Le's personal story is as interesting as this innovation.

Jamil: That's right. She **grew up** in Australia, but her family **comes from** Vietnam. Life was not easy when she was young, but her mother and grandmother encouraged her never to **give up**. Her experience really helped her to **get ahead**, way ahead!

[1] **pioneer:** a person who leads the way into a new area of knowledge or invention
[2] **portable:** can be carried or moved around
[3] **wheelchair:** a chair that allows people who cannot walk to move
[4] **application developer:** a computer professional who develops specialized software or applications

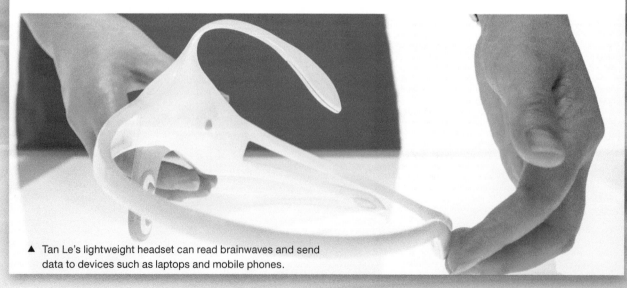

▲ Tan Le's lightweight headset can read brainwaves and send data to devices such as laptops and mobile phones.

2 CHECK. Read the statements. Circle **T** for *true* or **F** for *false*.

1. Tan Le's invention is large and heavy.   **T**   **F**

2. Tan Le's system can interpret people's thoughts.   **T**   **F**

3. Tan Le's system can only be used in hospitals.   **T**   **F**

4. Tan Le grew up in Vietnam.   **T**   **F**

5. Tan Le's family helped her succeed.   **T**   **F**

3 DISCOVER. Complete the exercises to learn about the grammar in this lesson.

A Look at the bold phrases in exercise **1**. Write the verb or verbs that come before each word.

about	ahead	from	out	up
talk				

B Work with a partner. Write one more word that you know in each column in exercise **A**. If you need help, see pages **A7–A9** for lists of phrasal verbs and their meanings.

A: *Another verb that goes with "out" is "watch," as in "Watch out!"*

B: *I think "look" with "out" is similar. It means "Be careful."*

  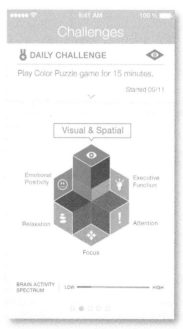

▲ Sample screen shots of brain activity and other information sent to headset users

LEARN

14.4 Phrasal Verbs

1. Phrasal verbs* usually have two words (a verb + a particle). Particles are small words (*about, over, on, in*) that look like prepositions. Unlike prepositions, however, they give a different meaning to the verb they combine with.	**Look out!** There's a dog in the road! *Phrasal Verb* I looked out the window. *Verb Prepositional Phrase* **look out:** be careful **out:** in a direction away from
2. Phrasal verbs are often used instead of single-word verbs that express the same meaning.	**call off** = cancel **go over** = review **find out** = discover, learn **hand in** = submit **get ahead** = succeed **run into** = meet (by accident) **give up** = quit, stop trying **talk over** = discuss

*See pages **A7–A9** for lists of phrasal verbs.

4 Underline the phrasal verb in each sentence. Then choose the correct definition. Refer to the lists on pages **A7–A9** for more phrasal verbs and their meanings.

1. Tan Le wants to <u>find out</u> more about how brains work.

   a. ask   ⓑ discover

2. As a child, Tan Le learned never to give up.

   a. stop trying   b. make mistakes

3. If you want more information, you can look up Tan Le's company online.

   a. find   b. contact

4. People are thinking about the different ways to use the new technology.

   a. are considering   b. are remembering

5. Some people do not like new technology, but it isn't going to go away.

   a. continue   b. disappear

6. The world cannot go back to an age without computers.

   a. advance   b. return

7. The scientist had to call off his research because his equipment was damaged.

   a. cancel   b. repeat

8. The researcher finished the test and turned off the machine.

   a. stopped   b. started

▶ A woman looks at a flying object with Emotiv Insight

14.5 Transitive and Intransitive Phrasal Verbs

	Phrasal Verbs	Direct Object	
Transitive	Jen and Joe **got on** They **talked over**	the flight their plans	to Beijing. for the trip.
Intransitive	Nancy **showed up** Her car **broke down**	— —	ten minutes late. on the way.

1. Some phrasal verbs are transitive.* They are followed by a direct object (DO).	We **called off** the party. DO
2. Some phrasal verbs are intransitive.* They are not followed by a direct object.	✓ Our car **broke down**. ✗ Our car broke down it. ✗ They broke down <u>the car</u>.

* See pages **A7–A9** for lists of phrasal verbs.

5 READ & WRITE.

A Circle the correct particle to complete each phrasal verb.

Riverwatch
Keeping Our Rivers Clean!

Dear Neighbor,

We all live in an area that used to have beautiful rivers and ponds. Have you noticed how the standard of these areas has been going (1) **over / down** for the last few years? Some people throw (2) **off / away** their garbage carelessly, and a lot of it ends (3) **out / up** in the river. I went to town hall to talk (4) **out / over** the problem with the town officials. They clearly don't have enough staff to clean (5) **up / away** these areas on a regular basis.

That's when I had the idea to set (6) **in / up** an organization to help. This is a new idea for our community. We're called Riverwatch, and we are already making a BIG difference!

Every weekend, we send (7) **away / out** teams to pick (8) **up / on** garbage from one of the rivers. It's clear that the problem of dirty rivers and ponds will not go (9) **away / down** on its own. If you are concerned about the area you live in and can spend a few hours with us once a month, come (10) **over / by** our next meeting.

Sincerely,
Pat Siever

B Seven of the phrasal verbs in exercise **A** are transitive. In your notebook, write six more phrasal verbs from the letter and their direct objects.

throw away their garbage

14.6 Transitive Phrasal Verbs: Separable and Inseparable

Transitive Phrasal Verbs	
Separable	Jack **looked up** the word. He **looked** the word **up**. He **looked** it **up**.
Inseparable	✓ Jill **thought about** the essay. ✓ She **thought about** it. ✗ Jill thought the essay about. ✗ She thought it about.

1. Most transitive phrasal verbs are separable.* The direct object (DO) can come after the phrasal verb or between the verb and the particle. Here are some common separable phrasal verbs:
 	
call off   find out   look up   set up
figure out   hand in   put on   talk over
	I **turned off** the light. → I **turned** the light **off**.
	        DO DO
	
	I **tried on** the coat. → I **tried** the coat **on**.
	       DO DO

2. **Be careful!** When the direct object of a separable phrasal verb is a pronoun (*me, him,* . . .), it must go between the verb and the particle.	✓ She didn't **pick** it **out**. ✗ She didn't pick out it.

3. Some transitive phrasal verbs are inseparable.* The direct object must come after the particle. Here are some common inseparable phrasal verbs:
 	
call on   come up with   go over   run into
come from   get on   look into   think about
	I **ran into** an old friend.
	          DO
	
	I **ran into** her at the store.
	        DO

4. **Be careful!** When the direct object of an inseparable phrasal verb is a pronoun, it still must go after the verb and the particle.	✓ I **came across** it while doing research. ✗ I came it across yesterday.

*See pages **A7–A9** for lists of phrasal verbs.

6 Complete the phrasal verbs in the students' responses to the professor's question. Use chart 14.6 and the lists of phrasal verbs and their meanings on pages **A7–A9** to help you.

Professor: What qualities do you need to be an innovator?

1. You have to be able to _____*go*_____ over a lot of notes and ideas.

2. You need to be good at finding _____ what people need.

3. It helps if you come _____ a family of innovators.

4. It's an advantage if you enjoy trying to _____ out solutions to problems.

5. You have to be patient. Sometimes, if you go to sleep thinking _____ a problem, you will _____ up with a solution.

6. To find the best solutions, you may need to talk _____ your ideas with other people.

7 Choose the option with the correct word order to replace the bold phrase in each sentence.

1. We **turned on the TV**. (a.) turned it on b. turned on it

2. The professor **called on Linda**. a. called her on b. called on her

3. We had to **call off the meeting**. a. call it off b. call off it

4. Don't **hand in your work** late. a. hand it in b. hand in it

5. **Put your shoes on**. It's time to go! a. Put them on. b. Put on them.

6. When did you **run into José**? a. run him into b. run into him

7. I can't **figure out the answer**. a. figure it out b. figure out it

8. I need to **look up the word** *portable*. a. look it up b. look up it

PRACTICE

8 Circle the correct words or phrases to complete the e-mails. Sometimes both answers are correct.

Hi Frank,

My trip was terrible! I was scheduled to fly to Houston to give a speech at a conference about innovation in the workplace. When I woke (1) **up / out** on the day of my flight, there was a terrible storm. I had to look (2) **the flight status up / up the flight status** on my phone because my computer wasn't working. There was no change, so I drove to the airport. The storm got worse, and my plane took (3) **off / away** three hours late. Then there was a problem with the conference schedule, and they had to call (4) **off my speech / my speech off**. I didn't find (5) **out / out it** until I received a text from the conference organizers when I arrived in Houston!

Hi Silvia,

You were asking about Penny. I ran (6) **into / over** her last week at the train station. She invited me to come (7) **over / over to** her apartment for dinner. We had a great time, but she's not very happy at work. She has a new boss, and the company didn't talk (8) **it over / over it** with her first. Hopefully, they will get (9) **along / up**.

9 Complete each sentence with the phrasal verb from the box that has the most similar meaning to the bold verb. Use each phrasal verb only once.

~~hand in~~	talk about	talk over	think over	turn down

1. Anyone interested in the job may **submit** an application.

   I need to _____ hand in _____ my application by tomorrow. I should get busy!

2. Please **consider** the job offer. We could use talented people like you.

   Hey, Tammy. Did you _____ the job offer? What did you decide?

3. Mr. Clark, Tamara may **refuse** the offer. Other companies have offered her more money.

   What's your decision, Tammy? Are you going to _____ the job offer?

4. Mr. Clark, I'd like to **discuss** offering more money to Tamara. What do you think?

   The boss and I will _____ the possibility of offering more money to Tammy.

5. The boss will see all employees individually to **discuss** any problems.

   Ken, can we _____ the problem with this design? I'd like to find a solution.

REAL ENGLISH

Phrasal verbs are more common in informal speaking and writing. The single word verb is sometimes used in a more formal situation.

Formal: *You must **submit** your essays no later than 5 p.m. on Friday.*
Informal: *Hey Jon, when do we have to **hand in** our essays?*

---

10 LISTEN.

CD4-15

A Listen to the excerpt from a lecture about inventors. Complete the text with the phrasal verbs you hear.

People like to believe that inventors are brilliant people who (1) _____ dream up _____

new ideas on their own. In movies about innovation, an inventor often

(2) _____ with the perfect solution to a problem. At times these

inventors (3) _____ problems, but they never

(4) _____ . They (5) _____ trying to make

our lives better, and eventually they succeed.

In fact, these popular ideas about inventors are far from the truth. In reality, most inventions

(6) _____ a community of people who are all trying to

(7) _____ the answer to a problem.

For example, people often (8) _____ the name of Thomas Edison

when (9) _____ innovation. Many people believe that Edison

(10) _____ the light bulb without any help. However, Edison's light bulb was

not completely new. He was just the first one to produce something that people could buy and use.

B Look at your answers from exercise **A**. Choose the best meaning for each phrasal verb. Refer to pages **A7–A9** for lists of common phrasal verbs and their meanings.

1. a. invent   b. want   c. own
2. a. arrives at work b. stops sleeping   c. goes home
3. a. make   b. offer   c. meet
4. a. stop   b. change   c. wait
5. a. work   b. continue   c. win
6. a. start with   b. affect   c. belong to
7. a. describe   b. avoid   c. solve
8. a. forget   b. mention   c. criticize
9. a. discussing   b. reporting   c. finding
10. a. created   b. stole   c. changed

11 APPLY.

A Put the words in the correct order to make questions with phrasal verbs.

1. you / any problems / into / have / recently / run

   _____Have you run into any problems recently?_____

2. new ideas / think / you / do / up / how

   _____

3. you / what / about / found / have / out / inventors

   _____

4. up / what words / you / looked / have / in this lesson

   _____

5. count / who / do / for advice / on / you

   _____

B Work with a partner. Ask and answer the questions you wrote in exercise **A**. Then ask follow-up questions to learn more about your partner.

A: *Have you run into any problems recently?*

B: *Yes, I ran into a few problems with phrasal verbs.*

A: *Oh, which ones?*

Charts
14.1–14.6

1 Circle the correct words to complete the conversation. Sometimes both answers are correct. See pages **A7–A9** if necessary.

Melanie: My brother Rob (1) **sent to me** / **sent me** an interesting article last night. He's (2) **working an assignment** / **working on an assignment** about a Japanese space project called *Ikaros*.

Ross: *Ikaros*? What's that?

Melanie: It's a spacecraft that uses solar power[1] instead of rocket fuel. It has a huge sail that (3) **takes in energy** / **takes energy in** from the sun and stores it. The sail measures just over 46 square feet (14.1 square meters). Light from the sun (4) **hits to the sail** / **hits the sail** and bounces off. This allows *Ikaros* to (5) **move** / **move in** through space.

Ross: Wow! I'm sure *Ikaros* didn't get into space on its own, though . . .

Melanie: No, *Ikaros* couldn't (6) **take off** / **take away** from Earth on its own. It was launched on a rocket in 2010 and when it (7) **arrived space** / **arrived in space**, the sail (8) **carried out its task** / **carried its task out** perfectly.

Ross: And where is *Ikaros* going?

Melanie: It's already taken photos of Venus and now it's (9) **going back** / **going ahead** to the sun . . . Anyway, back to Rob — he's probably finished his assignment and he wanted me to (10) **look over it** / **look it over** for him.

[1] **solar power:** power from sun

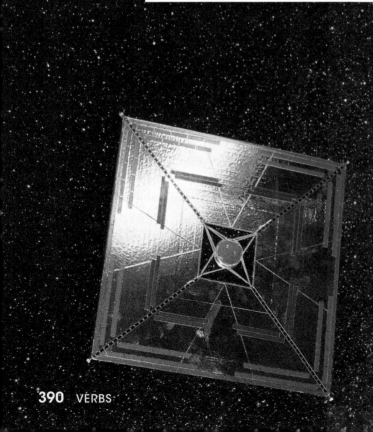

◀ The solar yacht *Ikaros* uses a large, square sail to travel from Earth to Venus and the sun.

2 **EDIT.** Read the posts about 3D printers from a technology website. Find and correct seven more errors with transitive, intransitive, and phrasal verbs.

Printing in 3D

[posted @ 10:20 pm by techwizard33]

A few days ago, a friend showed ~~to~~ me his 3D printer. I wanted to see it because I might buy for my son one. The printer was smaller than I expected. It cost my friend a lot of money, too, but apparently the price is coming down. He turned on it, so I was able to see how it worked. My friend uses his computer to design items for other companies. To test his ideas, he needs to try out them. Making an item to test used to be a long process, but now my friend can make one quickly with his 3D printer. It seems incredible! I think I will buy one!

▲ A 3D printer prints a model plane.

[posted @ 10:33 pm by kbb4210]

I agree. These sound great. The other day I ran a friend into when I was downtown. She does research on historical objects. She does a lot of work to the Smithsonian Institution in Washington, DC. In the past, she had to travel twice a month to examine the real objects at the Institution, but recently she also bought a 3D printer. Now the Institution sends to her the exact measurements of an object and she prints out it at home. It's great!

3 **LISTEN & SPEAK.**

CD4-16

A Read the questions. Then listen to a student present her invention to her class. In your notebook, take notes about each question.

1. What did the student invent?
2. What do you use it for?
3. Who did she create the product for?
4. How did she come up with her idea?
5. Did she run into any problems?
6. Has her invention taken off?

B Work with a partner. Discuss your answers to the questions in exercise **A**.

Connect the Grammar to Writing

1 READ & NOTICE THE GRAMMAR.

A What are some innovative products you know about? Discuss your ideas with a partner. Then read the article.

Would you take a pill to remember your passwords?

Nowadays, you need a password for almost everything. Trying to remember numerous passwords is a challenge for almost everyone. Why can't it be easier?

Well, now it can. The Motorola company has come up with a pill that will remember your passwords for you. When you take the pill, it reacts with the acid in your stomach. By doing this, it is able to send an electronic signal, or "password," to your phone, laptop, or other digital device. Your device reads the signal, and automatically logs you in to your accounts. Your body *becomes* your passwords. You no longer have to write your passwords down.

This seems like the perfect product, because people hate having to remember so many passwords. But will they like the idea of a password pill? The FDA[1] has approved the pill for sale in the United States, so we may soon find out. Products come and go—will the password pill take off and be a success, or will it be just one more failed invention?

[1] **FDA:** Food and Drug Administration

GRAMMAR FOCUS

Verbs have patterns. In addition to learning the meaning, it's a good idea to record the different patterns (for example, verb + object; verb + prepositional phrase). Notice the patterns of these verbs from the article in exercise **A**.

Transitive (with object)	Verb:	*Nowadays, you **need** a password . . .*
	Phrasal Verb:	*The Motorola company has **come up with** a pill . . .*
Intransitive (no object)	Verb:	*Products **come** and **go**—*
	Phrasal Verb:	*—will the password pill **take off** and be a success . . .*

B Read the article in exercise **A** again. Underline the verbs or phrasal verbs that you want to learn more about. Write each verb and its pattern in the chart.

Verb/Phrasal Verb Pattern	Pattern
1. *react*	*verb + prepositional phrase (intransitive)*
2.	
3.	
4.	

C Complete the chart with information from the article in exercise **A**. Then work with a partner and compare your answers.

What is the problem/need?	people have too many passwords to remember
Who invented the product?	
How does it solve the problem?	
When is it useful?	every day, whenever you are online, using a digital device
Why is (or isn't) it a good idea?	

2 BEFORE YOU WRITE.

A Work with a group. Brainstorm a list of innovative products you know about or ideas you have for a new innovation. Use the innovations from the unit or your own ideas.

B Choose one of the innovative products from your list in exercise **A**. In your notebook, draw a chart like the one in exercise **1C**. Write answers about your product.

3 WRITE two or three paragraphs about the innovative product you chose. Write an introduction describing the problem. Then use the information from your chart in exercise **2B** and the article in exercise **1A** to help you.

> **WRITING FOCUS** Choosing a Good Title
>
> A title is an important part to any piece of writing. The title of the article about password pills questions a new idea. Asking a question is one way to give your writing a good title.
>
> A good title:
> * catches the readers' interest
> * begins with a capital letter
> * does not have a period at the end, but may have a question mark (?) or an exclamation mark (!) at the end for emphasis

4 SELF ASSESS. Read your text. Underline examples of transitive and intransitive verbs or phrasal verbs. Then use the checklist to assess your work.

☐ I used transitive and intransitive verbs correctly. [14.1]

☐ I used direct and indirect objects with *to* and *for* correctly. [14.2, 14.3]

☐ I used transitive and intransitive phrasal verbs correctly. [14.5]

☐ I used separable and inseparable transitive phrasal verbs correctly. [14.6]

☐ I chose a good title for my essay about an innovation. [WRITING FOCUS]

Passive Voice and Participial Adjectives

▶ Rapa Nui National Park, Easter Island

EXPLORE

CD4-17

1 READ the article about a group of people who lived in South America long ago. Notice the words in **bold**.

The Moche of Northern Peru

Peru
SOUTH
AMERICA

From around A.D. 100–800, mysterious people inhabited[1] northern Peru. Recently, archaeologists[2] have made some important discoveries about these people. They **are known** as the Moche. Visitors to Peru can see the remains of their pyramids, which **are called** *huacas*. For a long time, little **was understood** about Moche society or culture, but that situation has changed since some important tombs[3] **were discovered**.

One of the most interesting tombs **was found** in 2013. Archaeologists uncovered the body of a Moche woman in a large room around 20 feet (6 meters) beneath the ground. The tomb clearly belonged to an important person.

Artifacts[4] in the tomb helped to explain the woman's position in society. For example, a tall silver cup **was found** beside her body. Moche art shows that similar cups **were used** in religious ceremonies. Archaeologists believe the woman was a priestess, or an important woman who performed religious ceremonies. They think that Moche society **was ruled** by women, or at least some Moche areas were. They believe that priestesses such as this one were queens of their people. Archaeologists hope that more secrets of this fascinating culture **will be uncovered** in the future.

[1] **inhabit:** to live in an area
[2] **archaeologist:** a person who studies the past by looking at items such as buried houses, tools, pots, and so on
[3] **tomb:** a grave; a place where a dead body is buried
[4] **artifact:** an object used by humans a very long time ago

► Experts carefully uncover objects from a Moche tomb.

2 CHECK. Make true statements according to the article. Match the beginning of each statement with the correct ending.

1. *Huacas* are _____.   a. in religious ceremonies

2. In 2013, researchers found _____.   b. some Moche areas

3. The priestess's tomb was 20 feet _____.   c. an important tomb

4. Silver cups were important _____.   d. beneath the ground

5. Women probably ruled _____.   e. Moche pyramids

3 DISCOVER. Complete the exercises to learn about the grammar in this lesson.

A Find these sentences in the article from exercise **1**. Write the missing words.

1. They _____ as the Moche.

2. For example, a tall silver cup _____ beside her body.

3. Moche art shows that similar cups _____ in religious ceremonies.

4. Archaeologists hope that more secrets of this fascinating culture _____ in the future.

B Look at the sentences from exercise **A**. Complete the chart with the words you wrote.

Verb Form	Passive Voice: *Be* + Past Participle
Present	
Past	
Future	

◄ Dos Cabezas, the site of an important Moche *huaca* (or pyramid) in northern coastal Peru

LEARN

15.1 Active and Passive Voice

Active and Passive Voice	
Active:	A guard **locked** the doors.
Passive:	The doors **were locked** by a guard.

1. In the active voice, the subject is the *agent* or *doer*. It performs the action of the verb. The object is the receiver of the action of the verb.

   In the passive voice, the subject is the receiver of the action of the verb.

   Active: Scientists **discovered** a lost city.
   Subject/Agent   Object/Receiver

   Passive: A lost city **was discovered** by scientists.
   Subject/Receiver

2. A sentence in the passive voice has a form of *be (not)* + the past participle of a verb.

   Oranges **are grown** in Florida.
   The lost objects **haven't been found**.
   Coal **was used** to heat buildings.

3. Only transitive verbs (verbs that can be followed by a direct object in the active voice) can occur in the passive voice.*

   Intransitive verbs (verbs that are not followed by a direct object in the active voice) cannot be used in the passive voice.

   They **saw** bears at the camp today
   Bears **were seen** at the camp today.

   ✓ Our taxi **arrived** early.
   ✗ Our taxi was arrived early.

4. Sometimes *by* + the agent comes at the end of a passive sentence.

   A lost city was discovered **by scientists**.

*See Chart 14.1 on page **374** for information on transitive verbs.

4 Write **A** if the underlined verb form is *active*, and **P** if it is *passive*.

__P__ 1. Moche society around San José de Moro was ruled by women.

_____ 2. Interesting objects were discovered in the tomb.

_____ 3. Archaeologists found a silver cup.

_____ 4. The priestess was buried in a special way.

_____ 5. She wore a simple necklace of local stones.

_____ 6. Several discoveries were made in Peru.

_____ 7. Today's lecture on Moche society was canceled.

_____ 8. The discovery of the priestess has changed the way we think about the Moche.

_____ 9. Online videos about archaeology are watched by a lot of people.

_____ 10. Major new discoveries will be reported in the news.

> **REAL ENGLISH**
>
> Use the passive voice to emphasize what happened rather than who or what performed the action.
>
> *A cup **was found** on the ground.*
> *The plans **weren't understood**.*

5 Circle the correct form of the verbs to complete the article.

Egypt is full of incredible ancient sites, but the most famous is the tomb of King Tutankhamun (King Tut). He (1) **ruled** / **was ruled** Egypt from around 1332 B.C.–1323 B.C. Until his tomb (2) **discovered** / **was discovered** in 1922, many details about his life (3) **didn't know** / **weren't known**. King Tut's tomb (4) **found** / **was found** in the Valley of the Kings by archaeologist Howard Carter. Carter (5) **believed** / **was believed** that Tut's tomb had to be in the area because of other nearby discoveries. When he (6) **found** / **was found** a door, he (7) **knew** / **was known** something important was behind it. Photos (8) **took** / **were taken** of the door before it (9) **removed** / **was removed**. Behind the door, Carter and his team (10) **found** / **were found** hundreds of gold objects, as well as King Tut's preserved body, or mummy.

▲ Burial mask of King Tut

15.2 Passive Voice: Present, Past, and Future Forms

	Passive Voice			
	Subject	*Be (Not)*	Past Participle	
Present	That TV show These cars	is aren't	watched made	by millions. in Germany.
Past	The meeting The discoveries	was weren't	canceled. made	by Dr. Jones.
Future	Our special guests The plans	will be won't be	treated changed.	well.

1. To form the passive voice, use a form of *be* with the past participle of the verb.	Gravity **was discovered** by Newton. Your bags **will be checked** by security.
2. **Remember:** The past participle of regular verbs is the same form as the simple past (verb + *-ed*). However, many verbs have irregular past participles.*	Many homes were ruined. (ruin/ruined/**ruined**) The secret was **kept**. (keep/kept/**kept**) Russian **is spoken** here. (speak/spoke/**spoken**)
3. To form questions in the simple present and past, place the appropriate form of *be* before the subject.	**Was** this car **made** in Korea? Where **were** the cars **made**?
4. To form questions with the future, put *will* before the subject.	**Will** the food **be eaten**? Where **will** the food **be kept**?

*See page **A4** for a list of irregular past participles.

6 Complete the sentences with the words in parentheses. Use the simple present, simple past, or future passive form of the verbs.

1. Before electricity was available, candles ___*were used*___ (use) for light.

2. The ancient site _____ (discover) three years ago.

3. Many items _____ (remove) for scientific study.

4. Work on the site _____ (complete) next month.

5. The museum _____ (not own) by the government now.

6. A: _____ Egyptian artifacts _____ (display) here?

   B: Yes, they _____. You can find them on the second floor.

7. The opening date for the Moche exhibit _____ (not announce) until next week.

8. How _____ food _____ (prepare) in the Middle Ages?

9. Where in the library _____ the books about ancient Greece _____ (keep)?

10. Native American history _____ (not teach) by Professor Schulz anymore

PRACTICE

7 Complete the exercises.

A Read the information about a common archaeological procedure. Underline the verbs.

Archaeological Dig: Standard Procedure

When team members <u>find</u> an artifact, they follow a standard procedure.

- A student assistant places the artifact in a special container.

- The assistant writes the information about the artifact on the container label.

- The assistant records the artifact in the project's database.[1]

- Experts analyze the artifact at the laboratory.

¹**database:** a computer program for storing information

B Complete the presentation. Use the passive voice and the verbs in exercise **A**.

> Hello, my name is Liz Harrison, and I'm a team leader on the dig. I'd like to tell you a little bit about our working methods on this project. When an artifact (1) _____is found_____ by team members, a standard procedure (2) _____. First, the artifact (3) _____ in a special container, and information about the artifact (4) _____ on the container label. After the artifact (5) _____ in the project's database, it (6) _____ at the laboratory.

C Complete the conversation between two team members about something that went wrong on the project in exercise **A**. Use the simple past passive voice.

Erik: We had a problem with our new student assistants yesterday.

Kumiko: What happened?

Erik: Well, unfortunately, the standard procedure (1) _wasn't followed_ (not follow). Some of the containers (2) _____ (not label) properly.

Kumiko: Oh, that's not good. (3) _____ all the artifacts _____ (place) in containers?

Erik: No, and some small pieces of pottery (4) _____ (damage) as a result.

Kumiko: That's terrible! (5) _____ all the artifacts _____ (record) in the database?

Erik: Yes, that (6) _____ (do) correctly. On the bright side, the team discovered one very interesting object.

Kumiko: Oh, really? What (7) _____ (find)?

> **REAL ENGLISH**
>
> Sometimes, the passive voice is used when the speaker does not want to blame a person or people directly.
>
> *The procedure **wasn't** **followed**.*

D **WRITE & SPEAK.** Look again at the question Kumiko asks Erik at the end of exercise **C**. Write a possible reply in your notebook. Use your own ideas and three to four verbs from the box in the passive voice. Then work in a group and take turns reading your replies. Whose is the most interesting?

| analyze | break | clean | find | know | make | repair | sell | steal | take | use |

Erik: A long, dirty necklace was found. After it was cleaned, they saw that it was solid gold. We think it was made over 800 years ago in a small town in Italy. It might be worth over $500,000. The necklace will be analyzed early next week, so we should have more information then.

8 EDIT & SPEAK.

A Read the article about Angkor Wat, an ancient site in Cambodia. Find and correct five more errors with the passive voice.

A Restoration Success Story at Angkor Wat

The temple of Angkor Wat in Cambodia was ~~build~~ *built* in the 12th century by a Khmer king. It was the state temple and also the place where the king was buried. Many parts of the temple are damaged. Water and time have done much of the damage. But also, the temple constructed in a way that has not lasted. Recently, restoration work on one important part of the temple was complete by a team of specialists. Restoration is when a damaged building brought back to a good condition.

For this restoration, special techniques were required, and the Cambodian team was well trained for the job. Gradually, over a five-year period, important parts of the temple cleaned and dangerous cracks were filled. The project was a big success, and the team plans to continue its work on other buildings at the site. Hopefully, all of Angkor Wat will restore in an equally successful way.

▼ Sunrise at Angkor Wat, Cambodia

B Complete the passive questions. Use the verbs in parentheses and a correct form of the passive voice.

1. When _____ was _____ Angkor Wat _____ built _____ (build)?

2. Who _____ (bury) there?

3. How _____ it _____ (damage)?

4. _____ the rest of Angkor Wat _____ (restore) in the future?

C Work with a partner. Ask and answer the questions in exercise **B**. Find the answers in exercise **A**.

A: *When was Angkor Wat built?*   B: *In the 12th century.*

9 APPLY.

A Read Paul's story about an item from the past. Underline the verb forms that are passive.

> I have chosen a woodworking drill. It <u>was owned</u> by my grandfather and was used in his work as a carpenter on ships. Sadly, my grandfather was lost at sea when my father was a child, so I never knew him. His tools are kept carefully by my family. I like to do woodwork myself, so his drill is still used, and it works very well. I'm going to give the drill to my son. It's nice to think that my grandfather will be remembered through his tools.

▲ Hand drill

B Complete the chart with information from Paul's story.

	Item: Woodworking drill
Who was it owned by?	
How was it used?	
Where was it used?	
Other details	

C Choose an item from the past to write about. Complete the chart for your item.

	Item: _____
Who was it owned by?	
How was it used?	
Where was it used?	
Other details	

D In your notebook, write a short paragraph about your item. Use the passive voice where appropriate. Then read your story to a partner.

EXPLORE

CD4-18

1 READ the article about a ship that sank in 1865. Notice the words in **bold**.

A Treasure Ship Tells Its Story: The SS *Republic*

In October 1865, soon after the end of the American Civil War, the SS *Republic* left New York on a journey to New Orleans. Five hundred barrels[1] of goods and a reported $400,000 in coins were loaded onto the SS *Republic* in New York. The money was shipped **by bankers and businessmen**. Because of the situation after the war, which the southern states lost, coins from the northern states **could be used** in the South to buy almost twice as much as they could in the North.

Sadly, the SS *Republic* ran into a hurricane[2] near the Carolinas and sank about 100 miles off of the coast of Savannah, Georgia. Lifeboats and a raft were launched[3] **by the crew and passengers.** Most of the 80 people on board survived. The coins, however, sank to the bottom of the ocean along with the ship.

In 2003, the wreck of the SS *Republic* was discovered **by a company called Odyssey Marine Exploration**. Over 51,000 gold and silver coins were recovered. Thousands of everyday items were also found. Many of these items **can** now **be viewed** in public exhibitions and on Odyssey's virtual museum: www.OdysseysVirtualMuseum.com. Viewing these items is a great way to see how people lived in the 1860s.

[1] **barrel:** a large round container made of metal or wood
[2] **hurricane:** a storm with very strong winds and rain
[3] **launch:** to put a boat in the water

▶ Painting of the SS *Republic* by John Batchelor (courtesy of Odyssey Marine Exploration)

2 CHECK. Read the statements. Circle **T** for *true* or **F** for *false*.

1. The SS *Republic* carried only passengers and money.   **T**   **F**
2. The American Civil War was won by the southern states.   **T**   **F**
3. After the war, money could buy more in the South than in the North.   **T**   **F**
4. The SS *Republic* was sunk by an enemy ship.   **T**   **F**
5. Items from the SS *Republic* may be seen by the public.   **T**   **F**

3 DISCOVER. Complete the exercises to learn about the grammar in this lesson.

A Find these sentences in the article in exercise **1**. Write the missing words.

1. Five hundred barrels of goods . . . _____ onto the SS *Republic* in New York.
2. . . . coins from the northern states _____ in the South . . .
3. In 2003, the wreck of the SS *Republic* _____ by a company . . .
4. Over 51,000 gold and silver coins _____ .
5. Many of these items _____ in public exhibitions.

B Look at your answers in exercise **A**. Write them in the correct column.

Passive without Modal	Passive with Modal
were loaded	_could be used_
_____	_____
_____	

LEARN

15.3 Passive Voice with Modals

Active Voice	Passive Voice
You may return purchases with a receipt. You can't return them without a receipt.	Purchases **may be returned** with a receipt. They **can't be returned** without a receipt.

Passive Voice with Modals					
	Subject	Modal (*Not*)	*Be*	Past Participle	
Past	The ship	couldn't		seen	because of the storm.
Present	The topics	can	be	researched	online.
Future	The report	might not		finished	on time.

1. The passive voice is often used with modals* to talk about past, present, and future.	The test **can be completed** at home. Projects **must be finished** next week.
2. Use a modal + *be* + past participle to form the passive.	The building **might be closed**.
3. To form questions with modals in the passive, place the modal before the subject.	A: **Can** the test **be completed** at home? B: Yes, it can. A: **When should** the project **be finished**? B: Next week.

*See Units 12 and 13 to review the meanings and uses of modals.

4 Complete the information sheet with the correct passive form of the words in parentheses.

August Archaeological Dive: Information Sheet

Welcome to this exciting dive! Over the next two weeks, many interesting items

(1) _____ may be found _____ (may / find) at this site. Some important items

(2) _____ (might / recover) from the wreck, so care

(3) _____ (must / take) not to damage them. Please take note:

- Tools and diving equipment will be provided. Personal tools and equipment

  (4) _____ (may not / use).

- New discoveries (5) _____ (must not / move) without permission.

- New assistants (6) _____ (could / require) to complete a training

  course away from the main dive site.

- Identification (7) _____ (should / wear) at all times.

- Our dive doctor (8) _____ (can / consult) when necessary.

Thank you all for your cooperation, and welcome to the team!

15.4 Using the *By* Phrase

Passive Voice + *By* Phrase
The sunken ship was found **by some divers.**
The passengers were rescued near the coast **by the Coast Guard.**

1. Use a *by* phrase with the passive voice to indicate who or what performed the action.	Some errors were made **by the students.** Their house was destroyed **by a tornado.**
2. Use a *by* phrase when it is important to know who or what did the action of the verb.	Our class was interrupted **by a loud noise.** The researcher is paid **by the government.**

3. Do not use a *by* phrase if the agent is
   a. unknown
   b. understood from context
	a. The items **were stolen** late last night.
	 b. The new health laws **were passed** yesterday.

5 Read the paragraph about the discovery of the SS *Republic*. Cross out four more unnecessary *by* phrases.

Treasure Found on the SS *Republic*

The wreck of the SS *Republic* was discovered in 2003 by a private company called Odyssey Marine Exploration. The ship was found ~~by the company~~ at the bottom of the ocean 100 miles southeast of Savannah, Georgia.

The remains of the SS *Republic* were around 1700 feet (518 meters) deep. New high-tech equipment was used by Odyssey to aid in the exploration and recovery effort. For example, items were removed from the wreck by a robotic craft called ZEUS.

Over 51,000 gold and silver coins were recovered by the Odyssey team from the wreck. Everyday items such as shoes, cups, and bottles were also found by the team. Photos of these artifacts are displayed on the company's website. Facts and details are also given by the company on the site for anyone who wants more information.

► Coins from the SS *Republic*

6 WRITE & SPEAK.

A Write passive questions about the SS *Republic* with *by* at the end.

REAL ENGLISH

Passive questions with *who* and *what* ask about the agent. They often have *by* at the end.

I haven't heard of that book.
Who was it written by?

1. (who / the SS *Republic* / discover)

   <u>Who was the SS Republic discovered by?</u>

2. (who / the company / start)

   _____

3. (who / the new equipment / buy)

   _____

4. (who / the ocean / search)

   _____

5. (what / the research teams / attract)

   _____

B Work with a partner. Ask and answer the questions in exercise **A**. Use the information from exercise **5** on page 407 to give answers.

A: *Who was the SS Republic discovered by?*

B: *A company called Odyssey Marine Exploration.*

PRACTICE

7 Rewrite the sentences using the bold verbs in the passive. Add a *by* phrase only when necessary.

1. People **can see** many historic items in the museum's new exhibit.

   Many historic items _____ <u>can be seen</u> _____ in the museum's new exhibit.

2. Groups **can't buy** tickets.

   Tickets _____ .

3. Visitors to the museum **may not park** cars outside the building.

   Cars _____ outside the building.

4. Adults **must not use** cameras in the exhibit.

   Cameras _____ in the exhibit.

5. However, children on school visits **may take** photographs.

   However, photographs _____ .

6. Visitors **should leave** their coats and bags in the coat check.

   Coats and bags _____ in the coat check.

7. The museum **might change** the objects on display without notice.

   The objects on display _____ without notice.

8. You **can purchase** souvenirs in the gift shop.

   Souvenirs _____ in the gift shop.

8 READ, WRITE & SPEAK.

A Read the information sheet about a college anthropology project. Underline the verbs.

Anthropology Project

Project Preparation and Details

Theme	What <u>can</u> we <u>learn</u> from disastrous or mysterious events?
What to do	• Choose a historical event from any period.
	• You can write about any country or culture.
	• You can do the work alone or with a partner.
What to study	• Read accounts of the event soon after it happened.
	• Study artifacts from the site.
	• Research the opinions of archaeologists and anthropologists.
Resources to use	• Visit the college library.
	• Use the Internet.
	• Interview members of the faculty (for interviews, by appointment).

Project Tasks and Due Dates

Choose a topic	January 31: Professor Lopez has to approve all topics.
Complete outline	February 7: A faculty member must sign your outline before you begin your project.
Present project	February 26: Dr. Henderson will arrange exact times.

B Complete the sentences. Use the passive voice and verbs from the information sheet in exercise **A**. Complete the *by* phrases where indicated.

1. A disaster from any period in history may _____be chosen_____.

2. Any country or culture can _____ about.

3. The work can _____ alone or with a partner.

4. Accounts of events should _____ soon after they happen.

5. Artifacts found at the site should _____ and expert opinions

   should _____.

6. The Internet can _____ as a resource.

7. Members of the faculty may _____.

8. All topics must _____ by _____ on or before January 31.

9. Project outlines should _____ by _____.

10. Presentation times will _____ by _____.

C Put the words in the correct order to make passive questions. Add *by* where necessary.

1. (who / must / the outline / sign)

   Who must the outline be signed by? _____

2. (can / the work / do / with a partner)

   _____

3. (whose opinions / should / research)

   _____

4. (can / the Internet / use)

   _____

5. (who / must / the topic / approve)

   _____

6. (who / will / the presentations / arrange)

   _____

D Work with a partner. Ask and answer the questions in exercise **C**.

A: *Who must the outline be signed by?*

B: *A faculty member.*

9   WRITE & LISTEN.

A Complete the information about Pompeii. Write the *by* phrases from the box.

| by archaeologists | ~~by disaster~~ | by millions of tourists | by Mount Vesuvius |

In A.D. 79, the Roman city of Pompeii was struck (1) ___by disaster___. The city was buried when tons of burning ash, stone, and deadly gases were shot into the air (2) _____, the nearby volcano. Sixteen thousand people were killed in one night. The disaster happened so quickly that evidence of everyday life was perfectly preserved under the ash until the city was discovered (3) _____ 1700 years later. Now Pompeii is visited (4) _____ every year.

B Listen to two students discuss their project on the disaster that struck the city of Pompeii. Complete the summary of what each student says with the modal verbs you hear and the passive form of the verbs in parentheses. Add *not* where necessary.

1. Juan: The research _____can be shared_____ (share) if we work together.

2. Val: The stories in books and films _____ always _____ (believe).

3. Juan: Some of the photographs _____ (include) in the project.

4. Val: The people who died _____ (respect).

5. Juan: The cast of the dog _____ (show) on the official website.

6. Val: A lot of good information _____ (find) on the official website.

7. Juan: Pompeii _____ (choose) by a lot of students.

8. Val: Our project _____ (approve) if we don't hurry.

▼ A plaster cast of dog killed at Pompeii

10 EDIT. Read the extract from a student's project. Find and correct six more errors with passive modals and the use of the *by* phrase.

Mystery at Sea:
The *Mary Celeste*

I have chosen to research the mystery of the ship *Mary Celeste*. This famous story should ~~include~~ *be included* on any list of historical mysteries. In early November 1872, the ship left New York carrying goods to Italy. One month later, the ship was discovered in the Atlantic Ocean by another ship. There was no one on board, but the goods that the *Mary Celeste* was carrying were still on the ship.

There was no sign of trouble, but the sailors, the captain, and his family could not found. The ship's lifeboat was missing, and a long rope was attached to the back of the ship. Some versions of the story say that a fully prepared meal could see on the table, so maybe everyone left in a hurry. This, however, cannot be confirmed. Even now we don't understand exactly what happened, and the truth may never know.

In my opinion, the evidence should be examined again by people. New information might discover using modern technology. Many people don't agree with me, though. They think some things just can't be explain.

11 APPLY.

A In your notebook, brainstorm a list of rules or instructions for these places. Use passive modals.

- your school   *Textbooks must be purchased before classes begin.*

- a library   _____

- a museum   _____

B Work with a partner. Share your ideas from exercise **A**. In your notebook, write more instructions for the places in exercise **A**.

EXPLORE

CD4-20

1 **READ** the article about an aspect of daily life in ancient Rome. Notice the words in **bold**.

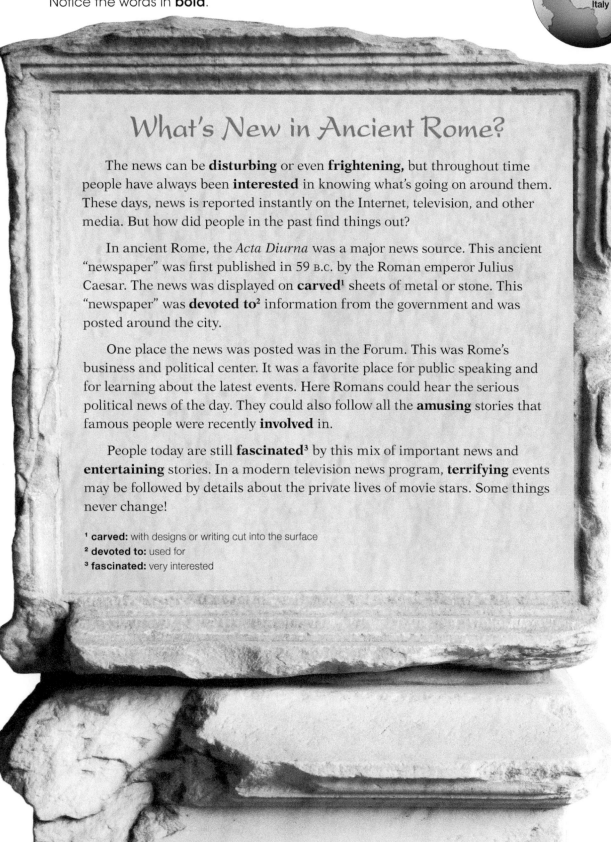

What's New in Ancient Rome?

The news can be **disturbing** or even **frightening,** but throughout time people have always been **interested** in knowing what's going on around them. These days, news is reported instantly on the Internet, television, and other media. But how did people in the past find things out?

In ancient Rome, the *Acta Diurna* was a major news source. This ancient "newspaper" was first published in 59 B.C. by the Roman emperor Julius Caesar. The news was displayed on **carved**[1] sheets of metal or stone. This "newspaper" was **devoted to**[2] information from the government and was posted around the city.

One place the news was posted was in the Forum. This was Rome's business and political center. It was a favorite place for public speaking and for learning about the latest events. Here Romans could hear the serious political news of the day. They could also follow all the **amusing** stories that famous people were recently **involved** in.

People today are still **fascinated**[3] by this mix of important news and **entertaining** stories. In a modern television news program, **terrifying** events may be followed by details about the private lives of movie stars. Some things never change!

[1] **carved:** with designs or writing cut into the surface
[2] **devoted to:** used for
[3] **fascinated:** very interested

2 CHECK. Choose the correct answer to complete each sentence.

1. According to the first paragraph, some news can be _____ .

   a. funny　　　　　　　b. scary　　　　　　　c. late

2. Compared with the news in ancient Rome, today's news _____ .

   a. includes greater detail　　b. comes in more different ways　　c. talks about different topics

3. In ancient Rome, people read the *Acta Diurna* _____ .

   a. in public places　　　b. only in the Forum　　　c. at home

4. The *Acta Diurna* reported on _____ .

   a. famous people's lives　　b. exciting stories　　c. official information

5. The news in the Forum was similar to modern news; it combined serious topics with _____ .

   a. amusing stories　　　b. political statements　　　c. government plans

3 DISCOVER. Complete the exercises to learn about the grammar in this lesson.

A Circle the correct words to complete the sentences from the article in exercise **1**.

1. The news can be **disturbed** / **disturbing** . . .

2. . . . people have always been **interested** / **interesting** in knowing what's going on around them.

3. The news was displayed on **carved** / **carving** sheets of metal or stone.

4. People today are still **fascinated** / **fascinating** by this mix of important news and **entertained** / **entertaining** stories.

B Look at your answers in exercise **A**. Check (✓) the true statements about the words you circled.

1. __✓__ They can come after *be*.

2. _____ They can come after a noun.

3. _____ They can come before a noun.

4. _____ They can be used as verbs.

5. _____ They can be used as adjectives.

▼ The Forum in ancient Rome was an important social center. Here many Romans probably received the first terrible news about the disaster at Pompeii.

LEARN

15.5 Past Participial Adjectives

1. The past participle* can be used as an adjective. The past participial adjective has a passive meaning.	The picture was painted by Da Vinci. ⎣___⎦ Past Participle (Passive) These rooms are already **painted**. ⎣___⎦ Past Participial Adjective

2. **Remember:** A past participle can be
  a. regular (the same as the simple past with –*ed*)
  b. irregular (different forms)
	a. amaz**ed**, interest**ed**
	b. brok**en**, forgot**ten**

3. A past participial adjective often describes a person's feelings.	People are **fascinated** by the news. Juan was **surprised** to see the story.
4. Past participial adjectives can come before a noun or after a linking verb such as *be, look, seem,* and *sound*.	The **excited** children began to scream. The children looked **tired**.
5. Past participial adjectives often occur with certain prepositions; for example: *surprised by* and *interested in*.	Bill seemed **surprised by** his promotion. The students are **interested in** history.

*****past participle:** the verb form used in the present perfect and the passive voice

4 Complete the exercises.

A Complete the e-mail with past participial adjectives. Use the verbs in parentheses. Then underline the prepositions that come after seven more of the participial adjectives.

Hi Franz,

Do you remember that summer job I was trying to get at the museum? I wasn't fully

(1) _____qualified_____ (qualify) <u>for</u> the job, and I was (2) _____ (frighten) of saying the wrong things in the interview. Well, guess what? I got the job!

I've just started, and I am already (3) _____(involve) in setting up an important exhibit on ancient Rome. I'm a little (4) _____ (surprise) by the responsibility my boss has given me. I was put in charge of displaying some examples of the *Acta Diurna*. They are really valuable and very heavy! My boss seems

(5) _____ (satisfy) with me, but I am (6) _____ (exhaust)!

Everything is more or less ready, and I'm very (7) _____ (excite) about next week. The exhibit opens on Wednesday, and the first two weeks are already

(8) _____ (sell out). I know you are (9) _____ (interest) in ancient Rome. You definitely won't be (10) _____ (disappoint) with the exhibit.

Hope to see you soon.

Penny

B Complete the extract from Penny's interview with the correct prepositions. Look at the prepositions you underlined in exercise **A**.

Interviewer: Why do you think you are qualified (1) _____for_____ this job, Ms. Browne?

Penny: I've been involved (2) _____ organizing several museum exhibits in previous jobs. My exhibits have always been popular, so the museums have been satisfied (3) _____ my work.

Interviewer: I see. And what personal qualities do you bring to your exhibits?

Penny: Well, I'm never frightened (4) _____ trying something new, so people are often surprised (5) _____ my ideas. I'm always very excited (6) _____ the exhibits myself, and I enjoy sharing that excitement with visitors. I don't want anyone to be disappointed (7) _____ their experience.

15.6 Present Participial Adjectives

1. The present participle (*-ing* form) can also be used as an adjective.	The story is **frightening.** That movie looks **terrifying.**
2. Use the present participial adjective to describe the characteristics of someone or something.	An **amusing** teacher makes a class fun. The exhibit at the museum was **interesting.**
3. Present participial adjectives can come before a noun or after a linking verb.	This is a **fascinating** movie. Her trip to China sounded **exciting.**
4. **Be careful!** When referring to people, past participial adjectives describe feelings, while present participial adjectives describe characteristics of the person.	We are **interested** in ancient history. The history teacher is **interesting.**

5 Complete Jana's blog with present participial adjectives. Use the verbs in parentheses.

My Blog about Chinese History

When I was a child, I loved to read about Chinese history, and I still do. On my blog, I talk about China's past and some of the (1) _____amazing_____ (amaze) objects that have survived to the present day. Last week, for example, I wrote about a cosmetics case I saw at the museum. Everyday objects are more (2) _____ (interest) to me than famous pieces of art. They show you how average people lived in ancient times.

▲ An ancient cosmetics case that was discovered in a Han dynasty tomb

I also review historical Chinese films on my blog. For example, the movie *The Last Emperor* is about the life of Pu-Yi, the last emperor of China before the Chinese

Republic. It's a (3) _____ (fascinate) movie. I sometimes review
(4) _____ (disappoint) movies, too. Some directors have made
(5) _____ (excite) events from Chinese history seem
(6) _____ (bore).

Every week, I post new content on my blog. It's (7) _____ (exhaust),
but I enjoy it. I let people make comments, too. Sometimes we disagree, but I enjoy
hearing other people's thoughts about my blog.

COMMENTS (1)

JTC59: I enjoyed reading the Chinese folktales you talked about last week. Thanks for an
(8) _____ (entertain) blog!

PRACTICE

6 Circle the correct participial adjectives to complete the article.

Lewis Chessmen Found 600 Years Later

In 1831, Malcolm Macleod was walking along the coast on the Isle of Lewis in
the north of Scotland when he found something special. Some unusual objects were
(1) **burying** / **buried** in the sand. When he looked closer, he made an (2) **exciting** / **excited**
discovery. Macleod found 78 (3) **carving** / **carved** figures. These figures are now
(4) **knowing** / **known** as the Lewis Chessmen.

The pieces are (5) **making** / **made** of ivory and date back to the 12th century. They
are (6) **interesting** / **interested** because of the expressions on their faces.

The figures have large, oval eyes and their expressions seem (7) **disappointing** /
disappointed or (8) **worrying** / **worried**. For this reason, they are (9) **amusing** / **amused**
to many people these days. Copies of these famous pieces are very popular with chess
players, and are even owned by people who think the game itself is (10) **boring** / **bored**.

▼ Lewis Chessman, from a collection
found on the Isle of Lewis, Scotland

7 LISTEN, WRITE & SPEAK.

CD4-21

A Listen to the three short conversations between students taking part in a special archaeology project. What type of project is it? Discuss your answer with a partner.

CD4-21

B Listen again. Circle the correct words.

Conversation 1

1. Jessie is **disgusted** / **disgusting**.

2. Tom is **annoyed** / **annoying**.

Conversation 2

3. Sue thinks the work is **interested** / **interesting**.

4. Dave thinks studying garbage is **bored** / **boring**.

5. Dave would like to do something more **excited** / **exciting**.

Conversation 3

6. Rick isn't **satisfied** / **satisfying** with the amount of work they have done.

7. Angela is **excited** / **exciting**.

8. Rick thinks their information is **surprised** / **surprising**.

C Write eight questions based on the sentences in exercise **B**. Use *Why* and the correct participial adjective.

1. _Why is Jessie disgusted?_ _____

2. _____

3. _____

4. _____

5. _____

6. _____

7. _____

8. _____

CD4-21

D Listen to the conversations again. In your notebook, take notes on the answers to your questions. Then work with a partner. Take turns asking and answering your questions from exercise **C**.

A: *Why was Jessie disgusted?*

B: *She didn't like the smell of the garbage.*

8 EDIT. Read the article about garbology. Find and correct five more errors with past and present participial adjectives.

Garbology: The Past through Trash

Most people think garbage is not very interesting, but archaeologists are ~~fascinating~~ *fascinated* by it. When archaeologists found 2000-year-old waste from Rome, they were excited about it. The waste taught them about the diet and daily life of people in ancient Rome. You can learn a lot about a culture by studying its trash.

Garbology can be described as the study of garbage to learn about a culture. Professor William Rathje and his students in Arizona invented the term when they were studying waste in modern America. Rathje and his students studied a number of landfill sites[1]. Sorting through garbage can be a tired and sometimes disgusted activity, but when the information from their research was collected, they were not disappointing with the results. The project led to some interested discoveries. It was clear that some popular ideas about modern American garbage were mistaken. For example, the team discovered that almost half of the garbage in the landfills is paper—a fact that many people found surprised.

[1] **landfill site:** a place where garbage is taken and buried

9 APPLY.

A Brainstorm all the things that you and people you know throw away. Then write short answers to the questions.

1. Are you surprised by the amount of trash you or others throw away? Why, or why not?

2. Are you worried about the amount of plastic or electronics you throw away?

3. What might people find fascinating about our trash in 100 years?

4. What topic in this lesson (or unit) did you find the most interesting?

B Work in a group. Discuss your answers to the questions from exercise **A**.

A: *I am surprised by the amount of trash my family throws away. We throw away a lot of plastic and food.*

B: *In my country, we reuse things a lot more. Everything is recycled.*

Charts
15.1–15.4

1 Complete the sentences with the words in parentheses. Use the active or passive form of the verbs.

1. Theories about history ___should be supported___ (should / support) by evidence.

2. This TV series about the Romans _____ (make) last year. It _____ (film) all over Europe.

3. Last night, Dr. Canas _____ (give) a lecture about the Middle Ages.

4. Your assignment on Gandhi _____ (must / complete) by Friday.

5. I _____ (might / finish) the job today.

6. _____ (the mail / deliver) before noon? I'm expecting a package.

7. Bikes _____ (must not / leave) outside the library.

8. Students _____ (can / obtain) further information from the dean's office.

9. Unfortunately, my watch _____ (can't / repair).

10. Where _____ (you / keep) your garbage bags?

Charts
15.1–15.6

2 **EDIT.** Read the article about unusual artifacts in Costa Rica. Find and correct seven more errors with the passive voice and participial adjectives.

An Ancient Mystery from Costa Rica

The giant stone balls of Costa Rica are one of the
                    fascinating
most ~~fascinated~~ human artifacts. The balls made in

prehistoric times and are perfectly round. The stone

comes from local mountains. It's likely that stone tools

were use to make the balls. The biggest ball is eight feet

across and it is weighed 16 tons.

Unfortunately, we may never be discovered the true

purpose of the stones since only a small number of

stones can be studied in context. Many of the stones were

removed from their original place.

Archaeologists are annoying about this situation.

They say that when artifacts are found by members of the

public, they must not be moved. Photos can take, but the

artifacts should not be pick up.

3 **WRITE & LISTEN.**

A Use the words to complete the questions for a history quiz show. Use the simple past passive.

1. where / the first public baths / build _____ *Where were the first public baths built?* _____

2. when / the first moon landing / complete

_____

3. where / scissors / invent _____

4. when / the first airplane / fly _____

5. who / popcorn / invent / by _____

6. when / the first CDs / sell _____

CD4-22

B Read the questions from exercise **A** and choose the answer you think is correct. Then listen to an extract from a quiz show and check your answers.

1. a. India   b. Ancient Greece   c. Ancient Rome

2. a. 1967   b. 1968   c. 1969

3. a. Ancient Egypt   b. Japan   c. Germany

4. a. 1898   b. 1903   c. 1907

5. a. Native Americans   b. Australians   c. Europeans

6. a. 1975   b. 1979   c. 1982

C Review the answers to the questions in exercise **A** and write a passive sentence in your notebook about each item or event.

1. *The first public baths were built in ancient Rome.*

4 **WRITE & SPEAK.**

A In your notebook, write answers to the questions. Then write three similar questions to ask your classmates. Write about the topics in this unit.

1. What was displayed in the Forum in ancient Rome?

2. Can the ruins of Pompeii be visited?

3. What are the giant balls of Costa Rica made of?

4. Which story in this unit were you most interested in?

5. Which story was the least interesting?

B Work in a group. Take turns answering the questions from exercise **A**.

1 READ & NOTICE THE GRAMMAR.

A Can you remember a special event that happened to you when you were a child? Tell a partner about the event. Then read the text.

My Grandfather's Gift

When my grandfather was a boy in Poland, fountain pens[1] were used for writing. All of his school work was done with a fountain pen. His first short story was written with a special silver fountain pen that his mother, my great grandmother, gave him for his tenth birthday. His name was engraved[2] on the pen. Sadly, his mother was killed in a car accident soon after this birthday. He was raised by his father. In an old photograph, my grandfather is dressed in a school uniform, and his fountain pen can be seen through the front pocket of his shirt. It seems he was rarely without his pen.

No one was really surprised when Grandpa became a writer. Now, most of his work has been translated from Polish to English. His stories can now be enjoyed by people all over the world, including me.

When I was ten, my mother and I went to Poland to visit him. It was an exciting time for me. He showed me his writing desk, and I remember deciding then that I wanted to be a writer, too. On the last day of our visit, my grandfather asked me to close my eyes. He gently placed his pen in my hands. I was stunned[3] and incredibly happy. I will never forget the connection I felt with my grandfather that day. It is one of the most important memories of my life.

[1] **fountain pen:** a type of pen that is filled from an ink bottle
[2] **engraved:** carved into; names or initials are often engraved in jewelry or other metallic items
[3] **stunned:** surprised or shocked

GRAMMAR FOCUS

In the text in exercise **A**, the writer uses the passive voice without the *by* phrase to focus on <u>objects or events</u>, not the agents.

> *When my grandfather was a boy in Poland, <u>fountain pens</u> **were used** for writing. <u>All of his school work</u> **was done** with a fountain pen.*

The writer uses the passive voice with the *by* phrase when the information about the agent is necessary.

> *He was **raised** <u>by his father.</u>*

B Look at the chart. Find each example of passive voice in the text in exercise **A**. Is the agent in the text or not? Check the correct column and complete the information. Then look at paragraph 1 of the text again, and add two more examples to the chart.

Passive Voice	Agent in text (necessary information)	Agent not in text (clear from context)
1. fountain pens were used 2. his name was engraved 3. his mother was killed 4. he was raised 5. his stories can . . . be enjoyed		✓ (by people)

C Complete the chart with information from the text in exercise **A**. Discuss your answers with a partner.

	Event: *Receiving gift from grandfather*
What is the memory?	*Receiving a special pen from my grandfather*
Why is this event important?	
Details	

2 **BEFORE YOU WRITE.** Decide on an event from your past to write about. Make a chart like the one in exercise **1C** in your notebook. Complete the chart with your own ideas.

WRITING FOCUS   Writing Strong Concluding Sentences

It is important to end each paragraph with a strong sentence. This lets the reader know the paragraph is ending and a new idea is coming. A good concluding sentence often states an opinion or makes a summary statement about the ideas in the paragraph. Notice the examples from the text.

It seems he was rarely without his pen.
His stories can now be enjoyed by people all over the world, including me.
It is one of the most important memories of my life.

---

3 **WRITE** two or three paragraphs about the memory you selected. Use the information from your chart in exercise **2** and the text in exercise **1A** to help you.

4 **SELF ASSESS.** Read your paragraphs and underline examples of the passive voice. Then use the checklist to assess your work.

☐   I used the passive voice correctly. [15.1, 15.2]

☐   I used the passive voice with the *by* phrase correctly. [15.4]

☐   I used the passive voice with modals correctly. [15.3]

☐   I used present and past participial adjectives correctly. [15.5, 15.6]

☐   I wrote strong concluding sentences. [WRITING FOCUS]

Noun Clauses and Reported Speech

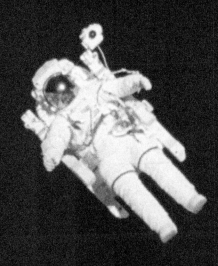

▲ Before 1984, astronauts on spacewalks used a long, thick wire called a tether to attach themselves to their spacecraft. In February 1984, astronaut Bruce McCandless left the space shuttle *Challenger* and performed the very first untethered spacewalk.

EXPLORE

1 READ the article about the discovery of a long lost Egyptian city. Notice the words in **bold**.

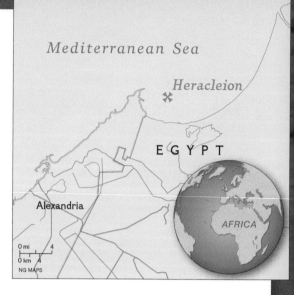

Discovering a Lost City

History books sometimes tell us about towns and cities that no longer exist. Where did they go? Stories suggest **that some of these places are lost beneath the sea**. Franck Goddio is a French underwater explorer who has discovered such places. His work has shown **that these lost places can be found**.

One of Goddio's most important discoveries is the Egyptian port of Thonis-Heracleion. At one time, historians thought **that Thonis and Heracleion were two separate cities**. However, Goddio and his team proved **that they were in fact two different names for the same city**. It is now accepted **that *Thonis* was the Egyptian name and *Heracleion* was the Greek name**.

Historians think **that the city was founded[1] in the 8th century B.C.** It was a center of trade and had religious importance because of its many temples. Experts believe **that the city was hit by several natural disasters** before it finally sank into the Mediterranean Sea in the 8th century A.D. In the ruins of the city, Goddio's team found statues, jewelry, coins, and inscriptions[2] that have added greatly to our understanding of life in ancient Egypt.

[1] **found:** to start or create a city or organization
[2] **inscription:** a piece of writing carved into an object

▲ Franck Goddio with an inscribed Heracleion stone from B.C. 378-362

2 CHECK. Choose the correct answer to complete each statement.

1. Franck Goddio has _____.

   a. found cities under the sea

   b. written stories about lost cities

   c. discovered a lost city on land

2. Thonis and Heracleion _____.

   a. were two separate cities

   b. were very close to each other

   c. were the same place

3. According to historians, Heracleion _____.

   a. was founded in the 8th century B.C.

   b. experienced only one disaster

   c. had no important buildings

4. The ruins of Heracleion _____.

   a. contained nothing of interest

   b. provided a lot of information

   c. were difficult to explore

3 DISCOVER. Complete the exercises to learn about the grammar in this lesson.

A Look at the chart. Find the sentence in the article that contains each clause with *that*. Then fill in the subject and verb.

Subject	Verb	Clause with *That*
Stories	suggest	that some of these places are lost beneath the sea.
		that these lost places can be found.
		that Thonis and Heracleion were two separate cities.
		that the city was founded in the 8th century B.C.
		that the city was hit by several natural disasters . . .

B Check the one true statement about the clauses with *that* in exercise **A**.

1. _____ They take the place of a verb.

2. _____ They take the place of a noun.

3. _____ They take the place of an adjective.

4. _____ They take the place of an adverb.

▶ An archaeologist measures the feet of a giant red granite statue at the site of Heracleion

LEARN

16.1 Noun Clauses with *That*

Noun as Object of Verb	Noun Clause as Object of Verb
Jennifer realizes the problem. 　　　　　　　　Noun	Jennifer realizes **that her grades are falling**. 　　　　　　　Noun Clause

1. A noun clause takes the place of a noun in a sentence. *That* can introduce a noun clause.	Louis believed **the professor**. S　　V　　Noun/Object Louis believed **that the professor was telling the truth**. S　　V　　Noun Clause/Object
2. **Remember:** A clause always has a subject and a verb.	Ann forgot **that her sister had borrowed** her keys. 　　　　　　　S　　　　V
3. A noun clause often follows verbs that suggest thinking or mental activity, such as *decide*, *think*, or *believe*.	I've **decided** that I will work harder next year. 　　　　　　Noun Clause
4. In speaking and informal writing, *that* is often omitted.	I dreamed **that I was flying**. I dreamed **I was flying**.

4 Read the sentences. Underline the noun clauses with *that*. Then circle and label the subject and verb of each noun clause.

　　　　　　　　　　　　　　　　S　　　V
1. Explorers always hope that (they) (will make) discoveries.

2. Goddio decided that he wanted to look for Heracleion.

3. He thought that he and his team could find the city.

4. They discovered that the city was near the coast.

5. The team realized that the ruins were very old.

6. The divers noticed that the ruins contained statues and jewelry.

7. Archaeologists know that the site is very important.

8. They believe that it will help our understanding of ancient Egypt.

> **REAL ENGLISH**
>
> Here are more verbs that suggest thinking or mental activity.
>
> | | | |
> |---|---|---|
> | *discover* | *hope* | *realize* |
> | *dream* | *know* | *remember* |
> | *find out* | *learn* | *suggest* |
> | *forget* | *notice* | *understand* |

5 Complete the exercises.

A Put the phrases in order to make complete sentences. Add *that* to the beginning of the noun clauses.

1. the lecture on ancient Egypt / found out / the students / was canceled

 The students found out that the lecture on ancient Egypt was canceled.

2. the city / learned / archaeologists / was important

_____

3. discovered / were over 2000 years old / the statues / scientists

_____

4. I / found a lost city / dreamed / I

_____

5. hope / some explorers / will be famous / their discoveries

_____

6. believe / I / has information on ancient Greece / her book

_____

B Work with a partner. Cross out *that* in the sentences in exercise **A**. Take turns reading each sentence with and without *that*.

REAL ENGLISH

As in relative clauses, the pronunciation of *that* in noun clauses is often reduced. The /æ/ is pronounced /ə/.

6   WRITE & SPEAK.

A Complete the noun clauses with the words in the box.

~~it is under the sea~~	it has improved a lot
they are the same	it was a little boring

1. What do you remember about Heracleion?

   I remember that __it is under the sea_____.

2. What did you learn about Thonis and Heracleion?

   I learned that _____.

3. What did you think about history when you were younger?

   I thought that _____.

4. What have you realized about your English recently?

   I've realized that _____.

B Use the information in the article from exercise **1** on page 426 and your own ideas to complete the noun clauses in exercise **A** in a different way. Write the sentences in your notebook, and then share them with your classmates.

1. I remember that Heracleion was hit by several natural disasters.

16.2 Noun Clauses with *That*: More Expressions

1. A noun clause with *that* can follow *be* + certain adjectives that express how someone feels, such as:
 	
be afraid   be happy   be surprised
be certain   be glad   be sure
be disappointed be sorry   be worried
	The students **were afraid** that the test was today.
	                      Noun Clause
	
	We **are sorry** that you didn't find your necklace.
	                    Noun Clause
	
	I'm sure that my answer is correct.
	            Noun Clause

2. A noun clause with *that* can follow certain common expressions, such as: a. *It is true . . .* b. *It is a fact . . .*	a. **It is true** that he worked in Egypt. b. **It is a fact** that Egypt is in Africa.
3. **Remember:** In a noun clause, *that* is often omitted.	Students were afraid **that the test was today.** Students were afraid **the test was today.**

7 Read the conversation. Underline seven more noun clauses and insert *that* in the correct place.

                                 that

Ben: Is it true <u>you're leading the search tomorrow</u>?

Lucia: Yes, it is. I'm surprised you know about it already.

Ben: News travels fast! Anyway, I'm glad you've been chosen. You'll be a great team leader. Dave doesn't have enough experience. I was afraid we were going to get lost today.

Lucia: I know. I was worried someone might get lost when he split us up into pairs. In my opinion, we should all stay together.

Ben: Yes, I agree. Professor Kim is disappointed we haven't found any sign of the city yet. He's sure we're in the right place, though.

Lucia: Well, it's true people have been looking for it for years . . .

8 **SPEAK.** Complete each sentence with a noun clause with *that*. Use your own ideas. Then share your sentences with a partner.

1. I am afraid _____

2. I am glad _____

3. I am sure _____

4. I am disappointed _____

I'm glad that tomorrow's Friday.

PRACTICE

9 READ, WRITE & SPEAK.

A Look at the photo and read the caption. Then read the conversation. Find seven more noun clauses (without *that*) and underline them.

Professor:	Great dive, everyone! So what do you think after seeing the Yonaguni monument for yourselves? Do you think <u>it's natural or man-made</u>? Is it a pile of rocks or the remains of an ancient civilization?
Kenji:	Well, I can understand all the excitement. It's true the rocks look like they have been carved. The edges are so straight . . .
Pam:	I agree. And I'm sure I saw some steps. They seemed to lead to the top of the monument.
Michaela:	Hmmm. I'm not sure I agree. The rocks looked natural to me.
Kenji:	What about the head-shaped rock? Did you see that, Michaela?
Michaela:	No, I had to go back to the surface because I had a problem with my diving equipment. I was afraid I didn't have enough air.
Pam:	I'm sorry you didn't see it.
Kenji:	I know there are some Japanese scientists who agree with us, Pam.
Michaela:	But the Japanese government doesn't agree. Don't forget the monument is officially considered a natural site.

▼ Divers explore the Yonaguni Monument off the coast of Japan.

B Complete the sentences about the students in exercise **A**. Use the information in the conversation and your own words.

1. Kenji and Pam seem to believe _that Yonaguni was man-made_

2. Michaela thinks _____

3. Kenji suggests _____

4. Some scientists are sure _____

5. The students' professor hopes _____

6. The professor is happy _____

7. I believe _____

8. My partner thinks _____

C Work with a partner. Compare your answers from exercise **B**. Then share your opinions about Yonaguni with your class.

I believe that Yonaguni was once on land. My partner thinks so, too. We aren't sure whether it's natural or man-made.

10 LISTEN & WRITE.

CD4-24

A Listen to a podcast about exploring the ancient city of Machu Picchu in Peru. For each statement, circle **T** for *true* or **F** for *false*.

1. Machu Picchu was built by Europeans.   **T**   **F**

2. Archaeologists first visited Machu Picchu over 100 years ago.   **T**   **F**

3. The number of visitors per day is limited.   **T**   **F**

4. Walking the Inca Trail to Machu Picchu takes ten days.   **T**   **F**

5. The only way to the city is on foot.   **T**   **F**

B Read the questions. Then listen to extracts from the podcast. How would the speaker answer the questions? Take notes on the answers in your notebook.

1. What is the best time of day to visit?

2. What is the quietest day to visit?

3. When is the best time to buy your ticket?

4. Is it difficult to get to Machu Picchu?

5. What is the best way to get to Machu Picchu?

C Write sentences in your notebook based on your notes in exercise **B**. Use noun clauses. Begin with *The speaker believes . . .* , *The speaker suggests . . .* , or *It is a fact that . . .*

The speaker believes that early morning or late afternoon is the best time.

11 APPLY.

A Complete each sentence with a noun clause with *that*. Make true statements about yourself.

1. I'm sure <u>that I will visit Machu Picchu one day</u>.

2. I was disappointed _____.

3. It's a fact _____.

4. When I was young, I dreamed _____.

5. My friends are sometimes surprised _____.

6. In ten years' time, I hope _____.

B Work in a group. Share your sentences from exercise **A**. Ask your classmates questions about their sentences.

A: *I'm sure that I will visit Machu Picchu one day.*

B: *Why do you want to go there?*

EXPLORE

CD4-26

1 **READ** part of a lecture about early exploration around the world. Notice the words in **bold**.

The Voyage of the *Kon-Tiki*

Professor: Today we're going to discuss **where the people of the Polynesian Islands came from**.

Chen: Excuse me, Professor, I'm not sure **where the Polynesian Islands are**.

Professor: They are way out in the Pacific Ocean. Anyhow, in the mid-20th century, most scientists believed they knew **where the islanders came from**. They thought the first islanders arrived from Asia over 5000 years ago. However, one man wasn't convinced. He was an explorer named Thor Heyerdahl.

▲ Thor Heyerdahl's craft, the *Kon-Tiki*, at sea

Indira: I've heard of him, Professor, but I don't remember **whether he was Norwegian or Danish** . . .

Professor: Norwegian, Indira. Heyerdahl had a theory that the Polynesian Islanders actually came from South America. He wanted to see **if his theory was possible**. So, in 1947, he sailed his balsa wood[1] boat, the *Kon-Tiki*, west from Peru to Polynesia.

Chen: Why balsa wood?

Professor: Well, it was a light-weight material that was probably used by early South American boat makers. He wanted to demonstrate **how early South Americans traveled**. After 101 days, Heyerdahl successfully reached the Tuamotu Islands in Polynesia. However, many scientists still didn't believe that his theory was correct. But now, decades later, new scientific research shows that some early Polynesians had South American DNA.[2]

Indira: So he was right?

Professor: Well, actually, we still can't be sure **whether or not early South Americans sailed west to Polynesia**. It's possible the Polynesians sailed to South America, too.

[1] **balsa wood:** a very light wood from South America that floats well
[2] **DNA:** an acid that carries genetic information in the cells of each living thing

2 CHECK. Choose the correct answer to complete each sentence.

1. The Polynesian Islands are located in the _____ Ocean.

   a. Atlantic   b. Pacific   c. Indian

2. Most scientists thought the first people in Polynesia came from _____.

   a. Peru   b. South America   c. Asia

3. Thor Heyerdahl planned his voyage because he wanted to _____.

   a. test his theory   b. prove scientists were correct   c. visit the Tuamoto Islands

4. Heyerdahl used a balsa wood boat because he wanted to _____.

   a. have a slow journey   b. save some money   c. travel like the early sailors

5. Recent scientific research has shown that Heyerdahl _____.

   a. was wrong   b. was right   c. might be right

3 DISCOVER. Complete the exercises to learn about the grammar in this lesson.

A Find these sentences in the lecture from exercise **1**. Write the missing words.

1. Today, we're going to discuss __where__ the people of the Polynesian islands come from.

2. Professor, I'm not sure _____ the Polynesian Islands are.

3. He wanted to demonstrate _____ early South Americans traveled.

B Look at the sentences in exercise **A**. Circle the correct answers.

1. The words you wrote in exercise **A** are usually used in **statements** / **questions**.

2. The word order after the missing words is like a **question** / **statement**.

◀ Aerial view of Paoaoa Point and Marina
Point, Bora Bora, French Polynesia

LEARN

16.3 Noun Clauses with *Wh-* Words

Wh- Questions
How did you know that?
Where is the museum?
What did the guide say?

Noun Clauses with *Wh-* Words		
I don't understand	how	you knew that.
Do you know	where	the museum is?
No one knows	what	the guide said.

1. A noun clause can begin with a *Wh-* word: *when, how, which, where, who/whom, whose, why, what.*	I don't know **when she will arrive.** Did you notice **where I put my bag?** I forget **how this machine works.**
2. **Remember:** A noun clause takes the place of a noun in a sentence.	Find out her name. Find out **what her name is.** Noun Noun Clause
3. Use statement word order in noun clauses with *Wh-* words. Do not use question word order.	What did **he** say? ✓ I understood **what he said.** ✗ I understood <u>what did he say</u>.
4. **Be careful!** Be sure to change the verb form in the noun clause to match *do/does/did* in the question.	When **did** he leave? I don't know when he **left.** Where **does** he **go**? I'm not sure where he **goes.**

5. A noun clause with a *Wh-* word can be used in a statement or a question. <u>Do not</u> use a question mark when it is in a statement.	I don't know **when she will arrive.**
	    Statement
	Do you know **when she will arrive?**
	    Question

4 Circle the correct answers.

1. I'm not sure where **is Polynesia / Polynesia is.**

2. Can you remind me who **was Thor Heyerdahl / Thor Heyerdahl was**?

3. I don't know how **the *Kon-Tiki* was built / was the *Kon-Tiki* built**.

4. I've forgotten when **Heyerdahl sailed / did Heyerdahl sail** to Polynesia.

5. Can you tell me where **was Heyerdahl / Heyerdahl was** from?

6. Do you remember what **he was trying / was he trying** to prove?

7. Do you know which islands **the *Kon-Tiki* sailed to / did the *Kon-Tiki* sail to**?

8. I don't understand what **does the new research show / the new research shows**.

5 Complete the exercises.

A Complete the noun clause in each sentence. Use the underlined part of the questions.

1. <u>When did people start</u> living in Polynesia?

Do you know ___*when people started*___ living in Polynesia?

2. <u>Where are the islands?</u>

Can you show me _____ on the map?

3. <u>How many days did the *Kon-Tiki* take</u> to get there?

Do you remember _____ to get there?

4. <u>What did the DNA results show?</u>

Do you understand _____?

5. <u>Who do you believe?</u>

Have you decided _____?

B Work with a partner. Ask and answer the questions from exercise **A**. Use the map to help you.

A: *Do you know when people started living in Polynesia?*

B: *Over 5000 years ago. / No, I don't remember.*

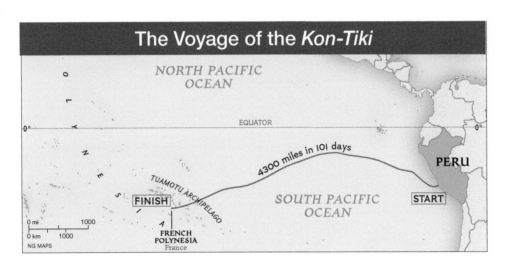

> **REAL ENGLISH**
>
> People often use noun clauses to be less direct and more polite when asking questions.
>
> *Excuse me. Do you know **what time it is?***

16.4 Noun Clauses with *If/Whether*

Yes/No Questions	Noun Clauses with *If/Whether*		
Are the workers busy?	I'm not sure	if whether	the workers are busy.
Did they see the e-mail?	We don't know	if whether	they saw the e-mail.

1. Use *if* or *whether* to change a *Yes/No* question to a noun clause.	Does she have class? I'm not sure **if she has class.** Do you know **whether she has class?**
2. Use statement word order with a noun clause beginning with *if* or *whether*.	✓ I don't know **if she is absent today.** ✗ I don't know if <u>is she absent today</u>.
3. When *if* or *whether* begins a noun clause, *or not* is sometimes added to the end of the clause. It is also possible to add *or not* directly after *whether*.	I don't know **if** he is right **or not.** I'm not sure **whether** she knows **or not.** I'm not sure **whether or not** she knows.

6 Finish each sentence by adding a period (.) or a question mark (?).

1. I can't remember whether Heyerdahl was Norwegian or not

2. Do you remember if the Polynesians came from South America

3. Mae wasn't certain if the lecture on Polynesia was canceled

4. I wonder whether Heyerdahl was right

5. Do you know if the professor wants us to write about Polynesia

6. Can you tell me whether the assignment is due this week

7 Complete the exercises.

A Look at the *Yes/No* questions. Then complete the noun clauses. Add a period (.) or a question mark (?) to the end of each noun clause.

1. Does Diego speak Japanese?

    Do you know whether *Diego speaks Japanese?*

2. Did I turn the TV off?

    I can't remember if _____

3. Is Alex on vacation?

    I'm not sure if _____

4. Was Joanne at the lecture?

    I wonder whether _____

5. Does the bus go to the park?

    Kai's not sure whether _____

6. Is the concert tonight?

    Can you tell me if _____

7. Did Shari leave?

    We're not certain if _____

8. Are they happy?

    No one knows whether _____

B Work with a partner. Take turns reading the completed sentences from exercise **A**. Add *or not* in an appropriate place.

Do you know whether or not Diego speaks Japanese?

PRACTICE

8 Read the questions about exploring the city of Mumbai in India. Change the questions to noun clauses to complete the sentences.

Mumbai (Bombay), India

1. Where is the Gateway of India?

    Jared wants to know ___where the Gateway of India is___ .

2. Is there time to explore the old part of town today?

    Joan isn't sure _____ to explore the old part of town today.

3. Is it a long way to the national park?

    Anna can't remember _____ to the national park.

4. How can we get to Film City?

    I don't know _____ to Film City.

5. Will we be able to see actors making a movie there?

    I wonder _____ actors making a movie there.

6. Which street goes to the harbor?

    Louise isn't sure _____ to the harbor.

7. Where is Crawford Market?

    Rick has forgotten _____ .

8. Do we need to bring the GPS?

    I want to know _____ to bring the GPS.

◀ The Gateway of India, Mumbai, India

9 LISTEN & WRITE.

A Look at the map and listen to the first part of a museum recording. Then listen again and choose the correct answers.

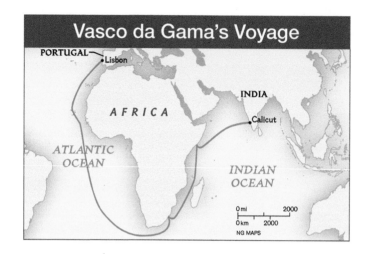

1. When did Vasco da Gama sail to India for the first time?   a. 1497   b. 1597

2. What country's king sent da Gama to India?   a. Spain   b. Portugal

B Read more questions about da Gama and his voyage. Guess the answers by choosing *a* or *b*.

1. What was the reason for the voyage?   a. trade   b. exploration

2. Where did da Gama sail from?   a. Portugal   b. India

3. Was da Gama Italian?   a. yes   b. no

4. How many ships did da Gama take with him?   a. two   b. four

5. What did da Gama discover?   a. a sea route to India   b. Indian spices

6. What else is da Gama remembered for?   a. his kindness   b. his cruelty

C Write sentences about the questions in exercise **B**. Use noun clauses and the expressions from the box.

| I'm not sure | I don't know | I don't remember | I'm not certain | I wonder |

1. I'm not sure what the main reason for the voyage was.

2. _____

3. _____

4. _____

5. _____

6. _____

CD4-28

D Listen to the complete recording and check your answers to exercise **B**.

10 WRITE & SPEAK.

A Use the words in parentheses to complete the polite questions.

1. (where / the zoo / be)

   Can you tell me _where the zoo is?_ _____

2. (how / I / can / get / to the theater)

   Could you tell me _____

3. (if / there / be / a good bookstore / near here)

   Do you know _____

4. (when / the bus to the castle / leave)

   Can you tell me _____

5. (what time / the stores / close)

   Do you know _____

6. (whether / the museum / be / open today)

   Could you tell me _____

B Work with a partner. Ask and answer your questions from exercise **A**. Use the information in Castletown Visitor Highlights to guide your answers.

A: *Excuse me. Can you tell me where the zoo is?*

B: *Sure. It's on Highway 15, just outside of town.*

Castletown Visitor Highlights
• Visit the castle at the north end of Castle Road. Free buses every hour, starting at 10 AM.
• See a play about a famous local explorer at Main Street Theater, Main St. & 7th Ave.
• Be sure to visit the famous Old Town Bookstore at Main Street and 4th Ave. Hours 10–8.
• Learn all about our town at Castletown Museum. Tues–Fri: 10–6; Sat–Sun: 9–5.
• For family fun, visit our local zoo! It's located just outside of Castletown, on Highway 15.

11 APPLY.

A In your notebook, draw a simple map of the place where you grew up or a place you know well. Mark an *X* on four places of interest, but do not tell your partner what they are.

B Work with a partner. Give your partner a list of the places and your map. Take turns asking and answering polite questions with noun clauses about each other's maps. Try to locate the places on the map.

A: *Can you tell me where the Museum of Modern Art is?*

B: *Sure, it's on 53rd Street, just off 5th Avenue.*

EXPLORE

CD4-29

1 READ the blog about space exploration. Notice the phrases in **bold**.

Is space exploration still a good idea?

▲ Valentina Tereshkova, the first woman sent to space, June 16, 1963, Moscow

Russian cosmonaut Valentina Tereshkova made the first space flight by a woman. She **said, "Once you've been in space, you appreciate how small and fragile[1] Earth is."** Several years after Tereshkova's three-day flight, my grandparents watched the first man walk on the moon. My grandmother **told me that it was an incredible moment**. She said that she remembered when Neil Armstrong **said, "That's one small step for a man, one giant leap[2] for mankind."** In those days, everyone thought that these were amazing achievements, but is space exploration still a good idea today?

Nowadays some leading politicians **say that space exploration is too expensive**. They **argue that the money should be used to deal with problems on Earth**. On the other hand, scientists **tell us that we have learned a lot from space travel**. Some people even **say the survival of humankind may depend on space exploration**. Obviously, the question is a serious one. In my opinion, the answer is clear. As Carl Sagan **said, "We have a basic responsibility to our species[3] to venture[4] to other worlds."**

[1] **fragile:** easily broken
[2] **giant leap:** a very big step
[3] **species:** a grouping of living things, such as the human species
[4] **venture:** to act with risk or possible danger

❝ We have a basic responsibility to our species to venture to other worlds. ❞
—**Carl Sagan**

◀ Astronaut Buzz Aldrich on the moon (July 1969)

◀ First-ever image of Earth from space, sent by *Voyager 1*

2 **CHECK.** Read the statements. Circle **T** for *true* or **F** for *false*.

1. Valentina Tereshkova was the first woman in space. **T** **F**

2. In the beginning, many people thought that space exploration was too expensive. **T** **F**

3. Some politicians think that problems on Earth are more important than exploring space. **T** **F**

4. Scientists believe that space travel has had practical benefits. **T** **F**

5. Carl Sagan thought that we should not explore space. **T** **F**

3 **DISCOVER.** Complete the exercises to learn about the grammar in this lesson.

A Circle the forms of *say* or *tell* in each of these sentences from the blog in exercise **1**. Underline the clause or sentence that follows.

1. My grandmother (told) me that it was an incredible moment.

2. . . . Neil Armstrong said, "That's one small step for a man, one giant leap for mankind."

3. . . . , scientists tell us that we have learned a lot from space travel.

4. Some people even say the survival of humankind may depend on space exploration.

5. Carl Sagan said, "We have a basic responsibility to our species to venture to other worlds."

B Look at the words you underlined in exercise **A**. Write the sentence numbers on the lines to complete the statements.

1. Sentences __2__ and _____ give the speaker's exact words.

2. Sentences _____ , _____ , and _____ have noun clauses.

LEARN

16.5 Quoted Speech

Exact Words
Rena: I feel sorry for you.
Chad: Where is Lucy going?
Tom: Is the train arriving soon?

Quoted Speech
Rena **said,** "I feel sorry for you."
Chad **asked,** "Where is Lucy going?"
Tom **asked,** "Is the train arriving soon?"

1. In quoted speech,* the speaker's exact words are written in quotation marks. Quotes are often introduced by the verbs *say* and *ask*.	He **said,** "The buses are running late." Lina **asked,** "Where is the bus stop?"
2. Notice the punctuation of quoted speech. a. Put a comma after the verb *say* or *ask*. b. Use quotation marks at the beginning and end of the exact words. c. Begin the quote with a capital letter. d. Put a period (.) or question mark (?) before the final quotation mark.	Quotation Marks Mr. Gomez said, "Math is not difficult." Comma Liam asked, "Where are we?" Capital *W* Before Final Quotation Mark
3. The phrase with *said* or *asked* can come at the end of the quoted speech. When it does, put a. a comma (not a period) at the end of a statement b. a question mark if the quote is a question	a. "Your paper is late," **the Professor said.** b. "Why are we here?" **they asked.**

* *Quoted speech* is sometimes called *direct speech*.

4 Read each pair of sentences. Then choose the sentence with the correct punctuation and capitalization.

1. a. Martin asked "Did you read the blog about space exploration?"

   b. Martin asked, "Did you read the blog about space exploration?"

2. a. Rita said, "Yes, I read it last night."

   b. Rita said, "yes, I read it last night."

3. a. Sally asked, "Have you finished your assignment about astronauts"?

   b. Sally asked, "Have you finished your assignment about astronauts?"

4. a. "Yes. It took me a long time." said Alfredo.

   b. "Yes. It took me a long time," said Alfredo.

5. a. "New photos of Jupiter have just been published," the reporter said.

   b. New photos of Jupiter have just been published," the reporter said.

6. a. "Have you seen the new photos, Mary," Alex asked.

   b. "Have you seen the new photos, Mary?" Alex asked.

5 Complete the exercises.

A Add the necessary capitalization and punctuation to complete the quoted speech.

1. Julie said, "I'd love to be an astronaut."

2. why is that Hector asked

3. Julie said I want to see the Earth from space

4. Hector said yes, that must be an amazing sight

5. are you worried about the dangers Ratna asked

6. it's worth the risk Julie said

7. Ratna said I don't like the idea of spacewalks

8. I think they sound amazing said Hector

B Rewrite the sentences from exercise **A**. Move the information about the speaker to the other end of the sentence.

1. "I'd love to be an astronaut," Julie said.

2. _____

3. _____

4. _____

5. _____

6. _____

7. _____

8. _____

◄ Astronaut Tracy Caldwell Dyson looks through a window of the International Space Station.

16.6 Reported Speech

Quoted Speech

Reported Speech		
Subject	Reporting Verb	Noun Clause

Quoted Speech	Subject	Reporting Verb	Noun Clause
Rena said, "Ben likes traveling."	Rena	said	(that) Ben liked traveling.
Tom said, "Jill's at home."	Tom	said	(that) Jill was at home.
Chad asked, "Where is Luz going?"	Chad	asked	where Luz was going.

1. You can report what someone says indirectly (i.e., without the exact words) by using a reporting verb + a noun clause.	Harry **said that the bus was late.** Jim **asked what time it was.**
2. If the main verb in quoted speech is in the present, it usually shifts to the past in reported speech.*	Julie said, "Running **is** great exercise." Julie said that running **was** great exercise.
3. Personal pronouns and possessive adjectives** often need to change in reported speech.	Joe: "I don't see **your** map." Joe said **he** didn't see **my** map.
4. **Remember:** In conversation and informal writing, *that* is often omitted. In academic or formal writing, *that* is often not omitted.	He said **that** the bus is late. He said the bus is late. The leader said **that** schools were important.

Reported speech is sometimes called *indirect speech*.
See Unit 4, pages **90–91 to review personal pronouns and possessive adjectives.

6 Complete the conversations. Change the quoted speech in parentheses to reported speech. Remember to shift the verbs from present to past, and to change the pronouns and adjectives as necessary.

1. A: Where is Sam?

   B: I don't know. He said that _____he was coming_____ .
   ("I am coming.")

2. A: Did you see the professor?

   B. Yes. I asked her if _____ .
   ("Is the assignment due on Friday?")

3. A: The weather doesn't look too good.

   B: No, it doesn't. Chris said that _____ .
   ("There's going to be a storm.")

4. A: What did you say to Larry on the phone?

   B: I asked him what _____ .
   ("What are you doing?")

5. A: Why didn't Diane help us yesterday?

   B: She couldn't. She said that _____ .
   ("I'm too busy.")

6. A: Did you ask Scott to come to the party?

   B: Yes. He said that _____ .
   ("I have too much work.")

7. A: Why did Irina go home?

   B: She said that _____.

   ("I'm not enjoying the movie.")

8. A: Is Juan going to Australia?

   B: He said that _____.

   ("I don't think so.")

7 **SPEAK.** Work with a partner. Imagine that you are in a noisy place. Repeat the question or statement using reported speech. Do not shift to the past tense.

A: *Do you want some coffee?*

B: *I'm sorry? What did you say?*

A: *I asked if you want some coffee.*

1. Do you want some coffee?
2. What time is it?
3. Are you enjoying the concert?
4. This restaurant is noisy.

16.7 Reporting Verbs

Subject	Reporting Verb	Object	Noun Clause
Larry	said		(that) it's time for lunch.
	told	them	
	asked		when we were starting.
	asked	us	

1. To report a statement, use
  a. *said* + a noun clause
  b. *told* + object + a noun clause
	a. Harry **said** (that) the bus was late.
	b. Jen **told me** (that) dinner was ready.

2. **Be careful!** You must include an object with *told*.	✓ Jen **told us** dinner was ready. ✗ Jen <u>told</u> dinner was ready.

3. To report questions and answers, use:
  a. *ask* + noun clause
  b. *ask* + object + noun clause
  c. *answer* or *reply* + noun clause
	a. They **asked** if the movie was still playing.
	b. They **asked Joe** if it was a good movie.
	c. He **answered** that it was.

8 Circle all correct answers. Sometimes both answers are correct.

1. Jerry (asked) / (asked me) what my book was about.

2. I **told** / **replied** that it was about early space travel.

3. He **told me** / **asked** he knew several astronauts.

4. I **asked** / **said** I didn't believe him.

5. Jerry **told me** / **said** his uncle worked on the space program.

6. I **asked** / **said** if he ever went to watch flights take off.

7. He **answered** / **told** that he did.

8. I **asked him** / **told him** which astronauts he knew.

9 Change the speakers' exact words to reported speech. Use an appropriate reporting verb in the simple past. Add or change pronouns as necessary.

1. **Will:** What are you watching, Mei?

   Will asked Mei what she was watching.

2. **Mei:** It's a video from the space station.

   _____

3. **Will:** Who's talking?

   _____

4. **Mei:** The mission commander is giving a report.

   _____

5. **Will:** Why is the woman's hair like that?

   _____

6. **Mei:** It's because of zero gravity.

   _____

▲ Astronauts Luca Parmitano (above) and Karen Nyberg (left) on the International Space Station, August, 2013

PRACTICE

10 Complete the exercises.

A Look at the photo and read the caption. Then read the conversation about insects in space. Rewrite the conversation as quoted speech.

Spidernauts?

Hong: What are you watching?

Tina: It's a video about insects in space.

Hong: Are you serious?

Tina: Yes, astronauts sometimes take spiders and ants into space.

Hong: Oh, why do they do that?

Tina: They study their movements and feeding habits.

▲ Nefertiti, the first jumping spider in space, spent more than three months in orbit and circled the Earth over 1500 times.

1. Hong asked, "What are you watching?" _____

2. _____ Tina replied.

3. Hong asked _____

4. Tina said _____

5. _____ Hong asked.

6. Tina said _____

B Review the conversation in exercise **A**. Then complete the reported speech.

1. Hong asked Tina _what she was watching_.

2. Tina replied that _____

3. Hong asked _____

4. Tina said _____

5. Hong asked _____

6. Tina said _____

A Work with a partner. Discuss the questions and make notes on your partner's ideas.

1. Do you know about other animals that have traveled to space?

2. Do you think that we can learn anything useful from these experiments? Explain.

3. Do you think that it's fair to send animals into space? Give your reasons.

B Report your partner's ideas to a small group or the class.

Maya told me that a cat went into space. She said that the cat was from France.

12 EDIT. Read the student's assignment. Find and correct six more errors with quoted and reported speech.

A Person I Admire

For this assignment, I watched an interview with Ellen Ochoa, who became the first Hispanic American woman in space in 1991. She went on to make several more flights and has spent over 950 hours in space.

When the interviewer asked her what ~~was~~ NASA training ^was like, Ochoa replied that everything was harder in training than in space. Next, the interviewer asked Ochoa how did it feel to float in zero gravity. She replied that it was fun to be weightless. She told there was really nothing to compare it to on Earth. She said the closest activity was probably swimming. Ochoa said her that astronauts had to prepare for all sorts of problems and accidents. The interviewer then asked the former astronaut did she miss her family when she was in space. Ochoa said it is difficult. She said the interviewer she used e-mail to communicate with her husband when she was in space.

▶ Launched in 1977, the Voyager 1 space probe is now more than 11 billion miles (18 billion kilometers) from the sun. It is the first spacecraft to leave the solar system.

13 LISTEN.

CD4-30

A Listen to two students discuss a project. Circle the correct answers.

1. Maria **asked** / **told** Phil how his research was going.

2. Phil told Maria that he **was reading** / **read** about the Voyager 1 space probe.

3. Maria **asked if** / **said that** it was a useful article for the assignment.

4. Phil **asked if** / **said that** the mission was at a very exciting stage.

5. Maria asked **why it** / **what** was exciting.

6. Phil **replied** / **told** that the probe was no longer in the solar system.[1]

7. Maria wanted to know **how** / **if** a man-made object was flying around the galaxy.[2]

8. Phil **told** / **answered** that it was the first time in history.

[1]**solar system:** the sun, the moon, the eight other planets, and moons that move around the sun
[2]**galaxy:** a large system of stars; Earth's solar system is in the Milky Way galaxy

B Use the sentences from the conversation in exercise **A** to write quoted speech. Remember to use the correct tense and punctuation.

1. Maria asked _, "How is your research going?"_ _____

2. Phil said _____

3. _____ Maria asked.

4. Phil said _____

5. Maria asked _____

6. _____ Phil replied.

7. _____ Maria asked

8. Phil said _____

CD4-30 **C** Listen again and check your answers from exercise **B**.

14 APPLY.

A Work with a partner. Ask and answer the questions. Take notes about your partner's answers.

1. Do you think space exploration is a good thing?

   _____

   _____

2. Do you think the money should be used for other things?

   _____

   _____

3. Do you want to go into space?

   _____

   _____

4. Do you think there is life on other planets?

   _____

   _____

B Form a group with another pair of students. Take turns reporting what your partner said on one of the topics from exercise **A**. Use reported speech.

I asked Rosa if space exploration was a good thing. She said it was worth the money and had many advantages for everyone.

Charts
16.1–16.7

1 Circle all correct answers. Sometimes both answers are correct.

1. I don't know **when** / **whether** the expedition left.

2. It is a fact **that** / **why** exploration is often a dangerous activity.

3. The explorer said, "I've found **the city".** / **the city."**

4. **I think** / **I'm not sure** if the mission was a success.

5. **I believe** / **I believe that** the report is true.

6. The clerk **said** / **told** the tickets were sold out.

7. Do you know **if** / **how** this machine works?

8. Can you tell me **if** / **whether** or not the train is on time?

9. Are you glad **why** / **that** you came back?

10. We **asked** / **asked them** whether they had a good vacation.

Charts
16.1–2,
16.5–16.7

CD4-31

2 LISTEN & WRITE.

A Look at the photo and read the caption. Then listen to two people talk about the Hang Son Doong caves in Vietnam. Choose the correct answers.

1. a. Brad said the pictures were fantastic.

   b. Brad asked Sylvie what she thought of the pictures.

2. a. Sylvie asked what was so special about the caves.

   b. Sylvie asked if the caves were special.

3. a. Brad asked if the caves were the largest anywhere.

   b. Brad said the caves formed the largest cave system anywhere.

◄ A caver explores the
Hang Son Doong cave
system in Vietnam.

4. a. Sylvie said she didn't agree with Brad.

    b. Sylvie said he was right.

5. a. Brad said that he didn't like going in caves.

    b. Brad said that he might go into a cave.

6. a. Sylvie said she disliked caves.

    b. Sylvie asked Brad why he disliked caves.

7. a. Brad said it was easy to have an accident.

    b. Sylvie told Brad that it was easy to have an accident.

8. a. Sylvie said that the risk didn't worry her.

    b. Sylvie told Brad the risk worried her.

B In your notebook, write a conversation using quoted speech between Brad and Sylvie. Use your answers from exercise **A** and your own ideas. Remember to use correct punctuation.

Brad said, "Hey, Sylvie, these pictures are amazing! Take a look." Then Sylvie said, . . .

C Work with a partner. Read your partner's conversation. Comment on anything that you think is incorrect.

Charts **3**
16.1–16.4,
16.5,16.6

EDIT. Read the student's presentation. Find and correct five more errors with noun clauses, quoted speech, and reported speech.

Why Are We Here?

Often we ask ourselves why ~~are we~~ *we* here. This semester, I have learned a lot about this question. After learning about fossils from different parts of the world, I am convinced that humans began a great journey out of eastern Africa around 60,000 years ago. Evidence shows that early humans explored all areas of the globe. How did they survive? Scientists say us that these early humans discovered plants and animals to eat and found ways to stay warm. But, they are not certain how did they move across wide oceans and over rough terrain. I'm sure many didn't survive.

The question is why they did it? I believe the reason is that humans have an innate desire to explore, learn, and take risks. The author T.S. Eliot said, "only those who will risk going too far can possibly find how far one can go." This suggests that being an explorer and taking risks helps us to survive and succeed. We should all ask ourselves, "What I am doing to improve life for the people who will live after me?"

The Human Journey

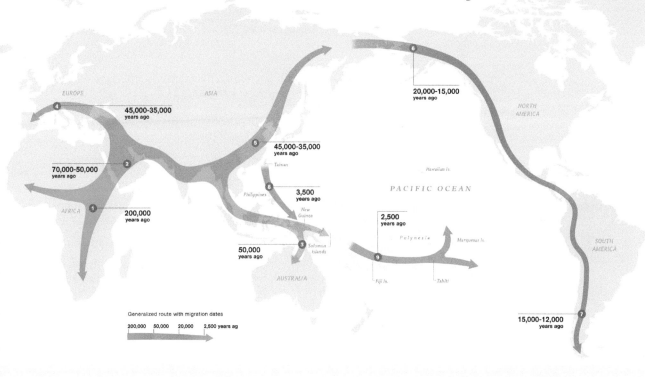

EUROPE

ASIA

4

45,000-35,000
years ago

6

20,000-15,000
years ago

NORTH
AMERICA

2

70,000-50,000
years ago

5

45,000-35,000
years ago

Taiwan

Hawaiian Is.

AFRICA

1

200,000
years ago

8

Philippines

3,500
years ago

New
Guinea

PACIFIC OCEAN

2,500
years ago

Polynesia

Marquesas Is.

SOUTH
AMERICA

50,000
years ago

3

Solomon
Islands

9

Fiji Is.

Tahiti

AUSTRALIA

15,000-12,000
years ago

7

Generalized route with migration dates

200,000   50,000   20,000   2,500 years ag

Charts
16.1–16.4,
16.6, 16.7

4 WRITE & SPEAK.

A Look at the map and review the student's presentation in exercise **3**. Then interview a partner about exploration and risks. Ask and answer these questions. Take notes in your notebook.

1. How long ago did the first humans settle in the place where your ancestors lived?

2. Do you think that people take fewer risks today than in the past? Why, or why not?

3. Do you consider yourself an explorer? Why, or why not?

4. What risks do you take? Give examples.

B Report your partner's ideas from exercise **A** to the class.

I asked Kerim if he thought people take fewer risks today. He said he thought so. He thought people in the past were more adventurous and willing to risk a lot.

▼ A camel caravan crosses the Danakil Depression. Eritrea, Africa, where our ancestors began their journey 60,000 years ago.

1 READ & NOTICE THE GRAMMAR.

A Think of a special trip or journey you have taken. Tell a partner the place and one thing you learned. Then read the text.

My Journey

One day my friend Bo asked me if I wanted to take a trip to Illinois. He said that some volunteers at the university were going to help people affected by a terrible tornado. Bo is a good friend and I could not say no.

My journey began on the plane. During the trip, I learned details of the storm. I also learned that we had a lot of work to do. From the plane, I saw the destruction of the storm. I was amazed that complete neighborhoods were flattened. I didn't have to ask if we were really needed. I knew we were.

We got to work right away. We cleared broken furniture, bricks, papers, and pieces of cars and household appliances. We moved branches and fallen trees. We talked with people whose homes were gone. I was surprised that many of them could still laugh. I couldn't imagine losing my home, my photos, my memories, but the people there really made me think. One man said, "My family is safe; nothing else really matters." An older woman said, "Life is too short to be sad for too long. We will rebuild and make new memories." I wanted to believe that I could be that strong. My journey was meant to help others, but I believe it helped me just as much.

GRAMMAR FOCUS

In the text, the writer uses noun clauses to describe thoughts and emotions. Noun clauses come after verbs, such as *learn, know, believe,* and after *be* + adjective.

> I also <u>learned</u> **that we had a lot of work to do.**
> I <u>was surprised</u> **that many of them could still laugh.**

The writer uses quoted and reported speech to tell the reader about conversations.

> One man said, *"My family is safe; nothing else really matters."*
> One day my friend Bo **asked me if I wanted to take a trip to Illinois.**

B Read the text in exercise **A** again. In your notebook, write an example of a sentence with a noun clause in each category:

1. after verbs of thought   3. reported speech

2. after *be* + adjective   4. quoted speech

1. I also learned that we had a lot of work to do.

C Complete the chart with information from the text in exercise **1A**.

Where did she go?	to Illinois, to a town hit by a horrible tornado
What did she do?	
What did she learn?	
Quotes	"My family is safe; nothing else really matters."

2 BEFORE YOU WRITE.

A Work with a partner. Choose a journey that taught you something. It can be a long trip (e.g., to another country) or a short journey (e.g., to a local museum). Discuss your idea with your partner and take notes.

B In your notebook, make a chart like the one in exercise **1C**. Complete the chart with information about your journey. Use your notes from exercise **2A** and the chart from exercise **1C** as a model.

3 WRITE about your journey. Use the information from your chart in exercise **2B** and the text in exercise **1A** to help you.

> **WRITING FOCUS   Using Quoted Speech to Add Impact**
>
> Writers use quoted speech for various reasons. One way is to make readers feel more connected or "in the moment." Notice the quotes in the text in exercise **1A**.
>
> *One man **said, "My family is safe; nothing else really matters."***
> *An older woman **said, "Life is too short to be sad for too long. We will rebuild and make new memories."***

4 SELF ASSESS. Read your text and underline the noun clauses. Then use the checklist to assess your work.

- ☐ I used noun clauses with *that* correctly. [16.1–16.2]
- ☐ I used noun clauses with *Wh-* words and *if* correctly. [16.3–16.4]
- ☐ I used quoted speech correctly. [16.5]
- ☐ I used reported speech and reporting verbs correctly. [16.6–16.7]
- ☐ I used quoted speech effectively. [WRITING FOCUS]

1   Spelling Rules for Verbs Ending in *-s* and *-es*

1. Add *-s* to most verbs.	like-like**s** sit-sit**s**
2. Add *-es* to verbs that end in *-ch*, *-s*, *-sh*, *-x*, or *-z*.	catch-catch**es** miss-miss**es** wash-wash**es** mix-mix**es** buzz-buzz**es**
3. Change the *-y* to *-i* and add *-es* when the base form ends in a consonant + *-y*.	cry-cri**es** carry-carri**es**
4. Do not change the *-y* when the base form ends in a vowel + *-y*.	pay-pay**s** stay-stay**s**
5. Some verbs are irregular in the third-person singular *-s* form of the simple present.	be-**is** go-**goes** do-**does** have-**has**

2   Spelling Rules for Verbs Ending in *-ing*

1. Add *-ing* to the base form of most verbs.	eat-eat**ing** do-do**ing** speak-speak**ing** carry-carry**ing**
2. When the verb ends in a consonant + *-e*, drop the *-e* and add *-ing*.	ride-rid**ing** write-writ**ing**
3. For one-syllable verbs that end in a consonant + a vowel + a consonant (CVC), double the final consonant and add *-ing*. Do not double the final consonant for verbs that end in CVC when the final consonant is *-w*, *-x*, or *-y*.	stop-stop**ping** sit-sit**ting** show-show**ing** fix-fix**ing** stay-stay**ing**
4. For two-syllable verbs that end in CVC and have stress on the first syllable, add *-ing*. Do not double the final consonant. For two-syllable verbs that end in CVC and have stress on the last syllable, double the final consonant and add *-ing*.	ENter-enter**ing** LISTen-listen**ing** beGIN-begin**ning** ocCUR-occur**ring**

3 Spelling Rules for Verbs Ending in -ed

1. Add -ed to the base form of most verbs that end in a consonant.	start-start**ed** talk-talk**ed**
2. Add -d if the base form of the verb ends in -e.	dance-danc**ed** live-liv**ed**
3. When the base form of the verb ends in a consonant + -y, change the -y to -i and add -ed. Do not change the -y to -i when the verb ends in a vowel + -y.	cry-cr**ied** worry-worr**ied** stay-stay**ed**
4. For one-syllable verbs that end in a consonant + a vowel + a consonant (CVC), double the final consonant and add -ed. Do not double the final consonant of verbs that end in -w, -x, or -y.	stop-stop**ped** rob-rob**bed** follow-follow**ed** fix-fix**ed** play-play**ed**
5. For two-syllable verbs that end in CVC and have stress on the first syllable, add -ed. Do not double the final consonant. For two-syllable verbs that end in CVC and have stress on the last syllable, double the final consonant and add -ed.	ORder-order**ed** HAPpen-happen**ed** ocCUR-occur**red** preFER-prefer**red**

4 Common Irregular Noun Plurals

Singular	Plural	Explanation
man woman tooth foot goose	men women teeth feet geese	Vowel change
sheep fish deer	sheep fish deer	No change
child person mouse	children people mice	Different word forms
	clothes groceries glasses jeans/pants/shorts scissors	No singular form

5   Spelling Rules for Adverbs Ending in -*ly*

	Adjective	Adverb
1. Add -*ly* to the end of most adjectives.	careful quiet serious	careful**ly** quiet**ly** serious**ly**
2. Change the -*y* to -*i* and add -*ly* to adjectives that end in a consonant + -*y*.	easy happy lucky	eas**ily** happ**ily** luck**ily**
3. Keep the -*e* and add -*ly* to some adjectives that end in -*e*.	nice free	nice**ly** free**ly**
4. Drop the final -*e* and add -*y* to adjectives that end with a consonant followed by -*le*.	simple comfortable	simp**ly** comforta**bly**
5. Add -*ally* to most adjectives that end in -*ic*.	basic enthusiastic	basic**ally** enthusiastic**ally**

6   Spelling Rules for Comparative and Superlative Forms

	Adjective/ Adverb	Comparative	Superlative
1. Add -*er* or -*est* to one-syllable adjectives and adverbs.	tall fast	tall**er** fast**er**	tall**est** fast**est**
2. Add -*r* or -*st* to adjectives that end in -*e*.	nice	nice**r**	nice**st**
3. Change the -*y* to -*i* and add -*er* or -*est* to two-syllable adjectives and adverbs that end in -*y*.	easy happy	eas**ier** happ**ier**	eas**iest** the happ**iest**
4. Double the final consonant and add -*er* or -*est* to one-syllable adjectives or adverbs that end in a consonant + a vowel + a consonant (CVC).	big hot	big**ger** hot**ter**	big**gest** hot**test**

7 Common Irregular Verbs

Base Form	Simple Past	Past Participle
be	was, were	been
beat	beat	beaten
become	became	become
begin	began	begun
bend	bent	bent
bite	bit	bitten
blow	blew	blown
break	broke	broken
bring	brought	brought
build	built	built
buy	bought	bought
catch	caught	caught
choose	chose	chosen
come	came	come
cost	cost	cost
cut	cut	cut
dig	dug	dug
dive	dived/dove	dived
do	did	done
draw	drew	drawn
drink	drank	drunk
drive	drove	driven
eat	ate	eaten
fall	fell	fallen
feed	fed	fed
feel	felt	felt
fight	fought	fought
find	found	found
fit	fit	fit/fitted
fly	flew	flown
forget	forgot	forgotten
forgive	forgave	forgiven
freeze	froze	frozen
get	got	got/gotten
give	gave	given
go	went	gone
grow	grew	grown
hang	hung	hung
have	had	had
hear	heard	heard
hide	hid	hidden
hit	hit	hit
hold	held	held
hurt	hurt	hurt
keep	kept	kept
know	knew	known

Base Form	Simple Past	Past Participle
lay	laid	laid
lead	led	led
leave	left	left
lend	lent	lent
let	let	let
lie	lay	lain
light	lit/lighted	lit/lighted
lose	lost	lost
make	made	made
mean	meant	meant
meet	met	met
pay	paid	paid
prove	proved	proved/proven
put	put	put
quit	quit	quit
read	read	read
ride	rode	ridden
ring	rang	rung
rise	rose	risen
run	ran	run
say	said	said
sit	sat	sat
sleep	slept	slept
slide	slid	slid
speak	spoke	spoken
spend	spent	spent
spread	spread	spread
stand	stood	stood
steal	stole	stolen
stick	stuck	stuck
strike	struck	struck
swear	swore	sworn
sweep	swept	swept
swim	swam	swum
take	took	taken
teach	taught	taught
tear	tore	torn
tell	told	told
think	thought	thought
throw	threw	thrown
understand	understood	understood
upset	upset	upset
wake	woke	woken
wear	wore	worn
win	won	won
write	wrote	written

8   Patterns with Gerunds

Verb + Gerund

They *enjoy dancing*.
She *delayed going* to the doctor.

admit	detest	mind	regret
advise	discuss	miss	remember
anticipate	dislike	permit	resent
appreciate	enjoy	postpone	resist
avoid	finish	practice	risk
can't help	forbid	put off	stop
complete	imagine	quit	suggest
consider	keep	recall	tolerate
delay	mention	recommend	understand
deny			

Verb + Preposition + Gerund

He *succeeded in winning* the prize.
Are you *thinking about taking* another course?

apologize for	concentrate on	object to	thank (someone) for
argue about	dream about/of	plan on/for	think about
believe in	insist on	succeed in	warn (someone) about
complain about	keep on	talk about	worry about

Noun + Preposition + Gerund

What's the *purpose of doing* this exercise?
I don't know his *reason for being* late.

benefit of	interest in	purpose of
cause of	problem with	reason for

Adjective + Preposition + Gerund

I'm *excited about studying* abroad.
Are you *interested in going*?

accustomed to	excited about	nervous about	tired of
afraid of	famous for	responsible for	upset about/with
bad/good at	(in)capable of	sick of	used to
concerned about	interested in	sorry about/for	worried about

9 Patterns with Infinitives

Verb + Infinitive

They need to leave.
I am learning to speak English.

agree	claim	know how	seem
appear	consent	learn	swear
arrange	decide	manage	tend
ask	demand	need	threaten
attempt	deserve	offer	try
be able	expect	plan	volunteer
beg	fail	prepare	want
can afford	forget	pretend	wish
care	hope	promise	would like
choose	intend	refuse	

Verb + Object + Infinitive

I want you to leave.
He expects me to call him.

advise	convince	hire	require
allow	dare	instruct	select
appoint	enable	invite	teach
ask*	encourage	need*	tell
beg*	expect*	order	urge
cause	forbid	pay*	want*
challenge	force	permit	warn
choose*	get	persuade	would like*
command	help**	remind	

*These verbs can be either with or without an object. (*I **want [you] to go**.*)

After *help*, *to* is often omitted. (*He **helped me move.*)

Verb + Infinitive or Gerund

I love to swim.
I love swimming.

begin	continue	love
(not) bother	hate	prefer
can't stand	like	start

Transitive Phrasal Verbs (Separable)

*Don't forget to **turn off** the oven before you leave the house.*
*Don't forget to **turn** the oven **off** before you leave the house.*

Phrasal Verb	Meaning	Example Sentence
blow up	cause something to explode	*The workers **blew** the bridge **up**.*
bring back	return	*She **brought** the shirt **back** to the store.*
bring up	1. raise from childhood 2. introduce a topic to discuss	*1. My grandmother **brought** me **up**.* *2. Don't **bring up** that subject.*
call back	return a telephone call	*I **called** Rajil **back** but there was no answer.*
call off	cancel	*They **called** the wedding **off** after their fight.*
cheer up	make someone feel happier	*Her visit to the hospital **cheered** the patients **up**.*
clear up	clarify, explain	*She **cleared** the problem **up**.*
do over	do again	*His teacher asked him to **do** the essay **over**.*
figure out	solve, understand	*The student **figured** the problem **out**.*
fill in	complete information	***Fill in** the answers on the test.*
fill out	complete an application or form	*I had to **fill** many forms **out** at the doctor's office.*
find out	learn, uncover	*Did you **find** anything **out** about the new plans?*
give away	offer something freely	*They are **giving** prizes **away** at the store.*
give back	return	*The boy **gave** the pen **back** to the teacher.*
give up	stop doing	*I **gave up** sugar last year. Will you **give** it **up**?*
help out	aid, support someone	*I often **help** my older neighbors **out**.*
lay off	dismiss workers from their jobs	*My company **laid** 200 workers **off** last year.*
leave on	allow a machine to continue working	*I **left** the lights **on** all night.*
let in	allow someone to enter	*She opened a window to **let** some fresh air **in**.*
look over	examine	*We **looked** the contract **over** before signing it.*
make up	say something untrue or fictional (a story, a lie)	*The child **made** the story **up**. It wasn't true at all.*
pay back	return money, repay a loan	*I **paid** my friend **back**. I owed him $10.*
pick up	1. get someone or something 2. lift	*1. He **picked up** his date at her house.* *2. I **picked** the ball **up** and threw it.*
put off	delay, postpone	*Don't **put** your homework **off** until tomorrow.*
put out	1. take outside 2. extinguish	*1. He **put** the trash **out**.* *2. Firefighters **put out** the fire.*
set up	1. arrange 2. start something	*1. She **set** the tables **up** for the party.* *2. They **set up** the project.*
shut off	stop something from working	*Can you **shut** the water **off**?*
sort out	make sense of something	*We have to **sort** this problem **out**.*
straighten up	make neat and orderly	*I **straightened** the messy living room **up**.*
take back	own again	*He **took** the tools that he loaned me **back**.*
take off	remove	*She **took off** her hat and gloves.*
take out	remove	*I **take** the trash **out** on Mondays.*
talk over	discuss a topic until it is understood	*Let's **talk** this plan **over** before we do anything.*
think over	reflect, ponder	*She **thought** the job offer **over** carefully.*
throw away/ throw out	get rid of something, discard	*He **threw** the old newspapers **away**.* *I **threw out** the old milk in the fridge.*
try on	put on clothing to see if it fits	*He **tried** the shoes **on** but didn't buy them.*
turn down	refuse	*His manager **turned** his proposal **down**.*
turn off	stop something from working	*Can you **turn** the TV **off**, please?*
turn on	switch on, operate	*I **turned** the lights **on** in the dark room.*
turn up	increase the volume	***Turn** the radio **up**, so we can hear the news.*
wake up	make someone stop sleeping	*The noise **woke** the baby **up**.*
write down	write on paper	*I **wrote** the information **down**.*

*We'll **look into** the problem.*

Phrasal Verb	Meaning	Example Sentence
come across	find something	*I **came across** this novel in the library.*
come from	be a native or resident of	*She **comes from** London.*
come up with	invent	*Let's **come up with** a new game.*
count on	depend on	*You can always **count on** good friends to help you.*
drop out of	quit	*Jin **dropped out** of the study group.*
follow through with	complete	*You must **follow through with** your promises.*
get off	leave (a bus/a train)	*I forgot to **get off** the bus at my stop.*
get on	board (a car/a train)	*I **got on** the plane last.*
get out of	1. leave (a car/a taxi) 2. avoid	1. *I **got out of** the car.* 2. *She **got out of** doing her chores.*
get together with	meet	*I **got together with** Ana on Saturday.*
get over	return to a normal state	*I just **got over** a bad cold. I feel much better now!*
go over	review	*Let's **go over** our notes before the exam.*
look after	take care of	*He has to **look after** his sister. His parents are out.*
look into	investigate	*The police **looked into** the crime and solved it.*
run into	meet accidentally	*She **ran into** Mai on campus.*

Intransitive Phrasal Verbs (Inseparable)

*My car **broke down** again!*

Phrasal Verb	Meaning	Example Sentence
add up	make sense	*What he says does not **add up**.*
break down	stop working	*This machine **breaks down** all the time.*
break up	separate	*Their marriage **broke up** after a year.*
dress up	put on more formal clothes	*He **dressed up** to attend the wedding.*
drop in	visit without an appointment	***Drop in** when you can.*
drop out	leave or stop	*She never liked school, so she decided to **drop out**.*
eat out	eat in a restaurant	*She hates to cook, so she **eats out** frequently.*
fool around	play with	*He **fools around** with old cars for fun.*
get ahead	succeed, improve oneself	*Now that she has a new job, she is **getting ahead**.*
get along	have a friendly relationship	*My coworkers and I **get along** well.*
get up	awaken, arise	*I **got up** late this morning.*
give up	stop trying	*I played the piano for seven years but then **gave up**.*
go ahead	begin or continue to do	*You can **go ahead**. We'll wait for Jane.*
go away	leave, depart	*The rabbits in the garden finally **went away**.*
go down	decrease	*Prices of cars have **gone down** recently.*
go on	continue	*How long do you think this speech will **go on**?*
go out	leave one's home	*Jon has **gone out**. He should return soon.*
go up	rise, go higher	*The price of gasoline has **gone up**.*
grow up	become an adult	*Our daughter has **grown up** now.*
hang on	wait	***Hang on** while I change my shoes.*
hold on	struggle against difficulty	***Hold on** just a little longer. It's almost over.*
look out	be careful	***Look out!** You'll fall!*
make up	agree to be friends again	*They had a fight, but soon **made up**.*
move in	go live in	*We **moved in** last week. We love the area!*
move out	leave a place permanently	*When is your roommate **moving out**?*
run out	use all of something	*Is there more paper for the printer? We **ran out**.*
sign up	join, agree to do something	*The course looked interesting so I **signed up**.*
sit down	seat oneself	*Let's **sit down**. Class is starting.*
speak up	talk louder	*Will you **speak up**? I can't hear you.*
stand up	get on one's feet	*The teacher asked the students to **stand up**.*
stay up	keep awake	*The student **stayed up** all night to study.*
take off	1. go up into the air 2. increase quickly	*1. After a long wait, the airplane finally **took off**.* *2. Sales of the new product have **taken off**.*
watch out	be careful	***Watch out!** There's a lot of ice on this road.*
work out	exercise	*The football player **works out** three times a week.*

11 Guide to Pronunciation Symbols

Vowels		
Symbol	Key Word	Pronunciation
/a/	hot	/hat/
	far	/far/
/æ/	cat	/kæt/
/aɪ/	fine	/faɪn/
/au/	house	/haʊs/
/ɛ/	bed	/bɛd/
/eɪ/	name	/neɪm/
/i/	need	/nid/
/ɪ/	sit	/sɪt/
/ou/	go	/gou/
/ʊ/	book	/bʊk/
/u/	boot	/but/
/ɔ/	dog	/dɔg/
	four	/fɔr/
/ɔɪ/	toy	/tɔɪ/
/ʌ/	cup	/kʌp/
/ɛr/	bird	/bɛrd/
/ə/	about	/əˈbaʊt/

Consonants		
Symbol	Key Word	Pronunciation
/b/	boy	/bɔɪ/
/d/	day	/deɪ/
/dʒ/	just	/dʒʌst/
/f/	face	/feɪs/
/g/	get	/gɛt/
/h/	hat	/hæt/
/k/	car	/kar/
/l/	light	/laɪt/
/m/	my	/maɪ/
/n/	nine	/naɪn/
/ŋ/	sing	/sɪŋ/
/p/	pen	/pɛn/
/r/	right	/raɪt/
/s/	see	/si/
/t/	tea	/ti/
/tʃ/	cheap	/tʃip/
/v/	vote	/vout/
/w/	west	/wɛst/
/y/	yes	/yɛs/
/z/	zoo	/zu/
/ð/	they	/ðeɪ/
/θ/	think	/θɪŋk/
/ʃ/	shoe	/ʃu/
/ʒ/	vision	/ˈvɪʒən/

Source: The *Newbury House Dictionary Plus Grammar Reference, Fifth Edition*, National Geographic Learning/Cengage Learning, 2014

12 Conversion Charts

Length

When You Know	Multiply by	To Find
inches (in)	25.44	millimeters (mm)
feet (ft)	30.5	centimeters (cm)
feet (ft)	0.3	meters (m)
yards (yd)	0.91	meters (m)
miles (mi)	1.6	kilometers (km)
Metric:		
millimeters (mm)	0.039	inches (in)
centimeters (cm)	0.03	feet (ft)
meters (m)	3.28	feet (ft)
meters (m)	1.09	yards (yd)
kilometers (km)	0.62	miles (mi)

Weight

When You Know	Multiply by	To Find
ounces (oz)	28.35	grams (g)
pounds (lb)	0.45	kilograms (kg)
Metric:		
grams (g)	0.04	ounces (oz)
kilograms (kg)	2.2	pounds (lb)

Volume

When You Know	Multiply by	To Find
fluid ounces (fl. oz)	30.0	milliliters (mL)
pints (pt)	0.47	liters (L)
quarts (qt)	0.95	liters (L)
gallons (gal)	3.8	liters (L)
Metric:		
milliliters (mL)	0.03	fluid ounces (fl. oz)
liters (L)	2.11	pints (pt)
liters (L)	1.05	quarts (qt)
liters (L)	0.26	gallons (gal)

Temperature

When You Know	Do This	To Find
degrees Fahrenheit (°F)	$(F° - 32) \times \frac{5}{9}$	degrees Celsius (°C)
degrees Celsius (°C)	$1.8C° + 32$	degrees Fahrenheit (°F)

Sample Temperatures

Fahrenheit	Celsius
0	–18
10	–12
20	–7
32	0
40	4
50	10
60	16
70	21
80	27
90	32
100	38
212	100

GLOSSARY OF GRAMMAR TERMS

action verb: a verb that shows an action.
> He **drives** every day.
> They **left** yesterday morning.

active voice: a sentence in which the subject performs the action of the verb. (See *passive voice*.)
> Michael ate the hamburger.

adjective: a word that describes or modifies a noun or pronoun.
> She is **friendly**.
> Brazil is a **huge** country.

adjective clause: see *relative clause*.

adverb: a word that describes or modifies a verb, an adjective, or another adverb.
> He eats **quickly**.
> She drives **carefully**.

adverb clause: a kind of dependent clause. Like single adverbs, they can show time, reason, purpose, and condition.
> **When the party was over,** everyone left.

adverb of frequency: (see *frequency adverb*.)

adverb of manner: an adverb that describes the action of the verb. Many adverbs of manner are formed by adding *-ly* to the adjective.
> You sing **beautifully**.
> He speaks **slowly**.

affirmative statement: a statement that does not have a verb in the negative form.
> My uncle lives in Portland.

article: a word that is used before a noun: *a, an, the.*
> I looked up at **the** moon.
> Lucy had **a** sandwich and **an** apple for lunch.

auxiliary verb: (also called *helping verb*.) a verb used with the main verb. *Be, do, have,* and *will* are common auxiliary verbs when they are followed by another verb. Modals are also auxiliary verbs.
> I **am** working.
> He **won't** be in class tomorrow.
> She **can** speak Korean.

base form: the form of the verb without *to* or any endings such as *-ing, -s,* or *-ed.*
> eat, sleep, go, walk

capital letter: an uppercase letter.
> New York, Mr. Franklin, Japan

clause: a group of words with a subject and a verb. (See *dependent clause* and *main clause*.)
> We watched the game. (one clause)
> We watched the game after we ate dinner. (two clauses)

comma: a punctuation mark that separates parts of a sentence.
> After he left work, he went to the gym.
> I can't speak Russian, but my sister can.

common noun: a noun that does not name a specific person, place, thing, or idea.
> man, country, book, help

comparative: the form of an adjective used to talk about the difference between two people, places, or things.
> I'm **taller** than my mother.
> That book is **more interesting** than this one.

conditional: a structure used to express an activity or event that depends on something else.
> **If the weather is nice on Sunday,** we'll go to the beach.

conjunction: a word used to connect information or ideas. *And, but, or,* and *because* are conjunctions.
> He put cheese **and** onions on his sandwich.
> I wanted to go, **but** I had too much homework.
> We were confused **because** we didn't listen.

consonant: a sound represented by the letters *b, c, d, f, g, h, j, k, l, m, n, p, q, r, s, t, v, w, x, y,* and *z.*

contraction: two words combined into a shorter form.
> did not → **didn't**
> she is → **she's**
> I am → **I'm**
> we will → **we'll**

count noun: a noun that names something you can count. Count nouns are singular or plural.
> I ate an **egg** for breakfast.
> I have **six apples** in my bag.

definite article: the word *the*. It is used before a specific person, place, or thing.
> I found it on **the** Internet.
> **The** children are sleeping.

demonstrative pronoun: a pronoun that identifies a person or thing.
> **This** is my sister, Kate.
> **Those** are Jamal's books.

dependent clause: a clause that cannot stand alone as a sentence. It must be used with a main clause.
> I went for a walk **before I ate breakfast**.

direct object: a noun or pronoun that receives the action of the verb.
- ➤ Aldo asked a **question**.
- ➤ Karen helped **me**.

direct quote: a statement of a speaker's exact words using quotation marks.
- ➤ Our teacher said, **"Do exercises 5 and 6 for homework."**

exclamation point: a punctuation mark that shows emotion (anger, surprise, excitement, etc.) or emphasis.
- ➤ We won the game**!**
- ➤ Look**!** It's snowing**!**

formal: describes language used in academic writing or speaking, or in polite or official situations rather than in everyday speech or writing.
- ➤ Please do not take photographs inside the museum.
- ➤ May I leave early today?

frequency adverb: an adverb that tells how often something happens. Some common adverbs of frequency are never, rarely, sometimes, often, usually, and always.
- ➤ I **always** drink coffee in the morning.
- ➤ He **usually** leaves work at six.

frequency expression: an expression that tells how often something happens.
- ➤ We go to the grocery store **every Saturday**.
- ➤ He plays tennis **twice a week**.

future: a form of a verb that expresses an action or situation that has not happened yet. Will, be going to, the present progressive, and the simple present are used to express the future.
- ➤ I **will call** you later.
- ➤ We**'re going** to the movies tomorrow.
- ➤ I**'m taking** French next semester.
- ➤ The show **starts** after dinner.

future conditional: expresses something we believe will happen in the future based on certain conditions; the if-clause + simple present gives the condition, and will or be going to + the base form of the verb gives the result.
- ➤ If you don't go to practice, the coach will not let you play in the game.

gerund: an -ing verb form that is used as a noun. It can be the subject of a sentence or the object of a verb or preposition. See page **A7–A8** for lists of common verbs followed by gerunds.
- ➤ **Surfing** is a popular sport.
- ➤ We enjoy **swimming**.
- ➤ The boy is interested in **running**.

gerund phrase: an -ing verb form + an object or a prepositional phrase. It can be the subject of a sentence, or the object of a verb or preposition.
- ➤ **Swimming in the ocean** is fun.
- ➤ I love **eating chocolate.**
- ➤ We are thinking about **watching the new TV show.**

helping verb: (see auxiliary verb.)

if clause: a clause that begins with if and expresses a condition.
- ➤ **If you drive too fast,** you will get a ticket.

imperative: a sentence that gives an instruction or command.
- ➤ **Turn** left at the light.
- ➤ **Don't use** the elevator.

indefinite article: the words a and an. They are used before singular count nouns that are not specific.
- ➤ We have **a** test today.
- ➤ She's **an** engineer.

indefinite pronoun: a pronoun that refers to people or things that are not specific or not known. Someone, something, everyone, everything, no one, nothing, and nowhere are common indefinite pronouns.
- ➤ **Everyone** is here today.
- ➤ **No one** is absent.
- ➤ Would you like **something** to eat?

independent clause: a clause that can stand alone as a complete sentence. It has a subject and a verb.
- ➤ **I went for a walk** before breakfast.

infinitive: to + the base form of a verb.
- ➤ He wants **to see** the new movie.

infinitive of purpose: to + the base form of the verb to express purpose or to answer the question with why. (also in order to)
- ➤ Scientists studied the water **in order to learn** about the disease.
- ➤ We went to the store **to buy** milk.

informal: language that is used in casual, everyday conversation and writing.
- ➤ Who are you talking to?
- ➤ We'll be there at eight.

information question: (see Wh- question.)

inseparable phrasal verb: a phrasal verb that cannot have a noun or a pronoun object between its two parts (verb + particle). The verb and the particle always stay together.
- ➤ I **ran into** a friend in the library.
- ➤ Do you and your coworkers **get along**?

intonation: the rise or fall of a person's voice. For example, rising intonation is often used to ask a question.

intransitive verb: a verb that cannot be followed by a direct object.
  ➤ *We didn't **agree**.*
  ➤ *The students **smiled** and **laughed**.*

irregular adjective: an adjective that does not change form in the usual way .
  ➤ *good →better*
  ➤ *bad →worse*

irregular adverb: an adverb that does not change form in the usual way.
  ➤ *well →better*
  ➤ *badly →worse*

irregular verb: a verb with forms that do not follow the rules for regular verbs.
  ➤ *swim →swam*
  ➤ *have →had*

main clause: a clause that can stand alone as a sentence. It has a subject and a verb. (See *independent clause*.)
  ➤ *I **heard the news** when I was driving home.*

main verb: the verb that is in the main clause.
  ➤ *We **drove** home after we had dinner.*

measurement word: a word that is used to talk about a specific amount or quantity of a non-count noun.
  ➤ *We need to buy a **box** of pasta and a **gallon** of milk.*

modal: an auxiliary verb that adds a degree of certainty, possibility, or time to a verb. *May, might, can, could, will, would,* and *should* are common modals.
  ➤ *You **should** eat more vegetables.*
  ➤ *Julie **can** speak three languages.*

negative statement: a statement that has a verb in the negative form.
  ➤ *I **don't have** any sisters.*
  ➤ *She **doesn't drink** coffee.*

non-action verb: a verb that does not describe an action. Non-action verbs indicate states, sense, feelings, or ownership. They are not common in the progressive.
  ➤ *I **love** my grandparents.*
  ➤ *I **see** Marta. She's across the street.*
  ➤ *They **have** a new car.*

non-count noun: a noun that names something that cannot be counted.
  ➤ *Carlos drinks a lot of **coffee**.*
  ➤ *I need some **salt** for the recipe.*

noun: a word that names a person, place, or thing.
  ➤ *They're **students**.*
  ➤ *He's a **teacher**.*

noun clause: a clause that can be used in place of a noun, a noun phrase, or a pronoun.
  ➤ *I didn't know **that she was here**.*
  ➤ *I'm not sure **if the store is open yet**.*

object: a noun or pronoun that receives the action of the verb.
  ➤ *Mechanics fix **cars**.*

object pronoun: a pronoun that takes the place of a noun as the object of the sentence: *me, you, him, her, it, us, them*.
  ➤ *Rita is my neighbor. I see **her** every day.*
  ➤ *Can you help **us**?*

participial adjective: an adjective that is formed like a present participle (*-ing*) or past participle (*-ed*) form of a verb.
  ➤ *Martin had **tired** eyes.*

particle: a short word that combines with a verb to form a phrasal verb; examples include *on, out, over, into, up, through,* and *back*.
  ➤ *I looked **up** the definition.*
  ➤ *The students ran **into** their teacher at the store.*

passive voice: when the focus of a sentence is on the object of the verb instead of the subject. Active voice focuses on the subject.
  ➤ *My wallet **was stolen**.*

past participle: the form of the verb used in perfect and passive. It usually ends in *-d* or *-ed*.
  ➤ *Jemila has **worked** here for a long time.*

past progressive: a verb form used to talk about an action that was in progress in the past.
  ➤ *He **was watching** TV when the phone rang.*

period: a punctuation mark used at the end of a statement.
  ➤ *She lives in Moscow**.***

phrasal verb: a verb and a particle that function as a single verb. See pages **A9–A11** for lists of common phrasal verbs.
  ➤ ***Turn off** the light when you leave.*
  ➤ *She's **figured out** the answer.*

phrase: a group of words that go together but are not a complete sentence (i.e., does not have both a subject and a verb).
  ➤ *He lives **near the train station**.*

plural noun: a noun that names more than one person, place, or thing.
  ➤ *He put three **boxes** on the table.*
  ➤ *Argentina and Mexico are **countries**.*

possessive adjective: an adjective that shows ownership or a relationship: *my, your, his, her, its, our, their*.

➤ **My** car is green.

➤ **Your** keys are on the table.

possessive noun: a noun that shows ownership or a relationship. To make most singular nouns possessive, use an apostrophe (') + *-s*. To make plural nouns possessive, add an apostrophe.

➤ **Leo's** apartment is large.

➤ The **girls'** books are on the table.

possessive pronoun: a pronoun that shows ownership or a relationship: *mine, yours, his, hers, ours, theirs*. Possessive pronouns are used in place of a possessive adjective + noun.

➤ My sister's eyes are blue. **Mine** are brown. What color are **yours**?

preposition: a word that describes the relationships between nouns. Prepositions show space, time, direction, cause, and effect; often they occur together with certain verbs or adjectives.

➤ I live **on** Center Street.

➤ We left **at** noon.

➤ I'm worried **about** the test.

prepositional phrase: a phrase that has a preposition + a noun or a noun phrase.

➤ I live **in New York City**.

➤ We saw the movie **at the new theater**.

present continuous: (see *present progressive*.)

present participle: the form of the verb that ends in *-ing*.

➤ She is **sleeping**.

➤ They are **laughing**.

present perfect: a verb form that connects the past to the present.

➤ I **have washed** the dishes.

➤ John **hasn't called** today.

present perfect progressive: a verb form used for a situation or habit that began in the past and continues up to the present or an action in progress that is not yet completed.

➤ I've **been getting up** early.

➤ **Have** you **been waiting** for a long time?

present progressive: (also called *present continuous*.) a verb form used to talk about an action or event that is in progress at the moment of speaking; the form can also refer to a planned event in the future.

➤ That car **is speeding**.

➤ I **am taking** three classes this semester.

➤ We **are eating** at that new restaurant Friday night.

pronoun: a word that takes the place of a noun or refers to a noun.

➤ The teacher is sick today. **He** has a cold.

proper noun: a noun that names a specific person, place, or thing

➤ **Maggie** lives in a town near **Dallas**.

punctuation: a mark that makes ideas in writing clear. Common punctuation marks include the comma (,), period (.), exclamation point (!), and question mark (?).

➤ John plays soccer**,** but I don't.

➤ She's from Japan**.**

➤ That's amazing**!**

➤ Where are you from**?**

quantifier: a word used to describe the amount of a noun.

➤ We need **some** potatoes for the recipe.

➤ I usually put **a little** milk in my coffee.

question mark: a punctuation mark used at the end of a question.

➤ Are you a student**?**

quoted speech: a statement that includes the exact words someone said. Quotation marks ("/") are used around the exact words.

➤ She said, **"I'm not feeling well."**

regular: a noun, verb, adjective, or adverb that changes form according to standard rules.

➤ apple ⟶ apple**s**

➤ talk ⟶ talk**ed**/talk**ing**

➤ small ⟶ small**er**

➤ slow ⟶ slow**ly**

relative clause: a clause that describes a noun or indefinite pronoun in a sentence. It comes after the noun or pronoun it describes. It is also called an *adjective clause*.

➤ The student **that I am sitting next to** is from Peru.

➤ I know everyone **who lives in my building**.

relative pronoun: a pronoun that introduces a relative clause. Common relative pronouns are *who, whom, whose, that,* and *which*.

➤ We met the woman **who** owns the shop.

➤ Here's the book **that** you were looking for.

reported speech: a statement of what someone said that does not have quotation marks.

➤ Adele said **that she was sick**.

reporting verb: a verb used to report what people say, either in quoted or reported speech (*say, tell, ask*).

➤ Tomo **said**, "Hi, how are you?"

➤ Jennifer **asked** if we were busy.

sentence: a thought that is expressed in words, usually with a subject and verb. A sentence begins with a capital letter and ends with a period, exclamation point, or question mark.

> ➤ *The bell rang loudly.*
> ➤ *Don't eat that!*

separable phrasal verb: a phrasal verb that can have a noun or a pronoun (object) between its two parts (verb + particle).

> ➤ **Turn** *the light* **off.**
> ➤ **Turn off** *the light.*

short answer: a common spoken answer to a question that is not always a complete sentence.

> ➤ A: *Where are you going?*
> ➤ B: **To the store.**

simple past: a verb form used to talk about completed actions.

> ➤ *Last night we* **ate** *dinner at home.*
> ➤ *I* **visited** *my parents last weekend.*

simple present: a verb form used to talk about habits or routines, schedules, and facts.

> ➤ *He* **likes** *apples and oranges.*
> ➤ *Toronto* **gets** *a lot of snow in the winter.*

singular noun: a noun that names only one person, place, or thing.

> ➤ *They have* **a son** *and* **a daughter.**

statement: a sentence that gives information.

> ➤ *My house has five rooms.*
> ➤ *He doesn't have a car.*

stress: we use stress to say a syllable or a word with more volume or emphasis.

subject: the noun or pronoun that is the topic of the sentence.

> ➤ *Patricia is a doctor.*
> ➤ *They are from Iceland.*

subject pronoun: a pronoun that is the subject of a sentence: *I, you, he, she, it,* and *they.*

> ➤ *I have one brother.* **He** *lives in Miami.*

subordinating conjunction: a conjunction that is used to introduce an adverb clause, such as *because, since, even though,* and *although.* (See *conjunction.*)

> ➤ **Even though** *he ate all his dinner, he is still hungry.*
> ➤ *She is late* **because** *she got lost.*

superlative: the form of an adjective or adverb used to compare three or more people, places, or things.

> ➤ *Mount Everest is* **the highest** *mountain in the world.*
> ➤ *Evgeny is* **the youngest** *student in our class.*

syllable: a part of a word that contains a single vowel sound and is pronounced as a unit.

> ➤ *The word* **pen** *has one syllable.*
> ➤ *The word* **pencil** *has two syllables (pen-cil).*

tense: the form of the verb that shows the time of the action.

> ➤ *They* **sell** *apples.* (simple present)
> ➤ *They* **sold** *cars.* (simple past)

third-person singular: in the simple present, the third-person singular ends in *-s* or *-es.* Singular nouns and the pronouns *he, she,* and *it* take the third-person singular form.

> ➤ *She* **plays** *the piano.*
> ➤ *Mr. Smith* **teaches** *her.*

time clause: a clause that tells when an action or event happened or will happen. Time clauses are introduced by conjunctions, such as *when, after, before, while,* and *since.*

> ➤ *I have lived here* **since I was a child.**
> ➤ **While I was walking home,** *it began to rain.*
> ➤ *I'm going to call my parents* **after I eat dinner.**

time expression: a phrase that tells when something happened or will happen. Time expressions usually go at the end or the beginning of a sentence.

> ➤ **Last week** *I went hiking.*
> ➤ *She's moving* **next month.**

transitive verb: a verb that is followed by a direct object.

> ➤ *We* **took** *an umbrella.*

verb: a word that shows action, gives a state, or shows possession.

> ➤ *Tori* **skated** *across the ice.*
> ➤ *She* **is** *an excellent athlete.*
> ➤ *She* **has** *many medals.*

voiced: a sound that is spoken with the vibration of the vocal cords. The consonants *b, d, g, j, l, m, n, r, v, w, z,* and all vowels are typically voiced.

vowel: a sound represented in English by the letters *a, e, i, o, u,* and sometimes *y.*

Wh- question: (also called *information question.*) a question that asks for specific information, not *"Yes"* or *"No."*

> ➤ *Where do they live?*
> ➤ *What do you usually do on weekends?*

Wh- word: a word such as *who, what, where, when, why,* or *how* that is used to begin a *Wh-* question.

Yes/No question: a question that can be answered with *"Yes"* or *"No."*

> ➤ *Do you live in Dublin?*
> ➤ *Can you ski?*

Note: All page references in blue are in Split Edition B.

Text and Listening

234: Exercise 1. Source: http://newswatch.nationalgeographic.com/2013/02/25/carnivorous-plants-glow. **240:** Exercise 11. Source: http://www.desertmuseum.org/kids/oz/long-fact-sheets/Saguaro%20Cactus.php. **242:** Exercise 1. Source: National Geographic Magazine, April 2011. **250:** Exercise 1. Source: National Geographic Magazine, January 2011. **256:** Exercise 10. Source: http://news.nationalgeographic.com/news/2009/05/090504-sunderbans-tigers-video-ap.html. **260:** Exercise 1. Source: http://www.epa.gov/air/noise.html. **264:** Exercise 1. Source: http://news.nationalgeographic.com/news/2011/01/pictures/110105-underwater-sculpture-park-garden-cancun-mexico-caribbean-pictures-photos-science. **271:** Exercise 1. Sources: http://www.nydailynews.com/news/world/felix-baumgartner-broke-sound-barrier-skydive-article-1.1255164; http://www.euronews.com/2012/10/24/felix-baumgartner-life-on-the-edge. **279:** Exercise 1. Sources: https://www.youtube.com/watch?v=8lThsSJU328; http://www.nationalgeographic.com/explorers/bios/kakani-katija/. **286:** Exercise 12. Source: http://ngm-beta.nationalgeographic.com/archive/a-monkey-that-knows-no-bounds. **288:** Exercise 4. Source: http://www.nationalgeographic.com/explorers/bios/barrington-irving. **308:** Exercise 1. Source: http://www.bbc.co.uk/news/mobile/world-europe-isle-of-man-15773388. **210:** Exercise 1. Source: http://www.inspirationgreen.com/the-trash-people-of-ha-schult.html. **358:** Exercise 13. Source: National Geographic Magazine, May 2011. **376:** Exercise 6. Source: http://education.nationalgeographic.co.uk/education/thisday/jun3/father-canning-laid-rest/?ar_a=4. **376:** Exercise 6. Source: http://www.encyclopedia.com/topic/Nicolas_Appert.aspx. **382:** Exercise 1. Sources: http://www.nationalgeographic.com/explorers/bios/tan-le/; http://www.ted.com/talks/tan_le_my_immigration_story.html. **396:** Exercise 1. Source: http://news.nationalgeographic.com/news/2013/08/130808-moche-priestess-queen-tomb-discovery-peru-archeology-science. **399:** Exercise 5. Source: National Geographic Magazine, June 2005. **404:** Exercise 1. Source: National Geographic Magazine, September 2004. **417:** Exercise 6. Source: http://photography.nationalgeographic.com/photography/photo-tips/uig-bay-evening-richardson. **419:** Exercise 6. Source: https://sites.google.com/site/fatherofgarbology/garbology. **426:** Exercise 1. Source: http://www.franckgoddio.org/projects/sunken-civilizations/heracleion.html. **431:** Exercise 9. Source: http://news.nationalgeographic.com/news/2007/09/070919-sunken-city_2.html. **434:** Exercise 1. Sources: http://www.telegraph.co.uk/science/science-news/8582150/Kon-Tiki-explorer-was-partly-right-Polynesians-had-South-American-roots.html; http://www.cla.calpoly.edu/~tljones/polynesia.%20science%202010.pdf. **454:** Exercise 3. Sources: http://outofedenwalk.nationalgeographic.com/; http://www.outofedenwalk.com/. **454:** Exercise 3. Source: http://ngm.nationalgeographic.com/2006/03/human-journey/shreeve-text. **Definitions for glossed words:** Sources: *The Newbury House Dictionary plus Grammar Reference*, Fifth Edition, National Geographic Learning/Cengage Learning, 2014; *Collins Cobuild Illustrated Basic Dictionary of American English*, Cengage Learning 2010, Collins Cobuild/Harper Collins Publishers, First Edition, 2010; *Collins Cobuild School Dictionary of American English*, Cengage Learning 2009, Collins Cobuild/Harper Collins Publishers, 2008; Collins Cobuild Advanced Learner's Dictionary, 5th Edition, Harper Collins Publishers, 2006.

Photo

Inside Front Cover, left column: Dr. K. David Harrison/Living Tongues Institute for Endangered Language, ©Jim Webb/National Geographic Creative, ©Nav Dayanand, ©Claire Bangser, ©Michael Christopher Brown/National Geographic Creative, **right column:** ©Sandra Lynn Kerr, ©Mark Thiessen/National Geographic Creative, ©Marco Grob/National Geographic Creative, ©Australia Unlimited/National Geographic Creative, ©AFP/Getty Images.

232–233: ©Joel Sartore/National Geographic Creative; **234:** ©Werner Lang/imagebroker/Newscom; **235:** ©Helmut Hess/imagebroker/age fotostock; **240:** ©Nelson Sirlin/Shutterstock; **241:** © B Christopher/Alamy; **242:** ©Martin Rietze/age fotostock; **243:** ©imagebroker/Alamy; **248:** ©Galyna Andrushko/Shutterstock; **250–251:** ©Watt Jim/Getty Images; **256:** ©Steve Winter/National Geographic Creative; **259:** ©Mike Theiss/National Geographic Creative; **260:** ©AFP/Getty Images; **262–263:** ©Peter Essick/Getty Images; **264–265:** ©Jason deCaires Taylor; **271:** ©Red Bull Stratos/ZUMA Press/Newscom; **272:** ©Marco Grob/National Geographic Creative; **276:** ©LehaKoK/Shutterestock; **278:** ©Cavan Images/Getty Images; **279 top:** ©Mark Thiessen/National Geographic Creative; **bottom:** ©Norbert Probst/imagebroker/SuperStock; **280:** ©NASA Goddard Scientific Visualization Studio/National Geographic Creative; **286:** ©Harish Tyagi/EPA/Newscom; **287:** ©David Stoecklein/age fotostock; **288:** ©Marco Grob/National Geographic Creative; **289:** ©Ace Kvale/Aurora Open/Superstock; **290:** ©Juanmonino/Getty Images; **292–293:** ©LEMAIRE StÂ©phane/Getty Images; **295:** ©Richard Nowitz/National Geographic Creative; **299:** © Juan Soliz/PacificCoastNews.com; **301:** ©Anthony C. LoBaido; **302:** ©Karen Kasmauski/National Geographic Creative; **305 left:** ©Alan Tobey/Getty Images, **right:** ©Alex Treadway/National Geographic Creative; **306:** ©Tim Laman/National Geographic Creative; **307:** ©LaserLens/iStockphoto; **308–309:** ©Seb Rogers/Alamy; **313:** ©Hervey Garret/National Geographic Creative; **314:** ©Guido Bissattini/Shutterstock; **315:** ©1001nights/iStockphoto; **316:** ©Fotosearch/Getty Images; **318–319:** ©John Warburton Lee/Superstock; **320–321:** ©Lior Mizrahi/Getty Images; **323:** ©Gamma–Rapho via Getty Images; **327:** Courtesy of Yong Ho Ji; **328:** ©Robert Harding Picture Library Ltd/Alamy; **330:** ©Christian Kapteyn/Alamy; **331:** ©Hamza Djenat; **332:** ©Lonely Planet Images/Getty Images; **335:** ©CulturalEyes—AusGS2/Alamy; **336–337:** ©JTB Photo/Glow Images; **341:** ©Blend Images/Getty Images; **342:** ©Granamour Weems Collection/Alamy; **344:** ©Inger Hogstrom/Danita Delimont Photography/Newscom; **346:** ©Moviestore collection/Alamy; **348–349:** ©Pete McBride/National Geographic Creative; **350:** ©Atsushi Tomura /Getty Images; **351:** ©Xinhua/Landov; **353 both:** ©Xpacifica/National Geographic Creative; **357:** ©Ladi Kirn/Alamy; **358:** ©Bill Becher/ZUMAPRESS/Newscom; **359:** ©Rex Features via AP Images; **360:** Graham M. Lawrence/Alamy; **364:** © Frans Lemmens/SuperStock; **367:** ©NotarYES/Shutterstock; **368:** ©Mark Thiessen/National Geographic Creative; **370–371:** © Bruce Dale/National Geographic Creative; **372–373:** ©JG Photography/Alamy; **372 top:** © AFP/Getty Images; **375:** © John W Banagan/Getty Images; **376 top:** © Hulton Archive/Getty Images, **bottom left:** © Boyan Dimitrov/Shutterstock, **bottom right:** © Jean-Paul Barbier; **379:** ©AMAZON/UPI /Landov; **380 left to right:** © Hulton Archive/Getty Images, ©UIG via Getty Images, ©Sebastien Bergeron/Getty Images, ©North Wind Picture Archives/Alamy; **381 left:** ©North Wind Picture Archives/Alamy, **right:** ©AFP/Getty Images; **382–383 background:** ©Hyena Reality/Shutterstock; **382–383 all others:** ©Tan Le/National Geographic Creative; **384:** ©Tan Le/National Geographic Creative; **390:** ©Andrzej Mirecki; **391:** ©David Stock/Alamy; **392 left:** © Lana K/Shutterstock, **right:** ©mishooo/iStockphoto; **394–395:** © Jim Richardson/National Geographic Creative; **396 both:** © Kenneth Garrett/National Geographic Creative; **399:** ©Jacques Alexandre/age fotostock; **400:** © Michael Melford/National Geographic Creative; **402:** © Martin Gray/National Geographic Creative; **403:** ©Image Farm Inc./Alamy; **404–405:** Original Artwork by John Batchelor. Courtesy of Odyssey Marine Exploration; **407:** ©St Petersburg Times/ZUMAPRESS/Newscom; **411:** ©Christian Goupi/age fotostock; **412:** ©De Agostini/Getty Images; **413:** © Oligo/Shutterstock; **414:** © Romaoslo/iStockphoto; **416:** ©pzAxe/Alamy; **417:** ©Heritage Images/Glow Images; **419:** ©Denver Post via Getty Images; **420:** ©Chris Cheadle/All Canada Photos/SuperStock; **422:** ©Gamma/Glow Images;

(continued on page C2)

MAP